THE CITY OF PARKS

Memories of an Outsider

K C ARORA

authorHOUSE®

AuthorHouse™
1663 Liberty Drive
Bloomington, IN 47403
www.authorhouse.com
Phone: 1 (800) 839-8640

Published by AuthorHouse   06/08/2016

ISBN: 978-1-5246-1310-5 (sc)
ISBN: 978-1-5246-1308-2 (hc)
ISBN: 978-1-5246-1309-9 (e)

Library of Congress Control Number: 2016909218

Print information available on the last page.

Other Publications by K. C. ARORA:

Equal Opportunities for Ethnic Minorities in Work Related NAFE: Identifying and Developing Good Practice in Colleges (with others); Inner London Education Authority, January 1990.

Indian Nationalist Movement in Britain, 1930-49; Inter-India Publications, New Delhi, 1992.

Colonialism and the Decline of the Cotton Industry in the 19th Century India; University of Greenwich, 1993.

'Mahatma Gandhi on Communal Individuality'; The Good Society Review, July 1993

'Krishna Menon: A St. Pancras Councillor'; The Good Society Review, July 1995

'The Steel Frame: Indian Civil Service since 1860, Sanchar Publishing House, New Delhi, 1996

'V.K.Krishna Menon: A Brilliant Eccentric'; India Weekly, 3 May 1996, Imperialism and the Non-Alignment Movement, Sanchar Publishing House; New Delhi, 1998.

V.K.Krishna Menon- A Biography, Sanchar Publishing House, New Delhi, 1998. A Short Introduction to principles of Economics, Hamilton & Co Publishers Ltd. London, 2000

Forthcoming Publications:

Stagnation and Change: Economic Impact of British Raj in India, 1765-1947.

Gandhi's Communal Society: Exposition and Critique.

Acknowledgement

The City of Parks (Memories of an Outsider) 1965-2015, is the outcome of my diary maintained, over a period of five decades. I am grateful to a number of people who helped me to introduce this book to the readers. My thanks are due to my family, who encouraged me to make my views public, otherwise it would have remained in the private domain. My sincere thanks to my publishers, Author House, for presenting it to the public in a book form, as well as an E-Book. Their editorial department made valuable suggestions, which had been taken into consideration.

However, these are my observations, experiences and views which took shape over a period of time. I am responsible for my thoughts and actions.

PREFACE

The City of Parks invites readers to join the author on his life journey. This autobiographical account weaves together the personal experiences, observation, after- the-fact reflections, and numerous small explanations that help scenes and times, which may be unfamiliar because of the passing of the years and the far-flung locations of those places, to come to life. Those who have read the manuscript, they found it a good read, interesting and provocative because-of its content and the areas covered related to the common people.

This diary was started in 1970, but not written in rapid succession. Occasionally, I did not write for months. This was, however, a chronological account of events and incidents in Britain, India and the world generally. This was also an expression of my feelings, interests and observations on many subjects. It was, nevertheless, not a historical account of social change, political activities or a record of my psychological manifestation. Many of the descriptions, illustrated and stated had taken place in my life. Some had been recorded on the basis of personal accounts of my friends, colleagues and neighbours. The difficulties encountered by me and others during a span of over five decades were of general nature that occurred in the life of a person who moved to live in a new geographical location and social surroundings.

It was not my intention to find inadequacies in any person, country or system. All societies had their own traditions, customs, political and social institutions founded essentially on historical, cultural and other ancient wisdom. They operated within their own parameters. It was a human nature to demand more but it was scarce that people attempted to exploit others for no good reason. Some of the personality traits of hard work, happiness, greed, conflict, co-operation and jealousy had been examined in these observations. By accepting people as they were and allow them to hold their own views, led me to accumulate abundant positive energy which became the bed- rock of my success in many fields. The criticism by others was meditatively considered and often ignored or avoided in order to make way to move on and to continue to make irrefutable contribution to social, educational and economic progress and in order to attempt to adjust in the existing environment without any endeavour to alter the situations.

The past five decades had witnessed enormous physical changes in the City of Parks. The decline of industrial base in the East-End, North and West London, meant that new housing estates and warehouses came into existence to replace them. The introduction of shopping Malls led to a decline of small family shops. The emergence of Canary Wharf as a financial center maintained London as the Financial Capital of the world. It housed not only international banks but also investment banks and insurance institutions.

Britain's joining of the European Union (formerly European Economic Community) brought European food culture. Coffee bars and Pizza Huts had been set up on the High Streets of London. The Character of some of these places had substantially changed and they had become intrinsically unrecognizable.

This was, however, a story of hurdles and impediments in the life of an individual who did not want much except for living a simple life based on his principles and social norms. He, nonetheless, overcame these obstacles by sheer determination, hard work and affirmative thinking. All of us had to face our own circumstances. Others might not understand the ever changing situations and future actions. The author attempted to follow the dictum of the Gita that 'work is thy duty, result is not thy concern', because the consequence of a future action could not be visualized or foreseen.

A large number of themes had been covered in these observations in relation to the City of Parks and other parts of the world. A comparison had sometimes been undertaken between the advanced and the developing nations because it was from the developing countries that people moved to live in the developed countries in search of better job prospects and improved life. They, however, had to face a number of problems in their new countries.

The Indian nationalism and rationalism had been examined along with the question of Modernization versus Westernization. In this, the role, education was paramount. Changes in the attitude and behaviour of people had been considered with the fluctuations in population structure and ethnicity in London in the past half a century. Peaceful life in this great city had sometimes been disrupted by terrorist attacks and unsociable actions. This had become an international phenomenon in the 21st Century.

Like many other stories the author felt pleased at his personal accomplishments and contribution to society, despite obstructions and impediments. The entire five decade period was not the same or similar. It witnessed variations in accordance with the alterable contours of socio-political-economic landscape.

CHAPTER 1

Struggle and the Adjustment, 1965-75

It is long, since I promised to narrate my experiences and observations in some detail. However, there had been few occasions in my life which had left a permanent impact on my mind. Certainly my coming to England brought some changes in my living. The roots of this go back to January 1964, when I was fast asleep at our flat at Chirawa (Rajasthan), India. I heard a big knock at the door at about 4 am. This knock woke me up. I opened the door and found my younger brother standing there with a colleague of mine. While I was pleased to see him, it also surprised me because this was unexpected and I had not been informed about his programme to visit us. We all went to sleep and started to talk in the morning. During our conversation, it emerged that a neighbour in Delhi was going to England in April. He had been granted a work visa by the British government. I became curious and thought, I would also like to go abroad. But I did not have the means. I, therefore, did not think further in this field. In February 1964, we moved to live in Delhi. In April 1965, I made an application for an employment visa at the British High Commission in New Delhi. To my astonishment I received a letter, from the commission in May, that the work voucher, for which I had applied, had been received and that I should bring my passport in order to collect it.

I asked a relative to help me in obtaining a passport because in 1965, the Indian government did not easily issue passports. A number of guarantees were required and some one with an asset of ten thousand rupees should stand a security. My relative asked his employer to assist in this matter. He agreed on condition, that on reaching London, I would send him a new ford car. When we went to the land registry for an ownership certificate, he was furious because the certificate showed that he was insolvent for up to ten thousand rupees. He permeated the view that he was a very rich man and owned a large number of properties and land in north east Delhi. Anyway, I submitted my application form and received my passport within a fortnight.

Some of my relatives were not keen with my decision to go abroad and asked me questions, how shall I pay for my flight, and who will look after my little family? I, however, decided to fly to a country distant across the seas of which I knew little except the language. I could not visualize at that time what was in store for me in England. Although it was my burning desire to go to London, it was never designed the way it happened. I borrowed two thousand rupees for my air ticket and flew to London on 15th of October 1965, leaving my gentle wife and innocent children on their own to face their problems, as I was to struggle and solve my enigma in a strange land. I had left my family at the same flat where I had lived with them in Delhi, but a close relative did not like the idea of them living on their own when we had a large family. They were, therefore, moved to another relative's place where they did not want to live.

They, therefore, went to live with Santosh's (my Wife's) parents for a brief period. I did not know when they went there. A friend (with whom I stayed on my arrival) in London did not like this. He told me that you should know the where- about and welfare of your family. He, therefore, wrote to my relative that he was mature enough and clever enough to tell us that the children had gone to stay with their maternal grandparents. The person in India did not like that, and rather than replying to that friend, he wrote to me that I had prompted this man to write to him and if I was so worried about my children why did I go to London? I let the matter slip and did not care about his views and behaviour.

I had my own problems to solve in London and find a proper place to live and a job to earn some money in order to pay my rent and other bills. We did really face a number of problems in those early years. When my wife returned from her parent's house to Delhi, my relative's family made it difficult for them to live peacefully. My young children and wife had to live in a small kitchen. My father took them to the village but some younger members of the extended family made their life miserable. My wife and children had to come back to Delhi to face the same adversity. One night they had to spend standing under a balcony in order to protect themselves from rain. That was the worst period of our lives. This was like a scene in a Hindi movie displaying poverty and bad days.

It was, however, not to last long. The Almighty had tested us and He provided us with everything in years to come; with a house, good job and other resources to live a comfortable life. My grandchildren would never face what my children had to endure in their childhood. That was my determination. I worked for it and worked hard. Many people helped me in accomplishing my objectives. Despite many hindrances, we were successful in our goals. At these achievements, however, some people were jealous and uncomfortable.

I found England wet and cold. It was a cold country, temperature reaching minus eight or even minus twelve centigrade. It rained almost every day in winter. I did not see sun for many months. I found a small room in West London where many tenants were from India. They came from south, north, west and eastern states of the country. European tenants also lived in that house. It was the responsibility of the landlord to clean the rooms and keep the house tidy. He also maintained a garden and grew flowers. There were some trees. A park was near by. They called it Ealing Common. The main advantage of this house was that it was near a tube station. The metro or London train service is called the tube or London underground because so many trains run under buildings especially in central London. Though there were surface stations and railway track as well.

First, I found a job at a walking distance. From September to December 1966, I worked at Shepherds Bush, West London. Then, I started to work

3

in the Customs & Excise department of the British government. I used to travel by tube to the office. It was an hour long journey from home to office. The train did not stop at many stations. In between Acton Town station and Hammersmith station, there were four small stations. The train used to run fast, yet I used to peep through the window and look at the area. I saw that there was green space, parks and beautiful houses. It looked like a country side but it was the inner city suburb of Chiswick. The Bedford Park area of this district appealed to me most and I thought of living there at some stage. In the early months of my stay in London, I, however, continued to live at Hanger Lane and travelled from the North Ealing station to the city' Tower Hill station. There were some facilities near this house- a barber shop, a newspaper agent, and a launderette. The main shops were at the High Street, about one mile away from the house. This area was known as Ealing Broadway. I was perhaps lucky to live in a room on my own in this big house at Hanger Lane, also known as South Circular Road.

Those who migrated from the Indian sub-continent in 1950s and 1960s told me that up to six people lived in a room or twenty in a house. It was not easy to find accommodation in London. Secondly, people wanted to save money in order to purchase their own houses. Later I learned that in the Bengali community, people even rotated the use of the bed. They worked in shifts and slept for eight hours in a bed. Then another man would come and sleep in the same bed. Not many families immigrated to England from the sub- continent at that time. Only men came in search of work and their families joined them afterwards. The Indian community decided to settle in Southall, a suburb on the out skirts of West London. Many had jobs there. A few shops and restaurants were also opened for Indians to buy their food supplies.

Although I had never worked in an office, I settled down easily at the Customs & Excise Department. I was given two weeks training. I also went to South-End-on Sea, where the computer work was done. The computer in 1966 was very large and stuck along the wall. It used punched cards; a kind of code was required for all sorts of work. First, I was fascinated with this machine, but I realised I could not work on such a machine. I, therefore, continued to work at the Head Office at Mark Lane in the city of London. The office was overcrowded. Far more people worked there than were required. I had an eight-hour duty, but I could have finished my work within three hours. We had a tea club and fellow workers made tea them-selves, rather then going to canteen. We used to buy buns and butter from the canteen. We talked a lot but never involved in gossip or criticism of any body. We did not talk politics either.

I made some good friends and enjoyed my stay there. The Head of department was an old lady who was very impressed with my work and attitude. I told her that I was interested in studies and wanted to attend evening classes. She was glad to know that and encouraged me to study. At the end of one year she thought that I should gain experience in other fields. She transferred me to the Revenue Section, which dealt with oil duties and changes in laws and regulations. I used to keep records of some duties and allowances given for pilferage of oil. I also prepared monthly returns for the work done by all of us and type any changes needed in regulations. It was a routine work, which I used to finish quickly, and then sit at my desk and read files and books.

In London, I faced some fundamental problems, both – financial as well as social. I suffered a few setbacks but soon, I began to feel at home. Life was not a bed of roses for me in this highly industrialised city. Yet, I did not regret in leaving the places where I spent my childhood and boyhood. Some people took undue advantage of my simplicity. At the beginning I could not foresee the future happenings and did not realize the complexity of the environment. I was easily swayed. Consequently, I began to lose grip over my own circumstances and at times, I developed a lack of self-confidence and indecisiveness. It was, however, not too late when I regained control over my situations and the state of affairs. I was helped by my determination, truthfulness and frankness. I realized that people did not like openness. Neither did they appreciate the importance of real facts. They did not want to be treated in the same way as they themselves treated others. They wanted to preserve some privileges for themselves as if the rights were theirs and the duties were to be left to others. This was duplicity and a false philosophy, which could have no practical value.

We all came to earn our living and there were a few people who arrived in London from India much earlier than me and yet they expected me to help them financially. I did really help a man, three times, whom I barely knew in India. At one stage, I enquired if he could help me in my need but he refused saying that he did not have any cash available in his bank or at home. Yet, a few months later he again asked me to lend him a lot of money. I discussed this episode with some colleagues and friends who warned me that there were people who exploit for their own purposes and would not help you in your requirement. You could not do anything and possibly lose time and money and might be put under emotional pressure. I, therefore, decided not to lend money any further. This did not go well with some people who broke all connection with me. This was a dilemma in the posture and conduct of such people.

This drove me away from those who had been friends in the past. I almost became solos and secluded. I felt lonely but safe and happy. I must state that in times of need I was never alone. There was always some one to help me. I kept in touch with my books, which kept me alive and my brain fertile. I visited a few places in London and other parts of the United Kingdom. I went to almost every tourist spot in London- the Museums, the Trafalgar Square with its pond and open space, the Westminster Abbey and the Parliament Houses, the Oxford Circus, the Piccadilly Circus and of course the famous parks at Regents Street, South Kensington-park, Hyde-Park and Kew-gardens. I went to visit Shakespeare's birthplace, Stratford – Upon- Avon, the Isle-of-Wight, the coastal towns of South-end-on-Sea, Brighton, Hastings, Eastbourne and Bournemouth. Thus days passed, months went by and years began to slip.

In 1967, I moved from North Ealing to Pekham in South London where I lived in the back room of a thorough lounge which was divided by a door. There was no solid wall between my room and the front part of the room. In the front room a young couple, from St.Lucia in the West Indies lived, with their young baby daughter. They used to shout very loudly. The house was not very attractive. It was rather old and dirty. I lived there for three weeks. The land lord lived opposite the house in the same street. After two weeks, I went to his house to tell him that I was moving out and that I had found another room at New Cross Road not far from Peckam. He tried to persuade me to stay on and that he would reduce the rent. While we were talking, his wife brought some oranges for us to eat. The man asked me to Chugo (have it) in Punjabi. I could understand a few words of Punjabi but I had never come across this word for eating because Chugo in Hindi is used for birds to eat their grain.

At New Cross, I first lived in basement which had damp and I could smell the wetness. I was afraid about my health and I asked the landlord to move me to the top floor smaller- room. He agreed to do that. I lived in that house with the other tenants who came from the Punjab. We became close friends. I stayed there until April 1968, when my family arrived from India. The room was not sufficient for all of us. We, therefore, moved to live in Dalston part of Hackney. We had two rooms and used to cook outside the room in the lobby above the stairs. There was a sink on the first floor, above the stairs. The garden side window on the first floor was broken. It was never repaired while we lived there. The house did not have a bath. We used to go to public baths, either in the city or in Hackney. There was, however, a High Street where we bought our food. There were also stalls near Dalston station and we used to buy green vegetables from there. It had all the facilities. I used to go to my office by bus. The office was only about two miles away. We lived there for twenty months.

As stated above, in April 1968, my immediate family joined me. It did not bring many changes except that we were four instead of one. Each other to talk with, to help and to give solace and comfort when one felt dejected. As to the character of a woman, my wife always stood by my side, preaching against utter despair and too much happiness. I did not know whether I had been influenced by such ideals. I still feel dejected or pleased according to circumstances. I had, nevertheless, attempted to be at comfort though my life had been nothing more than a spontaneous routine.

Saneh (daughter) and Azad (son) started to attend the local school. I continued to work at the same office but in a different department. The colleagues were good and co-operated most of the time. I had always prayed for two things – I should not develop vanity and that I should not harm any-one. Reactions from others had not been reciprocal. Misunderstanding had often taken place because of unsound and biased communication and one-sidedness.

In December 1969, I fell ill and was sick for three weeks. I felt lonely and at that time. I regretted our living in London. Not so much for my own sake but for the sake of the children and my wife. What could they do here in London? Back at home in India someone would certainly have helped. During this period I lost my voice and my memory. I could not do anything but pray. Nevertheless, I recovered from my illness and received a few letters of sympathy from my friends and relatives in India and in London. In January 1970, we moved to live in Manor Park, where we bought a three-bed room house. It was not a nice area to live and we did not know much about it. It, however, had a school and transport facilities. Children started to study at their new school where they adjusted themselves easily. We did not have a telephone. Children used to stay on their own during holiday. At lunch time, I used to come home from office to see them. Some times only for a few minutes but I felt satisfied that they were safe and had no problems. I hardly ever felt tired. I used to run from station to home and back to reach the office within an hour.

I believed that people would struggle for survival as ordinary human beings. Honesty and simplicity were the best ways to live, however perilous that might be. In my case, action and contemplation existed simultaneously. Much of my time was spent on thinking, brooding and planning rather than on action. Money was a secondary factor. I had probably overcome this drive. I had always regarded money simply another branch of social life but I would not wish to depend on others for money.

Very often, I had compared my village in India with London. If I am not proud of my humble origins, I have never regretted being born in a tiny village in northern India where people of different standards, ideas, religions and castes lived together in peace. London had performed the functions of an industrial city – be it administrative, marketing, commercial, social, educational or residential, It was also a living place for people from various backgrounds in race and creed. It had become a confluence of cultures. I preferred to call it a city of parks and bridges.

In London, I had kept myself busy. I worked and studied simultaneously. In order to take the first year degree examination and to prepare for the examination, I applied for study leave through my section in-charge. It was customary that the employees, who wanted to enhance their qualification, they were provided financial assistance and time off for examination. But when I applied for leave and reimbursement of examination fee, the person in charge questioned me, how did I found out about this facility and why should I be given assistance? This showed his prejudice. He did not support my application and I was not given any time off or financial help. I, therefore, took my own annual leave to take examination and I paid my own fee. I passed the examination but found it difficult to work as well as to study for a degree course. I, therefore, decided to pursue my studies for part 2 of the B.Sc. Economics degree, of the London University, at the City of London Polytechnic, on full time basis. I was generally questioned as to what was I going to do after finishing the course?

It seemed difficult to decide the future activities at that early stage. Education was an investment and one day it could bring dividends of acquiring a qualification. I left it to circumstances which could provide me with an opportunity to do something. I sensed that people should study basically to improve their status, better job prospects and because of ambition and interests. Activities could be divided into two categories – one to enjoy and the other for the sake of doing them. Moreover, life was as you thought and wanted to make it. Smooth living was not very progressive. One got to struggle in order to accomplish one's goal and concentrate on the final objectives in life, bearing in mind that peace, stability, discipline and humility were the essential tenets of good human life.

The classes for my degree course were to start at the end of September 1970. I applied, to my department, for study leave without pay. The section Head was not present that day when I made my application. His deputy supported my application and sent-off to the personnel section. She frankly told me that the Head might not support it so we should send

9

it immediately for approval. My leave was sanctioned because it had the support of the Acting Head. I had applied for a study grant to my local education authority. It was approved. So I had the time and the financial support to study.

Going back to Polytechnic, was an experience. In the early stages I had to adjust myself. I had become accustomed to working. It was not easy to study with young people. There were two or three students of my age group. I had been a teacher and worked behind a desk. Now I had a different position. A couple of lecturers were younger to me. But I did not have any complex that I should not be taught by young lecturers. As time passed, I began to enjoy my course and studies. I liked it and it gave me an opportunity for intellectual exercise and brain activity. All lecturers were very learned, intelligent and gentle apart from one lady lecturer. She took her class at 4 o'clock and her teaching method was so boring that I often fell asleep. She used to bring typed lecture notes and read them quietly. She never used the board in order to write something or to draw diagrams in Economics. She also did not give any handouts.

Plato's "The Republic" was my set text. I had to study it in some detail and thoroughly. Plato was greatly influenced by the Bhagwat Gita and the teachings of the Buddha. His metaphysics and the theory of the soul were borrowed from Indian religions. I felt that Plato was influenced, through Socrates, by the Indian society of those days. He was fascinated by the caste system and the philosopher king who ruled the city state. In his opinion, the king should be the most intelligent person in the realm. He should not have lure for property and his rule should be for the benefit of the ruled. For Plato collective leadership of modern cabinet system was no substitute for the rule by the best. He argued that the kingdom would be defended by the Guardians. The merchants, artisans and the agriculturalists formed the next layer of society. In the lower category of the society were the servants and slaves who worked for the upper classes.

Plato laid emphasis on Justice, Education and the study of the Good. Only a just society could provide happiness to its people who lived an orderly life. The Republic was, however, a book of philosophy and political theory.

Plato divided the political system into aristocracy, oligarchy, democracy and tyranny. He visualized the decline of political system from aristocracy to tyranny which could create turmoil in the city state.

What was utopian for Plato was real in many parts of Northern India. But something had gone wrong with the ancient Indian culture, which had inspired foreign philosophers to think and write. The aristocracy still existed but its basis now was selfishness. People were greedy and the rulers enjoyed themselves and did not work for common good. The masses had been ignored for the benefit of the few. The few lived while the others existed. This type of Indian culture bred ignorance, disease, superstition and selfishness.

During the winter break in 1970, I worked at the post office in order to earn some money. I earned just enough to pay our council tax. The wages were low but most students worked during Christmas holiday. I also went back to my old department during summer holiday in 1971. I worked there for two months and then returned to my studies for the final year of the degree course. I stayed at the City of London Polytechnic for two academic years. I read books and did my course work, which was not accounted towards the examination. But it gave some essay writing practice. In all, I read one hundred and fifty books. It was rather essential to read these many books in order to cover the subject matter and prepare for the examination.

Apart from reading books and periodicals, I was constantly watching the British society and was not altogether detached from the events in India. Earlier I had compared the peaceful living in London with that of my village. But the fundamental differences remained between the British society and the Indian society. One was essentially an industrial society and the other was an agricultural country. Both had different problems. The industrial society was faced with the problems of industrial relations, inflation, discipline, delinquency and congestion. While an agricultural country like India was facing transformation. It was confronted with the concerns of over population, malnutrition, unemployment, standard of living and how to overcome the traditional chains of social customs and how to modernise without giving up the essentials of the national spirit and the basic institutions.

Let me explain something of the political system in Britain since politics transcend society. It also tells us about the social structure and customs. Britain had a two party system – where there was a tussle to acquire power at regular intervals of about five years. It was strange to note that the Conservative party and Labour party, changed hands without disrupting the administrative structure. The fact was that there was no place for extremism in this country and the civil service was politically unbiased. It advised the ministers and obeyed their orders without prejudice. The civil service functioned under the supervision of the Treasury. The office of the Parliamentary Commissioner for Administration was to check the deficiency of administrators. The Members of Parliament took up grievances of their constituents. Generally, the politicians did not meddle with the administrative machinery. Some policies such as foreign and defence were bi-partisan.

Today the Conservative party was not feudal or capitalist, nor was the Labour party, whole-heartedly a socialist party or a mouthpiece of organised labour. Though, the 1980s saw an economic revolution towards privatisation and anti-unionism. It could be observed that there was a scope for change and influence. Today the Prime Minister governed the country in consultation with his cabinet colleagues and higher civil servants. The pressure groups played a significant part because Britain was an open society. Some people had questioned the influence of pressure groups in a country where political parties were so disciplined and powerful and had to fulfil their plans and election pledges. It was, nevertheless, the way the government functioned and the society was run in Britain.

In Britain, most of the qualified people went to industry and commerce. Some sought government jobs or joined politics. While others preferred to stay in educational institutions. One strange thing to be noted was the amalgamation of feudalism, capitalism and socialism. Relics of the past still remained. The Queen was the Head of State and was respected by the capitalists and socialists alike, though islands of dissent remained who resented this institution. Sometimes, I had appreciated the practical mindedness of the British people but at times I had been disappointed with the bankruptcy of some British intellectuals who believed that their systems were right and others were wrong. They did that without considering the diversity of the Universe.

I had also pondered over the Indian system. After all it was the largest democracy in the world. The success was still to be seen. There had been upheavals in the developing countries, even across the borders in China and Pakistan. How did democracy survive in India for quarter of a century after independence in 1947, despite mass ignorance, immense poverty and vast unemployment? I had often thought that the Indian society could be more active and people could participate more freely. Some reforms would have to be introduced. Practical and useful education would have to be imparted. This was an anomaly in the developing countries that they could not utilize their educated people and yet they claimed to be short of technical personnel. India had twice as many engineers as the Western Europe and was supplying a pool of engineers to the United States of America. This was misallocation of resources. Brain drain had further handicapped economic progress. I thought mass higher education was unproductive. If proper employment could not be provided to people, it was a waste of resources both human and capital. Compulsory and practical education for all and job training for those who needed them could be a good and more useful system.

The problems should be solved and not brushed aside or put away that they would disappear one day. One very important point to be noted was that the Indian problems could not be solved by European methods, though western technology should be applied to remove poverty. Social reforms were equally essential for economic progress. People should be open minded and prepared to give up some of the old customs and manners, while preserving the tradition of religious tolerance and folk-life. This was a vast field and there was no end to such problems. The solutions could be found, in the fields of agriculture, industry, economy, society and education. More vigilance, more understanding, mutual communication, fair mindedness and large heartedness were needed in order to make India a successful democracy and a modern state where every one could at least have an opportunity to express one's opinion and progress according to one's abilities and aptitudes.

After completing my course in June 1972, I returned to my department-Customs and Excise at Mark Lane, London. I started the same old job with the same old section of the Revenue Duties. There was hardly any change in my routine. I started to make applications for a job in industry. I also applied for a promotion in the department. But the Head of my department was not prepared to support my application. I, therefore, did not get a promotion. I sought an interview with the Principal Executive who agreed to look into it. But there was no change in the decision or policy. I, therefore, continued to work there as well as look for a job in other areas including teaching.

On 8 February 1973, Mrs. Indira Gandhi, the India Prime Minister, delivered a speech at the All India Political Science Association, Calcutta. This speech was published in the India News. I read it with great interest and enthusiasm. I appreciated her nationalism and nationalist ideas. While I was prepared to accept that every country had unique features based on its history, culture, philosophy, art, literature and social customs, there were some common practices and problems in most countries. Politics were not only about power struggle but were to seek reconciliation between conflicting interests. Political Science, moreover, was not only concerned with history of a political party or constitutional structure of a state, it was a constant process in search for better life in economic and social areas.

It was, Sociology and attempted to find a relationship between man and society. It was a study of government, which could be based on constitutional and administrative laws dealing with public administration and legalising and controlling the private sector in order to stop monopoly and private gains. Above all politics were a matter of thought, a Philosophy, which visualized the relationship between leaders and the led. It was a Psychology attempting to discover the attitudes and patterns of people's moods and changing patterns of voting behaviour so that a prediction could be made into the form of a future government. It was an instrument of social change leading towards something good, taking right decisions at the right time.

I, therefore, was not prepared to accept an attack on the comparative approach to the study of politics and government. Surely the European society was different from the Indian society. However, some of the institutions had developed on similar patterns. Monarchy existed in many countries and in the 20th Century most countries moved towards democracy. The Indian Parliament with two Houses was designed on the pattern of the British Parliamentary system, though both differ in their constitutional structure. Likewise, other institutions had been developed by following the other countries. There was a need for value judgement, differentiation and whether one particular example could be followed in certain circumstances. A blind following and imitation was bad and perhaps disadvantageous if not harmful.

A wide study of different countries was needed and was indeed carried out in many countries. The Universities of Sussex, Hull, London and Birmingham in England had developed specialised departments of Indian politics and society. They conducted higher degrees research work on various aspects of Indian politics including the non-violence of Mahatma Gandhi. In the United States, the study of different countries' political sociology and political behaviour including Geo-politics was a flourishing industry. It could probably be proper to mention here that the Indian constitution was written after a careful study of the United States', the USSR', the British and the French constitutions. On the US constitution basis, the Indian constitution begins 'we the people of the independent sovereign republic of India'. As I mentioned earlier, various institutions were planted into India from other countries. Today the need was not to give up something that had been achieved but to develop those institutions for common good and make the best use of them.

So far as the success of Indian democracy was concerned, it was an open question and how one defined democracy. Western writers, who were born and brought up in industrial societies, had seen an improvement in living standards; tend to think that industrialisation was the foundation for the success of democracy. Moreover, there was no single definition of democracy or the reason for its success. It differed from country to country. Gone were the days when people used to get together in order to enact laws for them-selves, decide their trade-relations and could also pass judgement. In today's national and continental states, the concept of public participation was unrealistic. People did not want to get involved in all such affairs. Because of the technicality of subjects and secrecies of policies in foreign and defence- affairs, the common man would not like to get involved and portray his opinion. Majority rule and representative governments were also not sufficient foundations for democracy, because they posed questions of information and consultation.

The success of democracy, whether liberal, totalitarian, socialist or communist, depended on who held power or the source of power. If a handful of persons had all the wealth, only a few had political, civil or military power, it was an oligarchy and not democracy. If most people had a reasonable standard of living, where there was a large middle class, people did not depend on others for food, it could to be identified as democracy. If these characteristics were found in Indian society we could call it a democracy. Otherwise how could one distinguish oligarchy from democracy? Simply an emotional call for national unity or showing unity at the time of foreign aggression, being exaggerated by the mass media communication; no change of a political party in power or non-existence of a revolutionary mood, was not a sign of success of democracy.

I had been writing about India for some time. In the above context and after staying in London for many years, I thought of a short visit to India to see my relatives and friends. I brought together my annual leave for two years and decided to go to India for six weeks. We left for Delhi on 21 March 1973. On this morning a friend, who drove us to central London, saw us off. From there we took a coach to airport. We went by Kuwait Airways. Our plane was delayed because of industrial action at the London Heathrow airport. The plane took off exactly at one o' clock. The flight was pleasant and interesting because we were curious to go home. The service was good. We stopped at Paris, Rome and Kuwait airports for about an hour each. The Kuwait airport was not very attractive. The grey colour did not suit an international airport. Some of the passengers behaved in the same way as in a village. They were simple people and worked in factories in England but originally came from villages in the Punjab. They removed their trousers to go to washroom in the plane. They had neither modernised nor westernised themselves. We reached Delhi-Palam airport at 6.30 a.m. Indian standard time.

There, we were received by a host of relatives including my father. We drove home. On the way we saw many physical changes in New Delhi and old Delhi. It was a sign of progress but disparity existed. Huts and palatial buildings stood side by side. The rich and poor walked shoulder to shoulder. Despite prohibition, begging continued. Increased transportation had led to over-crowding and congestion on roads. We stayed in north-east Delhi for three days. People who- knew came to visit us. They were curious and asked about our personal life in London, our incomes and expenditure, savings and so on. They also enquired about the attitude of the British people towards the Indian community. Various questions were asked about the British way of life, society and customs.

I also went to my old school in Khari-Baoli in old Delhi, for an informal conversation with my ex-colleagues. The school Headmaster invited me for a formal talk when the teachers could ask me their inquisitive questions; increase their knowledge and understanding of the West. I availed this opportunity just before returning to England. I first explained the educational system and the social structure in Britain and then answered their questions. Some of the questions were relevant, while other questions did not look proper to me. For example, one gentleman asked me 'what good attributes did you see in the Indian society and what shortcomings did you find in Britain?' Actually, it was difficult to answer such a question. I was not there to judge goodness or badness in societies. I was neither a moral philosopher nor a religious sociologist. It also depended on one's liking or disliking. I had always believed that nothing was good or bad but thinking made it so. Many things were good at a place in certain circumstances while they looked awkward in other situations in different countries as visualised by other people. Therefore, we should be very careful when we undertook a comparative approach in our analysis of different systems.

My view was that these types of questions transcended limited knowledge and shallow outlook. Different civilizations had progressed differently in accordance with their climatic conditions, social and historical factors. There was always something good in one system as well as the other. Such questions also reflected the personality of the person who asked them. I had expected some curiosity and intellectual maturity from teachers. Still the discussion was very lively. It also provided me an opportunity to meet my old friends and colleagues and some new comers.

I had thought that my ex-colleagues and neighbours would be curious to know about the living conditions, social customs, economic and technological progress, cultural activities, theatres, cinemas and television programmes. They would ask me how I adjusted myself in London. Instead, their curiosity was confined to bread and butter issues. They had firm convictions, beliefs and ideas. It reflected that India was still fighting a war for freedom from the clutches of British colonialism and that the British were still imperialists involved in racial and colour prejudices. I acknowledged, that there were prejudices and I had suffered on many occasions due to this reason and there was a lack of equality of opportunity in Britain in the early 1970s. But they also related to problems faced by immigrants in a new country.

I spent three weeks in my village in Uttar Pradesh. It was good. My village folks came to visit me. I also went to see them. The climate was good. It started to get hot because of the summer season. I fell sick for a few days. But I enjoyed my stay in the village after a long time. From our village we went to visit our in-laws. They were all delighted to see us. My father-in-law invited all his sons and daughters to his village. We, therefore, stayed there for a week. One day we went to see an Indian film in a near by town. I had an opportunity to see some of the new relatives. On returning from UP, we stayed for a week in Delhi, We went to the Zoo, and also visited other parts of old Delhi and New Delhi. I also went to my brother's office at

Scindia- House. I must stress that over all our stay in India was refreshing and good.

This short visit to India was a survey and perhaps an experience. I imagine that India had taken a mould in her history. People though tied to traditions were economically aggressive and were prepared to work hard in order to improve their living standards. It looked as if one could have a future if determined and ready to move and undertake adventure. He could make his life happy, secure and sociable.

After returning to London, I decided to change my employment. I applied for various jobs in industry without success. I felt a bit disappointed and perhaps frustrated but a ray of hope kept me active. I did not stop sending applications in the hope, 'if winter comes shall spring be far behind'. Some of my friends suggested that I should apply for a teaching post. I made about thirty applications to schools and local Education Authorities between May and July. I attended an interview at Loxford School, Ilford. They could not tell me straight away and never sent me a letter either way. The Newham education department wrote to me at the end of July that they were ready to consider my application for a History teacher at a comprehensive school, if I wished to be considered. I consented for this by phone on 3 August 1973. On the 4th, I received a letter for an interview, which took place on 8th August.

Early in the morning that day, I went to Stratford (East London), where I was seen by an Inspector for Schools. He explained to me certain things and then expressed that he was prepared to offer me a temporary post of History teacher at Little Ilford School in Manor Park, which was about five minutes walk from my house. He spoke to the Head of that school who said that he (the Head) would be delighted to have me on his staff. He, therefore, offered me my first teaching job in London. Now, I could only imagine that a feeling of ecstasy passed through my heart and I was overjoyed. I, however, controlled my emotions.

I entertained the view that I was right in my thinking that there was a time for everything. Every one accomplishes one's objectives. It could take some time. One should always be optimist and determined and make effort. In the end success would be achieved. Apparently my philosophical ideas had been translated into action. I never gave up an expectation and a feeling of advancement. After the interview, there was nothing special for the next few weeks. Though, my friends and colleagues used to ask me 'how would you like teaching after such a long break?' I, however, looked to the day when I was to join the school.

In the mean- time, I had been pondering about the socio-political trends in India in relation to nationalism and rationalism. These two trends could be observed in the Indian political thinking that seemed to divide people in their expressions and activities. For a long time, India had been a stagnant society and there was very little opportunity for cultural inter-course with the outside world. Yet an elitist group was rising with western thinking and another group was attempting to revive the glory of ancient Indian civilization. These two groups were still seen in the form of rationalists and nationalists. Rationalism had been identified with Westernism and nationalism with the attitudes and customs of a nation. Every one had its own national identity because of its specific features with regard to historical background, social structure and philosophical outlook. But the past one hundred and fifty years had witnessed enormous changes in the world. There was hardly any country, which had remained isolated and had maintained its sophistication. All had seen external influences.

The West and the western traders, administrators and military personnel, had politically dominated the world. The others had carried the message of western culture and philosophy to far and distant countries. The western education system had been planted into non-western states. European languages had been introduced. The economic and political institutions had been designed on western patterns. Even religious beliefs had been accepted as superseding their own. In other words the world has moved towards unity with the leadership of the West. However, because of geographical and historical reasons, it had not been a successful attempt. It had led to differences and deviations and sometimes conflict. It was rather difficult to change the minds of men and women. The well-known views to the German philosopher Hegel – of a thesis, an anti-thesis and then of synthesis find an echo and perspective approach to the determination of world dynamics. If we consider westernism or rationalism as a new thesis then nationalism should be considered as an anti-thesis and some compromising factors as synthesis or a basis for collaboration, co-operation and co-existence. In this context we should analyse how far one aspect or the other had dominated the 20th Century politics in India.

After the collapse of the Indian power in the form of the Mughal Empire or the Maharajas, the British took over the political reigns of India and then the western influence began to penetrate into the Indian society. Obviously the host community resented but at the loss of power, politically it was in a weaker position. However, many social organisations sprang up around the country. The leaders started to examine the reasons for the defeat. They looked to the ways to revitalise the society. They discovered the drawbacks in their own social structure and set out to eradicate their frailties. Some of them appealed to the ancient culture and civilization, while others wanted to introduce some new methods perhaps influenced by the West or borrowed from the West. They believed that it was rather difficult to revive the past and that India had a future role to play in the international arena. It should, therefore, modernise without westernising itself. They thought that the Indian agricultural society would gain little from the industrialised west except administration and technology for economic development.

It would not be proper, however, to say that political parties did not exist in India prior to the birth of the Indian National Congress. Associations existed as social and religious organizations for the welfare of the people and to awaken the conscience of the nation. Still they did not work as political forces or as pressure groups. Their functions were confined to social reforms and preaching. The political awareness and development came in the early years to the 20thCentury. Because of lack of mass following the Indian political parties remained elitist middle class establishment. A political organisation could be successful only when it had touched the heart of the people and had aroused an identity among the masses, opened opportunities and membership to all.

21

Before Gandhi ji took over the leadership of the Indian National Congress, it was a middle class elitist structure. It was the Mahatma who asked people in villages and towns to work for the Congress. He made the Congress a mass party. Under his leadership different systems operated simultaneously. He normally appealed to the hearts and minds of the people. He was, therefore, revered by all except a few leftists who believed that with mass support and following he should have carried a revolution instead of negotiations with the British authorities. Some activists like Vinova Bhave and Jai Prakash Narayan with different attitudes turned to Gandhism in the later years. They saw a religious and social appeal in the Gandhian philosophy. People like Nehru and Menon who differed profoundly in their thinking and outlook, also called them- selves, the followers of Gandhi. Gandhiji's was a democratic approach with a slight bend towards spirituality and oriental leaning.

It was a paradox that rationalists identified themselves as true nationalists and criticized the West. Whereas the nationalists accommodated well with the West and often had close co-operation with those countries. However, many people had accepted the Committee system, parliamentary democracy, decentra-lisation of power and administration, and small-scale industries. While some were bent for drastic changes, others were prepared for a slow process. They wanted to keep some of the old systems but also wanted to move forward. This was of-course diversely accepted or rejected by both the nationalists and rationalists. Any particular form of nationalism was not shared by all. It differed from provincialism to internationalism, socialism and democracy, non-violence, political and economic equality. These values probably belonged to the ruling group rather than to the society as a whole. The top Congress leaders, administrative services and the military, might have shared these values but many intellectuals did not share them. Neither were they accepted by a substantial majority of the lower middle classes.

For many people the integration of Indian and Western thinking was a problem. They found it difficult to reconcile the materialistic development and spiritual aspects of life. Some rejected industrialisation which was considered as a symbol of problems like slums, juvenile delinquency and crime, mass cultural vulgarity, the break down of religious values, loss of intimacy of the communal life and the break- up of the joint family system. Others were prepared to sacrifice these norms for quick material development. The spiritualism of India had provided an alternative to mass demands for materialism of the West. Only a limited number of people had kept themselves satisfied with minimal needs. Others had rejected this notion and would be glad to see India a mass consuming and materially developed society.

India's dichotomy – the ancient values and the material growth was possible. In order to solve this parody, the techniques of social scientists and social philosophers should be utilized. It was a pity that their services had not been used to find integration and to get the better of the two worlds. Anti-power feeling, non-institutional framework should be discouraged. Religion should be confined to influences and values of spiritualism and rituals. While every day need should be fulfilled by the use of technology and by developing social, economic and political institutions.

Thus far, I have expressed my thoughts on India which sound prescriptive. Now I intend to record some of the experiences of teaching at a comprehensive school in East London. There was very little teaching in the way I was trained or I had practised in the past. The children were of mixed ability, different races and gender. Some of them were determined to study and work hard, while others thought they were being forced into the school system. They were not only anti-academic but also noisy and disruptive. Some- times, I was dismayed and disappointed at the classroom atmosphere and considered that the concept of education was miles away from the practice. The education as a source of development of mind, spirit and morality was a mere utopia. The schools were merely child minding places. Though the education system was child centred. The child had to take an initiative and had to do his work. Every child was given individual attention, encouragement and sometimes punishment. There was, however, little scope for talking sensibly in a class- room atmosphere where the teacher could explain the theme. The children could, nevertheless, copy any thing from the board and answer questions from the text- books.

In my opinion the whole purpose of schooling was not to produce intellectuals but to provide education as a social service and educate children for citizenship so that they could play their part in the social and economic life of the country. From this point of view, it was not a bad idea to educate children in large comprehensive schools. This, however, did not accomplish the real aims and objectives of education for personality development. A child stayed at school for about eleven years, and yet entered his adult life as an uneducated person. What amazed me most was that some children could not read or write. Not because of any language problem but because they had either escaped the attention of the teacher in the class or were not encouraged to read and write at any stage. I thought that such children should be encouraged to write any thing. To my satisfaction some of them began to show improvement in their performance.

A host of subjects were taught at a comprehensive school. The basic aim of comprehensive education was to provide a choice. The whole system was geared to achieve uniformity and equality of opportunity. It was a good concept but its non- academic approach could not have positive results. I would have liked to see an educational atmosphere in the classroom, children listening attentively to their teachers and participating in discussions, It was not contradictory to the principles of liberty or individuality. It was advantageous for all and the real meaning of education could be discovered and cohesion between school and society could be established.

It was strange that a country which has had free and compulsory primary education for over one hundred years, still had three million people who could not read or write (in 1973) especially among the working class. Some young people knew that as manual workers they could earn more money than some educated folk. There was, therefore, little incentive to acquire formal qualification. The middle class strata had moved out of the inner London boroughs. The place, where I started to teach, was predominantly a working class area, with a high proportion of ethnic minority groups whose children had their own problems. The teachers were themselves divided and did not make a coherent group in order to provide a good service. The right wing racist teachers were unhappy to see ethnic minority children in the school. The moderates tolerated the situation but they were not prepared to promote multiculturalism. The radicals and the trade unionists were, however, prepared to eradicate racism in the school.

The difficulties, however, remained in the education system. In the early years' of a child's education, especially in the Infant schools, emphasis was laid on playing. Very little effort was made to encourage a child to read a book or create an interest in books. Consequently some children became escapers and went undetected. They were later neglected because of large groups and for the benefit of willing and intelligent children. Consequently, the poor child started his social life without any comprehension or knowledge of books. Some obviously found it difficult to adjust themselves in the developed industrial society. A personal approach studded with tact and tolerance on the part of a teacher could, however, have brought fundamental changes in the education methods and communication methods.

In February 1974, the general election took place in Britain. The election issues were inflation and the miners' strike which brought down the Conservative government of Edward Heath. It also produced a new situation in British politics. A minority Labour government was formed after fifty years. By now I also gained a reasonable experience of teaching in London and had come in contact with the facts and events of school life, attitudes and behaviour of pupils. But I did not want to go in to details about these topics. I would rather like to write about "Happiness", a philosophical theme and what could make me happy? It was very difficult to define happiness. With rationality and maturity, however, I could be happy. A job satisfaction, fulfilment of necessities, healthy environment at home, a good social atmosphere and even changes in behaviour in accordance with the circumstances could make me happy. I had no desire to be a big man or a rich man or accomplish a high social status. I believe that the society was an organic whole. Therefore, every person was important and had a role to play. Any parochial cause should not degrade human beings.

I found it difficult to work at that school despite some support. I, therefore, decided to leave the school. I did not regret it, though I would miss some friends. I spent only one year at that school. It was not bad but it was not easy either. It was hectic despite the fact that it was near our house. My summer holiday started in despair and dissipation but I was not sorry to have left that school where I had become disenchanted. I was pretty hopeful that I would get a job before too long. I made many applications but attended only three interviews and was selected by the Inner London Education Authority.

Before I proceed any further, I must write some thing about my beliefs. Though I am not a superstitious person, I am inclined to believe the dictates of the stars. I did not want to become a fatalist, and yet I would like to record two forecasts predicted on my birth stars.
'Throughout August and September, the influence of planet mars was strong in your solar horoscope. This would give you "get up and go"; incline you to have to take up initiative. This applied especially in the business sphere. Due to discontent prevalent in recent months, you might try to force a business change or to start up a new activity or association which would be fruitful.' Of course, through out August this was the position.

I would be sitting and thinking and would get up, write letters, do decoration, go somewhere and do something or the other. At times, I was sad but I remained active. I was prepared to take quick decisions and act upon them.

The second prediction at a later date stated that 'throughout the remainder of September, set out to have a good time, to strengthen present relationships and develop new ones, to create good will. Some contacts and activities could be useful to you career wise and this was a time when, if you were outgoing, there would be a pleasing response from your companions'. This also proved right. I received four letters and two visits from friends in London. There was ample opportunity for social contacts, which proved advantageous. I joined an inner London School on 19th September as a full time teacher.

I used to travel from east London to south London to teach at the School. It took me more than an-hour to reach there. I had to take a bus, tube, change to another tube line at Monument station and again at Stockwell station, for another tube and then bus and walk about 200 yards. The school was generally fine. The department was well organised and well equipped. The other teachers were good and accommodating. There was an understanding between them and me. This was the sole basis of our friendship, attraction and my desire to work there. I still thought of moving to teach at a college. I, nevertheless, enjoyed myself at the school. I organised the teaching and liked the students. No major problems arose. Apart from teaching, I began to take part in academic administration. I was consulted about my timetable and classes, I would like to teach.

The Head of Department of Business and Public Administration, at Eastham College, also wrote that he would like to see me at the College for a talk. When I went to see him, he offered me a part-time teaching job in Economics which I accepted because it was an evening class on Mondays. I agreed to teach this class. At the Eastham College, I taught Economics and the Business Environment to ACCA (Association of Certified Accountants) Foundation class. I enjoyed it very much. I had to prepare lecture notes on Saturday morning, which was time consuming, but awarding. I had mature students between the ages of 19 and 42, from bachelor young people to married with children. The students also participated in discussions. This teaching continued only for two terms.

I, therefore, concentrated on my school teaching and some reading and writing. As a part of school fieldwork, I had a chance to stay in an English countryside with school students. The school had a rural study centre at Etchingham in Sussex. It was hectic but pleasant. We visited a few villages and farms. One of the farms was special in Britain. The cows were given artificial ancilation and were kept under special heating conditions. They gave birth to calves in nine weeks. The artificial breeding system was new to me. The cows at that farm were worth about twenty thousand pounds each in 1975.

CHAPTER 2

Road to Progress, 1976-85

The early 1976, witnessed a change in the leadership of the Labour party. I had thought that this would not alter the situation and policies would remain the same. But in May something strange bubbled up, possibly, due to a weak leadership. Such a predicament had not been seen for many years. A debate, in the House of Commons on 'Immigration and Race Relations,' aroused doubts in the hearts of the British people. The politicians and the mass media exploited it to their advantage. The newspapers were breathing fire and fury. The British news media often dramatized things. This time they behaved irresponsibly. People kept their heads down but arguments continued. This proved damaging for the society. Uncertainty persisted. A gloomy picture was painted of future of Britain. This became a political issue and in such circumstances minority communities suffered most. They suffered in many fields –social, economic and environmental. A strange whirl had been created in the smooth running of the social situations.

In these circumstances the sensitive issue of immigration flared up. Enoch Powell and Bob Mellish spoke of a possibility of rivers of blood in the cities of Britain. The media started a psychological attack. This also led to a belief of mass exodus from the Indian sub-continent. It was, however, unfounded as there was no primary immigration from India or other countries. But a secret report by a British foreign office official further fuelled the situation as it indicated that everyone from the sub-continent was planning to come to England.

The British people were very fond of praising themselves and wanted to be identified as the most tolerant and civilized society. The incidents of May 1976 portrayed a different picture, which showed that the minorities were not acceptable in Britain. Damages were inflicted on Asian properties. On a Friday night, two Arab students were attacked and killed in east London. After a week an Indian- youth was brutally knifed and killed in Southall, Middlesex. This boiled the blood of the Indian community in London. At the same time it put fear and suspicion in their hearts and minds. They even stopped walking alone at night and did not allow their children to play on the streets and in parks. Eventually, people decided to take action. Some youths vowed to take revenge. For the first time the Asian community was united for a cause. The Asian diplomats were united. The Indian press gave a correct and full coverage of the incidents. Some responsible British politicians came forward and deplored the state of affairs.

In the mean- time, other pressing incidents came to light and the matter began to subside. Nevertheless, this was not so simple and easy, but some calm emerged. The modality had changed a great deal. In the course of time, the heat of the matter also receded. Efforts were made to improve race relations especially by the socialists, the Labour party and the trade unions.

I now return to another theme related to my job. I have now started my third year at the school. I enjoyed my last two years and things improved a little in the field of discipline- especially with the younger students. Some older boys remained adamant and unchanged. Some other problems remained unresolved. In April 1976, I was accepted at the Brunel University to study for the Advanced Diploma in Education. This course was held on Wednesday afternoon, from 2pm to 7pm. I, therefore, needed some time off from the school. I brought this to the notice of the persons concerned. I was promised that care would be taken in designing my time table in order to give me free time to attend the classes at Brunel. But when the time table came out, I was given one last period free. This was unhelpful. I spoke to the Head of department and the Director of Studies. But no useful result emerged. I decided to use the only time available, though it hurt me a lot. It was hectic to attend lessons without proper time allocation. I was often late at the University.

At the end of 1976, my promotion prospects were marred through dirty politics and my study for the Advanced Diploma in Education at the Brunel University was hampered. The school did not keep its promise to relieve me to attend my lessons. On a Friday in November, the Head of Department came to the dining hall where I was having my dinner. He first sat down with me and then asked me whether I was applying for the post of Deputy Head of the Department. I asked for his opinion. He said that 'You should be kidding with yourself, if you thought that you would get that job'. I was shocked and surprised and told my friends and colleagues of this incident. The Headmaster himself said that he was untactful. If he did not want to support you, he should have kept quiet. The former Deputy Headmaster felt that an injustice had been done to me. Any way I did not waste much time on this. The National Union of Teachers obtained permission for me to attend my course at Brunel. I also decided not to work with a biased man and was transferred to Economics and Business Studies Department at the same school.

In January 1977, we were burglared again. Now we decided to move out of the area altogether. We looked for a house in north and west London and decided to move to Bedford Park, Chiswick. The house was not in a good shape but after renovation and redecoration it became quite attractive and comfortable. We moved to live in Chiswick in August 1977. Children were admitted in new schools and offered subjects of their choices. This part of London was very quiet. It was an inner city suburb. Parks on both sides of our street and of course the churches. It was perhaps ten years earlier when I used to travel from North Ealing to the city of London, I thought of living in this locality. Its quiet atmosphere and greenness appealed to me.

Bedford Park was the first inner city suburb not only in London but in the world. Some famous writers, judges, politicians and actors lived here.

Apart from front and back gardens, it also had good transport service. It was served by Chiswick Park station and Turnham Green station. Bus services on both sides of our Avenue could take us to central London as well as to outer London suburbs.

The year 1977, also witnessed a change of government in India when Mrs. Indira Gandhi and the congress party lost power after thirty years. A new party took charge under Morarji Desai. In Pakistan Prime Minister Zulfikar Ali Bhutto was deposed in a coup de tat and power passed into the hands of the military junta.

Every- thing was fine at school. We had a first year parents evening. I was first year tutor that year, though I did not teach my tutor-set. I had an opportunity to meet parents. I was a bit surprised to find that the boys did talk about me at their homes. Some parents mentioned it to me and next morning, the Housemaster sent me a note, expressing his thanks. He also stated that many parents had praised and appreciated whatever I had done for their children. Many children showed their gratitude at Christmas by giving me cards and season's greetings and wishing me all happiness in the New- Year.

I had hardly looked back to my early schooling. But at this time there were some occasions to recollect and think of my childhood. I also talked about it twice to my Advanced Level Economics students, how I left my primary school and my village at the age of nine and took my degree at eighteen. There was nothing fascinating about it and I felt no emotions. Others perhaps received some encouragement from such an account. The memories were vague. It was difficult to recall those scenes and incidents. Only some major happenings recurred in my mind.

The partition of India and the creation of Pakistan in 1947 meant that a large number of Hindus and Sikhs had to leave Western Punjab. They became refugees because the movement of people was not planned. Both the major political parties, the Congress and the Muslim League, agreed to look after the interests of the minorities in their countries. But violence in Punjab made it impossible for non-Muslims to live there. Many officials and local people also forced the Hindus and Sikhs to leave their villages and cities where they had lived for many generations and centuries. They left without their assets and belongings. Some of them had to leave in the clothes they were wearing.

On arrival of people from the Punjab, the Uttar Pradesh government and Delhi provided them residence and made arrangement for food and clothing in the short term and their rehabilitation in the long term. School classes were extended and some new tutor groups (classes) were created and students were accepted without school leaving certificates. Such a situation also arose at Khurja in UP, where my eldest brother was a student at a Higher Secondary School. He found out that there were places in the 1st year of the secondary school. He felt that I could be accepted as one of the students there and that I could cope with the academic work. Despite the fact that I had not completed my primary education and had not acquired sufficient knowledge and skills. This also left a few gaps in my learning especially in Mathematics.

I had become disenchanted with the village primary school because the teachers kept me in the lower classes, though I knew my numbers, time table, halves, three quarters, two and a half times. I could read, write and do maths. I almost taught these things to students in the school as a class captain. The school teachers, however, promoted students into next class not on the basis of qualification or passing the examination but on payment of five rupees. If some one paid five rupees every six months, a student could do two classes in one year. My father paid some money to teachers who considered, the payment was for my siblings. My father worked out, two rupees for me and three rupees for my sister and five rupees for elder brother were paid to teachers.

In July 1948, a new teacher arrived at our village primary school and he asked me to bring five rupees for my promotion into the upper class. I told my father of the teacher's demand. But he (my father) told me that he had already paid the money as in the previous years. I passed on this message to my teacher. I also told him that I had scored 98% marks in the examination, so why should I be required to pay any money. The teacher did not like my reply and was angry with me. He canned me once for answering him back.

On that day, I went home for lunch and never returned to school. I offered to go to a school in the nearby village. But that was not acceptable to my family. They questioned as to how would I travel alone to another village every day? Over the weekend, my eldest brother came home from Khurja. He advised the family that I should be sent to the city with him, which they did. I went to live in the city. I prepared my self for some tests and started to learn English. However, it was not that easy as it sounded. While waiting for admission at school, I used to stay at my brother's room and practice English writing and reading. One day when my brother returned from school, as he was a High School student himself, I was excited that I had learned writing small and big alphabets; I tried to show him, my written work in English. Without looking at the writing book, he slapped me and planted his fingers on my cheek, which became red. He also shouted at me that I was behaving like a child (and not like a nine year old man who had just left his parents, siblings, friends and the village). I was surprised at his behaviour and thought that I left my village school because I was canned by the teacher. Now after getting a slap on the cheek where shall I go? When we went to the village at the week-end, I told my grandfather about the incident. My grandpa told my brother not to hit me again.

At the High School, I was interviewed by an English teacher, a Hindi teacher and the class tutor. I was accepted to study at my brother's school. There was only one other student I knew, out of one thousand students at the school. I, nevertheless, started to attend my classes. One day, my village fellow was not in the class and I returned home because I felt lonely in the crowd. My brother asked me why was I back home so early? I simply replied that my friend was not in the class.

This was the beginning of my new life in city. I had to leave my village, my family and friends in order to pursue my education. In the course of time, I became used to this life and made some new friends. I developed good relationship with my peer group and teachers at the School and later at the College with my lecturers. I stayed at Khurja for nine and a half years. After the Bachelor of Arts (BA) degree, I did BT (Bachelor of Teaching), a teachers training at Kirodimal College, Bhiwani (Haryana) and taught at Chirawa High School in Rajasthan for more than three years and in Delhi for more than one a half years.

However, in class 8th, I could not do my annual examination because of long illness. I had scored good marks in the Half-yearly examination. I was, therefore permitted to proceed into 9th class. But I was out of touch with my studies in the intervening months and lost interest in many subjects including science. I chose 'Arts' subjects for my High School studies. My class friends questioned me for not studying sciences because most clever students opted for science subjects. My giving up of science subjects closed my doors for medicine and engineering courses which perhaps I wanted to do. Thus my fate was sealed at the tender age of twelve. While all doors were shut for me to study these courses, a window of opportunity remained open for me to study Social Science and Literature. Eventually, I studied thirty one subjects at various levels, from secondary education to Diploma and Degree level at colleges and universities.

+   +   +   +

Returning to the chronology of my life in London, the year 1978, I had a peaceful start.

I made my application for study leave. It was accepted with some amendments. I preferred the changes because I could concentrate for about five weeks on the examination work. I had to accept only thirty five days rather than forty days normally allowed in such situations. The only astonishing thing was that the Head of my former Department told me that the Headmaster had said that with this type of leave, he could not provide me a good testimonial. I did not quite believe him. When I saw the Headmaster, he did not give me that impression. I let the matter slip, assuming that I had behaved most conscientiously and professionally.

At the University of Brunel, I submitted my essays on comprehensive schools in Grouping and Curriculum Innovation, and for Educational

Technology. The other major decision I took in January 1977, was to buy three years added service for pension purposes. I would pay monthly instalments for the next ten years and three years- service would be added to my total teaching service at the end of my career.

I had also been pondering over the world scene, which had been the consequence of the decisions of great many years. The post- war trend had led nationalism to its peak. There had also been a move towards secularism. Surprisingly the states of Israel and Pakistan were created while the world was moving towards secularism. Racial politics was also gaining ground when the world was becoming smaller and there was hardly any country, which had a homogenous society. Britain itself was not a one race, one culture country. The South- East England and London had only one third of its population of British origin. It was still to be seen whether Britain would become a multi-cultural society, in the real sense where the people of different backgrounds could have equality of opportunity. So far it had been unsuccessful. On many occasions people from minority groups had been infuriated. Some political parties and pressure groups were amending their attitudes and approach, for their own ends to win the minority community's votes and sympathy.

In January 1978, the question of race and immigration came up again on the political scene of Britain. I did not know who started it. Possibly the mass media was trying to stir up, because there was no other theme for a debate in the community or possibly the Conservative party introduced it as an election gimmick in order to win the right wing votes because they had no alternative economic and social policies. The economic performance of the Labour government had been excellent. The value of sterling had begun to recover and the reserves were up by a billion pounds.

It was characteristic of the right wing conservatives to call themselves religious but the party was dogmatic and intolerant towards the minorities. It disliked any changes. From this point of view and bearing in mind that the British society was mainly a conservative society, the hostility towards the minorities was not unusual. This theme dominated the newspapers' front pages for many days. The Labour party totally rejected the idea of further control of immigration at that time because it was unrealistic and impossible, without inconveniencing the family life of many people resident in Britain as only the dependents were being allowed into this country.

I had my suspicions on the whole issue. It was possibly a question of cultural differences and many misunderstandings. India had accomplished economic progress during the recent past and India was now the 8th industrial power in the world. It had achieved not only self-sufficiency in agricultural products and some industrial goods but had acquired competitive advantage in the world markets, though her voice was not heard as loudly as it should have been. The Indian politicians had proved that they were fairly radical and determined at the same time. They were faced with gigantic problems on all fronts. Yet economic progress was visible. It was hoped that this could continue in the future. Then her people would be respected everywhere and not made a tool in electioneering idiosyncrasy in some countries.

I have mentioned something about the British conservatism. I have always thought that people from north Indian state of Uttar Pradesh were conservative in their conduct. They did not want to bring drastic alterations in the social structure. They did not even want to move from their homes or villages. If they went to other places to live, they had always pined for their past. They were traditionalists but they were not hostile towards their minorities, which had always been accepted as their own and as a part of society. Is there any similarity between these two groups of Uttar Pradesh (UP) and Britain? Perhaps, very little. The Indian conservatism taught tolerance but the British conservatism was possibly intolerant at that time. Both were, however, religious minded. The British conservatism had hardly ever initiated change. The Indian conservatives had provided leadership for change. Nationalism sprang up and grew in UP and it had provided six of the seven Prime ministers of India. In short, the Indian state of Uttar Pradesh was traditionalist but had witnessed modification. People were religious but no single religion dominated the state. Perhaps they believed in an organic concept of society.

I had been looking into the relationship between education and economic development with special reference to developing countries. The education contributed to economic growth and the economic base of society could be changed with education. Some countries could, however, be faced with a dilemma and might raise the aspirations of people but could fail to provide all facilities for education as well as employment for their educated people. The mass demand for education and increased educational provisions were associated with diversion in occupational structure and proliferation of middle class values. There could be a down grading effect of educational qualifications. This could also alienate people and threaten the fabric of society. A challenge to traditional culture and onset of modernisation might also lead to a break down of social system. Education though good for society might lead to rapid changes with unwanted consequences. The education leading to unemployment could also be socially and economically wasteful if not disastrous. The role of education should, however, be modernisation and to maintain traditional culture.

Personally, I had rarely made any permanent friends. It was not that I had a set pattern of life or that I held certain values. Whenever my views differed with those of others we fell apart, though I always attempted to respect others' opinion, I did not accept things being repeated and repeatedly said to me. The talk of money drove me away from comradeship. Such views had sometimes made me think about myself. It was seldom that I sat down to assess my own personality and characteristics. Whenever I experienced alienated from others, I asked myself whether I was selfish or had an inflexible attitude of mind. I could not find an answer to this question. I left it to others to judge.

I had, however, thought differently because of the environmental effects and my peculiar mixture of education. The thoughts of great philosophers had left some influence on me. Despite the fact that many others and I had been brought up under the same cultural conventions, we had interpreted the philosophy differently and possibly a range of ideals, both oriental and occidental, had guided me. This difference created difficulty in correlating our views and ideas. This was, nevertheless, a controversial theme and I had no intention of developing it further. I fear that it could take me away from realism to the world of imagination and fantasy.

In March 1978, the ILEA school's sub-committee published a report on 'Multi-Ethnic Education'. It reflected on the problem of minority groups and especially the children in the inner London area. This report was studied by many of us. We did not like the use of the term 'ethnic' because this could relate to racial groups or creed. My response was that people would not like to use multi-religion and polytheistic religion simultaneously. The question, however, was whether this word could be used in every day expression? Could we move towards a plural society and maintain ethnic groupings at the same time? As a matter of fact minorities provided the foundation for a plural society. The problem was how to stop one minority from exploiting the other minorities and lay the sound foundation for equality of opportunity in order to make a valuable contribution for economic development and social change.

The new 'Nationality Act' in Britain posed a major conundrum. It affected the rights of the Commonwealth citizens. The rights of children, born in Britain, could be withheld only because their parents were from non-white Commonwealth nations. The non- recognition of ethnic groups as a part of society could alienate them. This could also lead to all kinds of frustration and discrimination in housing, finance, education and employment. In such circumstances, the concept of a multicultural society was unattainable. Such a society could be accomplished only through education. An emphasis on cultural diversity was vital. The different cultures could not be studied independently but should be studied in conjunction with each other. This would eventually create a common-culture.

The teaching of social sciences and Humanities would facilitate this transition from a monolithic culture to multiculturalism. This, however, required an understanding and open-mindedness. We could not live in a closed society in this supersonic age when the distance had been narrowed and countries had drawn nearer. It was essential to develop the educational system in order to match these changes. We would have to gear our socio-economic and educational methods in order to accomplish our aims and objectives for establishing a multicultural society.

In May 1978, the English Department at the School (ILEA) invited me to talk about India. I first spoke about the two great civilizations which sprang up in India some five thousand years ago. One of them, the Indus-Valley civilization was famous for its trade, administration and architecture. The excavations of Mohan-Jodaro and Harappa towns in the states of Sindh and West Punjab, suggested that the people of these cities were fond of art, painting and sports. They had a good drainage system, swimming-pools and squared-houses. The other civilization flourished in the plains of the Ganga and Jamuna rivers. The people of these areas were literary minded and created the Vedas, Upanishads, the famous epics of the Ramayana and the Mahabharata, and of course the Gita. Many Gphilosophers, poets and mathematicians contributed to these cultures. Taxila in the Punjab, Banaras and Prayag (Allahabad) in Uttar Pradesh and Ujjain in Madhya Pradesh along with Patliputra in Bihar were the great seats of learning and had institutions of higher education. Sanskrit was the main language of these people.

The recorded history of India, however, began with the founding of the Maurayan Empire. Prior to that, city states and village republics had existed in India. The villages were not isolated from the main stream of social and economic life. India had no political unity but a common culture existed from Kashmir to Kerala and from Gandhar (now in Afghanistan) to Assam. People followed the teachings of the Vedas and attempted to seek a reality of life through discussions, thinking and meditation. Chandra Gupta Mauraya, the founder of the peacock throne, was the first emperor of the united India. His grandson, Emperor Asoka, was an excellent administrator. He turned to Buddhism in the later part of his life. He sent missionaries abroad to South East Asia, West Asia, Mongolia and central Asia. He dedicated his wealth to spread Buddhism.

After two hundred years of Asoka's death, however, there was a revival of the old Vedic religion, which had sometimes been identified with Hinduism. Buddhism and Sikhism were the offshoots of Hinduism.

Hinduism was not just a religion. It was a way of life. Any one person or a group of people did not found it. It had existed since the dawn of civilization. It was sanatan dharma (an eternal religion). Ancient Hindus had thought that their religion had always been there. It had no official beginning. It was a religion because it had values and rituals. It embraced social customs and traditions. All aspects of human life from birth to death and beyond were discussed in it. The main beliefs included cosmology, the doctrine of Karma, the concept of varnasharam-four stages of life and the philosophy of adhirakiveda or competence. My colleagues, in the English Department, appreciated this talk.

I had often believed that education psychology was mainly concerned with the theories of learning. But at Brunel University, where I studied for the Advanced Diploma in Education, I discovered that the study of 'personality' and knowledge of the 'self' had become an important theme for education psychology since the Second World War. Self was the product of social interaction and one perceived oneself as others saw him or her. Sometimes he/she had to adopt another person's role. Personality had been looked in many ways, traits and types. But Eyesenck's classification into introverts and extraverts, neurotics and stable person's, division of attitudes into conservatives and radicals, tender- minded and tough-minded, had been quite popular. His classification of 'character' into choleric, melancholic, phlegmatic and sanguine, appealed me most. I had also been looking into the attitudes, their formation and adoption, anxiety, drives and motivation and their academic achievement, personality development and so on. Those who had high self esteem of themselves tended to be adjustable. Inferiority complex, self- esteem, self- rejection led to maladjustment. I also attempted to analyse my own self-conception. I thought, I was an introvert but creative.

I had an opportunity to do a participant observation. I looked into the classroom action, reaction, between pupils and teachers and between pupils and pupils. This was a good experience for me. I made some objective observations but analysed them in a subjective fashion. I spent some time on thinking and working on educational planning with special reference to teachers training in England. I still believed that education had an important role to play in transforming the society. It, however, depended on what type of education was provided to students and how they received and responded to it?

The educational planning was not merely concerned with more places in higher education. It was related with the changes in the system, structure, curriculum and context. It could be looked in three related perspectives-the social demand approach, the manpower planning approach and the rate of return approach. As a country becomes rich, it could afford leisure time and costs. The demand for more education would, therefore, go up. Education was demanded for consumption as well as for improving the status and prestige. It was vital that specialists conducted planning and the planners should include intellectuals, philosophers, teachers, political-leaders and bureaucrats. In the advanced countries, planning affected the field of higher education in order to produce highly qualified people, though there was no co-relation between higher qualification and occupation. Qualified people were, moreover, required for professional jobs.

The education planning was not an easy task. It faced many social, political, economic and financial constraints. The efforts should, therefore, be made to overcome these impediments. The aims and objectives of planning should be clearly defined. The educational objectives should portray the society's commitment to the future. These ideas should embrace basic human-values. The planning should be short, medium or long term according to circumstances. A broad educational system should prevail. The science and engineering students should be taught Humanities and Social sciences; and the Humanities students should be taught natural sciences and technology at undergraduate level.

The complex problem of the changing world could be solved by an understanding and extensive knowledge in all fields and by an efficient and effective education. All the resources including human resources were scarce in the world. They should, therefore, be utilized in the cost effective way. The education system should produce the skills required by the economy and the society. Education should not, however, be treated as an extension of the 'on the job training'. It had other aims to accomplish. We should make full and efficacious use of the educated people. Under utilization was misallocation of resources and it would mean lesser returns from an investment in human capital.

The winter of 1979, witnessed the coldest weather in Britain for fifteen years. It snowed many times in the early months of this year. The temperature reached below freezing point and sometimes −8C at night. This kind of weather continued for two months. The country saw almost a general strike when the tanker drivers, the lorry drivers and the public employees took industrial action, and supported the Ford car workers at Dagenham. The strikes remained the headlines in the newspapers during this period. It challenged the five-percent norm for wage rise decided by the government. It was argued by the government that the country could afford only that much money. But the people of this country hardly realized that. The wages were rising by about sixteen-percent, which raised the rate of inflation. The main problem, however, was the lack of productivity and the lack of industrial growth. The workers were possibly not aware of all the situations and old technology was being used.

Britain's competitive position in the international market had deteriorated because of poor industrial performance. Britain had hardly ever been able to compete with other countries in the goods market. It had always had the balance of trade deficit. Invisible trade had often paid for goods and commodities, thus achieving the balance of payments. The British government intended to solve the problem of inflation through Monetary and Fiscal policies but these were secondary measures and were not substitutes for an Incomes policy. The government was trying to move towards a planned economy. The free collective bargaining and trade union powers racked the plan. This sort of industrial environment was unacceptable to the people of Britain. The government was blamed for industrial unrest. It, therefore, lost popularity. It was being argued that unless some thing drastic happened the Labour government would lose the general election that year.

There was nothing unusual in India at the end of the 1970s. But across the borders in Pakistan, Iran and other places various incidents were happening. It looked as if the old fashioned fanaticism was returning to these societies. The strangest thing was that these countries opposed change and progress. It was a human nature not to accept sudden changes. The technological progress had surpassed the social progress. In Pakistan, the life of Prime Minister Zulfikar Ali Bhutto was in the hands of the army council. It would be a pity and disaster for democracy if he was hanged. He was the man who worked twenty-four hours, a day and brought his country out of turmoil and was leading the nation towards economic and social progress. He was an intellectual and he failed to feel the pulse of the people in power. Later, he was hanged. It was difficult to identify the influence of foreign powers in his down fall and tragic end.

In Iran, a revolution took place through a civil war when thousands of people died. The people of Iran contravened the introduction of any new methods in social and political life. It was being argued that perhaps a republic would be set up there, as the Shah had become a symbol of Western influence and a puppet of the West. He had abdicated his responsibilities towards his people and his culture. An Islamic revolution succeeded in Iran and the Shah had to flee the country in April 1979.

In Britain, the general election was imposed due to a defeat of the government on a 'no confidence' vote. Prices, inflation and unemployment remained the main themes on the election agenda. All the major parties presented their arguments to the nation. The Labour party had many constructive policies but it lost the general election and the Conservative party won with a substantial majority. For the first time, Britain had a woman Prime minister.

During the summer months of 1979, I spent some time on thinking of the international scene. There was a great deal of competition not only in economic field but also in the fields of politics and culture. The western culture was dominant in the world. The other cultures looked like shadows. It was possibly due to their failure to maintain political power and enlighten social customs. For example during the last twenty years the dowry system had spread like a plague in Indian communities on the subcontinent and abroad. Surprisingly, the educated people had shown no understanding, changes in behaviour or an inclination to challenge this arrangement. They identified themselves with the society and were a part of this practice. They had accepted this unfair tradition. It was ironic that the higher the qualification of a young-man, more dowries was demanded by his parents. Perhaps they believed that they had educated their sons for a good marriage and more dowries and not for a high paid job. They did not understand the basic concepts of cost- benefit analysis of education and the rate of return approach.

Perhaps there was something wrong with the education system in India, which did not prepare young people for a professional and adult life but it encouraged them to lead a life in a society where their parents and grandparents had lived in serfdom, slavery and ignorance. I did not know whether I could call it ignorance or bankruptcy of ideas among the young who had to depend on their parents for financial support because of high unemployment and low incomes. But they could think carefully before taking a decision regarding marriage. The young people hardly had any say in this custom where parents of both parties did all the arrangements. It would, however, weaken the society and would become another custom like the 'suttee' when the woman was cremated live on the death of her husband. It could lead the society into darkness. I had no intention to write any more on this subject because it had no value, no ideology and no philosophy. It was ephemeral but its effects were permanent. I, therefore, wished for a strong political and legal frame work and action against the dowry system.

I would, however, like to write something about London. The glittering lights of London airport portray something about this great city but a full illustration was required to understand this conurbation. Built on the clay hills, London was divided by the river Thames into north and south, stretching many miles in each direction. Founded by the Romans as Londonium, it had expanded over the centuries. The various gates show that the Londoners had lived within the city walls, which was now known as the city of London. The old Tower and the markets surrounding it were the witnesses of this truth.

Even Hackney was a farming village in the Elizabethan times (16th Century). But London started to grow in the 18th Century and it had spread over 40 miles from east to west and 30 miles from north to south. It contained the glory of the British power on the world scene in the 19th Century and the decay in the later half of the 20th Century.

The most unique features of this city were the self-contained towns as if they were designed to serve their population. The city itself remained important as a business and finance centre with the Bank of England, the Stock Exchange, foreign banks, Insurance companies, the customs and excise department's headquarter, and the port of London to facilitate import and export of goods. Before the great fire of London in 1644, it had one hundred and sixty churches. The St. Paul's Cathedral and 43 churches still attract pilgrims to this city. These churches reflected the styles of English architecture of the years gone by.

The sister city of Westminster, was a political and diplomatic centre with High Commissions and embassies of many countries within its boundary. It also had the Houses of Parliament, the Westminster abbey and the Buckingham Palace. London was a seat of the British government and the centre of the Commonwealth of Nations, which had over fifty members now (1990). It houses the courts and the Fleet Street where all the major newspapers of this country were published. The West-end of London was famous for shopping and theatres. A theatre in Holborn was almost two thousand years old. The Royal Shakespeare theatre was situated opposite the India House in Aldwych.

The parks of London provided open space in this city and there were parks within easy reach of the residents. Sometimes, London was called the city of parks, with Hyde Park – the largest in the world and the Kensington Gardens. The Regents Park, St. James Park, Richmond Park and the Kew Gardens were of unequal beauty and glamour. There were parks in every locality.

The museums and bridges were some of the other quintessence of London. The British Museum, the Albert and Victoria Museum, the Natural History Museum, the Science and Geological Museums, were tourist attractions. The bridges did not only serve as a link between the two sides of the city, many of them were unique in themselves. The Tower- Bridge could be lifted high in order to give way for the ships coming and going from the London-port. The London-Bridge and the Westminster-Bridge were of historical importance. The London eye had added to its beauty.

London was also a centre of learning. The University of London and its colleges cater for thousands of students from home and abroad. The Institute of Education, the London School of Economics, the University College, the Chelsea College and the Imperial College specialize in different branches of learning. In 1992, the Polytechnics were made new universities. The Westminster University, the Middlesex University, the South Bank University, the Greenwich University, the East London University and the Metropolitan University provided facilities in business education, technology, sciences and social sciences. With the expansion of education in Britain since the early 1960s, the City University and the Brunel University had been set up. The Kingston University, the West London University and the Surrey University were within easy reach of London.

The higher education was quite good in Britain. The students studied full-time, part-time, day-release and sandwich courses. The Degrees and Diplomas were very popular and about 70% of all graduates proceeded for a postgraduate degree or other kind of professional qualification. Though professional qualifications were undertaken for specific jobs, degrees were accepted in many occupations, especially in public administration and in general management. Many changes had been introduced from time to time to meet the demand of the changing circumstances.

The examination procedures had been altered at various levels. The Essay type examinations were not sufficient to judge the knowledge and understanding of students. The Multiple choice questions and short answer questions had been introduced in examinations. The continuous assessment and case studies form an integral part in some business studies courses. The syllabuses had been changed to meet the needs of the time. The multi-ethnic education was gaining some momentum in British schools and universities. It was thought that there was a need to study various cultures and countries. It was because of the presence of young people of different ethnic backgrounds in schools especially in London. London was no more a homogeneous Anglo-Saxon city. There were people of various races and creed permanently resident here. They had kept their own cultures which provided them identity and self-confidence. People, however, mixed at jobs and on social occasions. They attempted to understand each other. There was a growing tendency to respect one another and to treat each other as they were; rather than to force them to assimilate.

The young Asians were in a different dilemma. They attended English schools, came in contact with their peers, often ate western food and listened to western music. They started to follow the western culture, participated in the Christian religious functions and identified themselves as British. It hurts them if someone called them otherwise. They thus became totally alienated from their hereditary cultures and sometimes from their own parents, especially if they spoke different languages. They were unable to analyse or synthesise the two cultures. The children were unable to do so because of lack of experience. Their parents were unable to do so because of lack of education. As the children grew up, they had their own experiences and developed self-realisation. The majority of them accepted themselves what they were and possibly were ready to live between the two worlds without adopting either of them. They were not self- rejecting. Some of them even dug out their own cultural greatness.

The academic achievement of Indian children remained hindered (though in 1990 a study by the Research and Statistics Unit revealed that in inner London area the achievement of Indian children was the highest and was better than that of the British children). Most of the Indian students and their parents were ambitious and perhaps very ambitious and had high visions. Many of them wanted to get on the ladder through professional qualifications. Some certainly succeeded. Still the problems of many Indian children remained on many fronts. Language was the very first of them. They had to overcome the perceived notion of their teachers about them. Nevertheless, those who were determined to accomplish their goals and did not easily give up; they would succeed in their mission. It was often suggested that the children brought up in Britain would face less problems than the adults who came to live here. It was possible that they could get some understanding from the people in order to achieve recognition. They would have to prove themselves and would have to work hard.

The Indians were a hard working people and they were also ambitious. They respected their cultural values but they had also become a part of the British society and had adopted some aspects of western way of living. They had made a valuable contribution to the British economy, especially in small businesses and in running small shops, which were very demanding and needed to be kept open from 6am to 10 pm.

If the British society became multicultural in the real sense of the term, it would be easy for people to manifest themselves and make progress. Otherwise a struggle to exist would continue. The same applied to a family life. If the parents and children were closer to each other, there would be less deviation and more openness. It would lead to progress and development in all dimensions. Any kind of narrow attitudes would breed dissension, misapprehension and ill judgement. It would be grossly unfair to limit the scope of success. The cultural customs and traditions should remain alive and therefore, subject to change.

In July we went on a coach trip to Malvern Hills. The weather was not good. It rained throughout the day. We did not enjoy as much as we would have liked. However, we liked the physical landscape of the area. We also saw Oxford and High-Wycombe. There was nothing unusual about these towns. They had the same kind of buildings and shopping centres as we saw in London. There had always been common elements throughout this country, though peculiarities were visible in certain places. For example Oxford had the oldest university in the country and High-Wycombe had a picturesque view and also a historical importance. The English countryside was beautiful. There were hills, ridges, forests, slopes, fields and farms of various types in different regions of the country.

On 2nd September 1979, my father-in-law passed away in his village in North- India. I was shocked to read his untimely death but his death hurt my wife most. It took her some time to recover from the shock and bereavement. The agony of his departure from this world persisted for a long time. I had not met him quite often, but I liked him very much. He was very shy to communicate with others. He never hurt any body's feelings, and never troubled any one. His demands were limited. He was not materialistic. Neither was he religious or superstitious. He struggled all his life. His mother died when he was very young and was brought up by his grandmother and his father.

He started to work even before graduating High School. He was sincere and hard working and worked efficiently until his retirement. His means were small but he educated his children. One of them took an engineering degree from the famous Roorkee University in India and two others graduated from Agra University. He was a family man and liked and loved his children. In the later part of his life he used to travel from one son's residence to the others'. He tried to please and help them all. Whenever, there was a function at one son's place, he was there to guide. He was determined and flexible at the same time. I was surprised to see all his children and grandchildren at his village in April 1973, when we visited India. His simple words were his commands. He was not an authoritarian person, yet he had an influence over his family and kept all his children aligned to each other. He was perhaps a joining link in the family. He would be deeply missed by the members of his family who loved him so dearly.

The end of 1979, witnessed a change in the world. In Iran, students occupied the American embassy and kept fifty people there for many days. They wanted the extradition of the Shah in exchange for those people. On 26th December 1979, the Soviet army occupied Afghanistan. This outraged the West. The West was worried about the Soviet intentions. If the Soviets moved further south to the Gulf States, the West would lose its supplies of oil and raw materials. It was very dramatic. There were television programmes. The newspapers carried similar headlines. The Soviets argued that they went to Afghanistan on the invitation of the communist government of that country. It was maintained that the West would attempt to destabilise Pakistan and obtain a change in leadership. Perhaps another military ruler would replace General Zia Ul Haque. The democracy would not be allowed to return to that country.

India held her elections on 3rd and 6th January 1980. It brought Mrs. Gandhi and the Congress party back to power. The people were perhaps unhappy with the performance of the right wing parties which could not stay together for more than two and half years. The elections were democratically held. The law and order, and inflation were the major issues. India again proved as a mature democracy. The West did not welcome the return of the Congress party and Mrs Indira Gandhi to power. Her younger son Sanjay Gandhi was also elected to Parliament. He had been unpopular in the intellectual circles and in foreign countries as an immature politician but his country folk voted for him.

In March 1980, the Cambridge Institute of Education organized a course for 'A' Level Economics teachers. I was interested in attending such a course. I, therefore, applied and was offered a place. The Head of Business Studies and the ILEA Inspector for Business Studies also wanted me to attend this course. It was to be held from 7th to 9th of March at the Hargrave Hall, in Suffolk. I packed my things early in the morning on Friday and went to school as usual, taught my first lesson and then started my journey. It was a mild weather albeit cloudy. I boarded a British Rail train from Liverpool Street station to Cambridge. I read a book during the journey. At Cambridge, I changed a train for Bury St Edmunds.

When I reached Bury St. Edmunds, I enquired for a bus for Hengrave Hall but there was no bus service until 4pm. There were no taxis either. I, therefore, started to walk to the Hall. It was a beautiful countryside, flat agricultural land all around. Soon it began to rain. I was drenched in the rain. Initially I enjoyed the walk but, I got tired, though not totally exhausted. The road was very busy and there was no pavement or footpath to walk on. Often I had to walk on grass and then move back to the road. I saw the farmers ploughing their farms and the others doing their work.

There was a ford tractor factory on one side. That was the only industry in the area.

The Hargrave-Hall, was in the northeast of the village. It was a huge building which looked like a fort from the distance. It had medieval architecture. In fact it was an Abbey and a Church with open land at the front and woodland further ahead and a water pool near the entrance gate. I reached Hengrave hall just before 3pm and went straight to the reception. The receptionist took me to my room where I changed my wet clothes. I made a cup of coffee and drank it in the room. I placed ten pence near the coffee jug as a contribution though it was not necessary to pay for the coffee. I then rested until 4pm.

The teachers gathered in the Hall. There was no formal introduction. All the teachers were given badges to hang at the collar of their jackets. David Whitehead, of the London Institute of Education, talked about the press reports on 'A' level Economics and the book reviews. He had done quite a few reviews himself and told us what should be looked for reviewing a textbook. The teachers were then divided into five groups and were given several books to review, i.e. the syllabus, index, format and price. Our group took four books. We reviewed one book each and reported our findings to the whole group. From the other groups one or two persons reported about their findings. Most of the time people criticized the textbooks in one way or the other, but some of the books were acceptable to the majority, as 'A' level textbooks. These covered the whole syllabus and were suitable for all types of students.

We had dinner at 7pm. We were served bread and butter and tomato soup. I had two slices of bread. Then we were given mushrooms in cheese and peas. Between 8 and 9 pm, we watched a film on poverty in Britain in the 1970s, and another on banking called 'bargain'. This film was a sort of advertising for the banking services. Just after 9pm, I retired to my bedroom. I could not sleep well as it was a new place for me. I woke up many times during the night. Next morning, I changed at 7.30 am and was ready for beak-fast at 8.30.am. After the break- fast, we had a session on gaming and simulation. There were various games in Economics with which I was already acquainted. We played the manager and the union game on pay rises and on redundancy. Then we played the card game on national income. I won the round within five minutes. We did not have much free time.

The lunch was at 1pm. It was not very tasteful from my point of view. No question of a choice. I had some jam cake. Then we had talks on teaching Economics to our students in various institutions. Every one relayed his or her experience. We all had similar experiences throughout the country. At 2pm I phoned home to enquire about the wellbeing of the family. After 2pm, a resident at the Hall took us around the building and to the church. He explained that this place was built between, 1525 and 1538, at a cost of three thousand pounds. Now it would cost about ten million pounds to build the same building. Many famous people, including King Henry the VIII and Queen Elizabeth I, had stayed in the Hall. There used to be a village at that sight. It was later moved to a nearby location. We had tea at 4PM. I enjoyed the tea, possibly because the lunch was not successful and I was hungry. Then we were given talks on the use of overhead projectors and making of overhead jells. We saw a film on banking and the history of money. It was quite good and enjoyable.

After a few minutes break, we had dinner of soup, bread, salad and an orange. The food was no tasty at all, but the company of other teachers was good. We watched a couple of videos on Economics and business life. One of the videos was on the brewery firm 'John Young'. I was rather surprised to learn that the firm gave out its profits to the National Front but employed black workers. Perhaps to exploit them and to make them pay the subsidies to a political party, which was against them? On the surface, it gave an impression that it did not discriminate in employment against the black people. They were offered jobs as porters and truck drivers.

We finished early and I decided to go to my room rather than to go to the pub. I could not sleep well again. It was worse than the previous night. Next morning we had our break- fast at 9am. Then we had a session on multiple choice- questions, data response and syllabuses and examination techniques. The discussions were quite useful. We all participated and presented our views. After lunch at 1 pm we left for our homes.

After the Easter holiday in 1980, there were some changes in the school. The Deputy Headmaster became Headmaster at another ILEA school. The Head of Business Studies became acting deputy Headmaster. In the meantime, I was promoted to become the Acting Head of Business Studies. This increased some of my work load. I had to prepare the departmental timetable and lists for new fourth year. I also started to teach the existing 4th Year because my students had finished their examinations. I still had some free time. Some people liked this promotion and were glad that the authorities had recognized my work and appreciated it. I managed the work without any difficulty. My old department was not very happy with my promotion. The students started to behave slightly better. I presented my first departmental report to the governors. We were proud of our 'A' level and 'O' level results.

There was no problem either at home or at school. So I thought of visiting my parents in India. I had not seen them since May 1973. There was an unusual feeling and sentiment. I had hardly been close to my parents but at this time, I felt that something was missing in my life. I had invited them to London on many occasions but they could not come to see us. I informed every one that I was planning a visit to India. They were all pleased and perhaps equally excited as I was. They all wrote back except for one. I received some more letters from those who were not even informed. I told some of my friends in London. They were keen to have first hand knowledge of mother India on my return. Three of my friends decided to have Christmas dinner at an Indian restaurant. We went to a West End restaurant and enjoyed ourselves.

I left for Delhi on 22nd December 1980. I reached Heathrow airport a little early, checked in my luggage and went through the security and immigration. The immigration officer enquired about my old passport, which had my residence status. This old passport was, however, destroyed by me long time ago. The immigration officer told me that there could be some questions on my return but there should be no problems. The flight was late by about thirty minutes and then we started our journey through Paris and Kuwait. We reached Delhi airport at the scheduled time. At the Delhi airport it took us three hours to get out.

There, a number of my relatives were waiting for me. Some of whom, I did not expect and some I could not recognize. Some waited at the airport all-night and slept rough or did not sleep at all. I was overjoyed and forgot all inconvenience faced earlier. I had two choices; either I could go to my brother- in- law's house in New Delhi or to my younger brother's place. I decided to go to north east Delhi in order to meet every one there. In the afternoon, I went to my brother- in –law's house and stayed overnight with his family. I could not believe that two of his brothers came to see me for a few hours only and spent a lot of time on travelling.

One of my nephews asked me if I could make myself available to talk to his university friends. We agreed on a mutually convenient time. I reached his house at 8.30 pm on Wednesday. I first explained the constitutional growth in England. We also looked at the social structure, the political system, the educational system and the economy. It took us quite a while to analyse all these points. The curious lads asked questions on current affairs, the virginity test and the treatment of Indians by the British. I attempted to answer in an objective fashion. They were all pleased. We finished the discussion at about 10 pm.

As it was my fact-finding and visiting tour, I also spent a lot of time in travelling from one place to another. At some places I stayed only for a few hours and spent many hours in the trains and on the buses. I enjoyed the company of my relatives. The two weeks passed happily and without any major incident. If there was one, I did not care. I was to return to London on Tuesday 6th January 1981. I reached at Delhi-airport, on time but the plane was delayed by ten hours. I had never been bored so much in my life as I was bored on that day. I felt lonely in a crowd of thousands of people because there was no one to talk with. We were further delayed at Kuwait and I arrived in London on Wednesday instead of Tuesday. I did not come across any difficulty at Heathrow airport. My family was waiting there.

So we came home and relaxed and discussed my visit to India. Every one was delighted to get their gifts.

On 18th January 1981, I received a phone call and later a letter from the London Regional Examining Board (LREB) informing me, that I had been appointed an Economics examiner. I was delighted at the news and shared the news with some of my colleagues and friends who were very happy to hear that. Some colleagues had mixed feelings. The Academic Term from January to April was easy. Teaching went on smoothly. For the next year, we had been allocated three groups for the 4th year and 15 periods for the sixth form. We suggested for dividing our 5th form into three sections. Our proposal was accepted by the school authorities. It was hoped that the number of students would go up in the Department.

During the summer of 1981, violence flared up in Brixton, South London. The real cause of this act was never discovered. It was, however, suggested that the police's mishandling of the situation coupled with existing economic and social grievances led to this violence. The situation calmed down soon. In July, there were racist attacks in Southall, mainly on Asians and their property. This led to burning and looting. The Southall riots spread to other parts of London and other cities in England, including Liverpool and Manchester.

At one stage it looked like a concerted action because it had similarities of action. This was repeated again and again over the weekends in August. The police and the youth confronted each other. After a few weeks the situation calmed down. The government set up a Commission of Enquiry and appointed a minister for inner cities to look into the problems. These tactics were, however, used to ease the situation.

The month of September was busy. The number of students in the Business Studies Department increased because-of good results in public examinations. Our results were the best in the school and well above national average. In October, I went to the school centre at Etchingham, in East Sussex. I enjoyed my time there.

I also got involved in a project on 'Gandhi's humanitarian philosophy. Consequently, I started reading books on Gandhi and related topics. Many new ideas came to light. I became interested in this area of study. It looked like a drama, which was staged over three decades from Gandhi's return from South Africa until his death. However, I intended to confine my research to his humanitarian aspects, which were formed by the culmination of the Indian religions and Western thinkers.

At the school, I developed good relations with the new Headmaster. There was a great deal of resentment among teachers to his proposals to introduce changes in the running of the school. This was understandable, especially when teachers were used to different sort of leadership. But subjective criticism was bad and rejection of his ideas when they made sense was worse. Last week, he invited me to his office to inform me that my position had been upgraded to scale three. It was a good thing and recognition of my work in the Department. I was, however, not excited, as I had been when I was offered my first teaching job in London or even when I was appointed the Acting Head of Department. There would be some more money which will be properly used. This extra resource had arrived because I did not have my part-time job this year. This increased my faith in God and a desire to live a happy life. I had not been able to live to the basic principles of simple living and high thinking. My expenditure was on essential goods only.

The weather was bad in December 1981 and January 1982. So much snow was not seen in London and the South-East for a long time. In other parts of the county, it snowed heavily which was followed by flooding when the snow melted. It made life uncomfortable if not harsh. Strikes by the British rail workers had not affected me personally but it made travelling difficult. The tubes were over crowded. I hoped for the life to return to normal in the near future and the travelling to become easy.

On 8th March 1982, I had my interview for the Head of Business Studies at the school. Although I was Acting Head for more than two years it was essential to confirm it. The interview itself was not difficult except that the Deputy Head master insisted that I should know the names of as many students as I could. The Chairman of the Governors of the school thanked me for the marvellous work I had done so far and wished me well. Regarding resources, I suggested that we should buy a Phillips machine. They all laughed at this suggestion. We did not have any celebration at home or at school. A number of ideas kept on creeping in my mind. I could not sleep until 4am. I was not excited on becoming Head of Department. I followed the teaching of the Gita in not distinguishing between pain and pleasure and gain and loss and to remain ever green. This was a right dictum under the circumstances.

I still brooded over the circumstances and how the situations could change. Only a few years ago the Head of my old Department told me that I had no future at the school. I should, therefore, try somewhere else. I was the person to have produced the best results in the school and it was recognized by the authorities. It was with the blessings of the elders.

In 1969, when the world celebrated Gandhiji's birth centenary, I told myself and my family that if I had to follow some one, I would follow Mahatma Gandhi. In my early years, I had scarcely read on Gandhi, only one chapter on the 'Apostle of Peace' in High School in the early 1950s. 'Ahimsa in Education' at Intermediate level at college at Khurja and the poems, like 'Bapu' and 'Walk Thou Alone' by Tagore. But in 1960, I edited a magazine at Chirawa High School on Gandhi's birthday. All articles and poems were related to the Mahatma. I myself wrote an article on 'Gandhi and Education'. After that, there was a pause. In London, I read Louis Fisher's biography of Gandhiji.

However, during my Master's degree course, I devoted 25% of the course to study the Gandhian philosophy. Gandhi to me was a philosopher who had a vision for a different kind of society than the one which existed. It was hardly recognized by the Indian masses who worshipped him. Having obtained knowledge of the West and the East, I decided to combine these two together and examined Gandhi's thoughts on communal individualism in relation to the western spiritual thinkers- Tolstoy, Thoreau and Ruskin. A large amount of literature existed on Ahimsa, non-co-operation, programme for constructive work, and his social, moral and educational philosophies. I wanted to contribute something new.

I was extremely busy in the months of May, June and July 1982. I used to go to libraries, mainly the London University Senate-House Library, the India Office Library and Records. By the end of May, I finished the first draft of my project and it was ready to be read by the supervisor. I further revised the dissertation which included the suggestions and amendments made by my supervisor. I asked a secretary to type my dissertation and paid her whatever she asked. I enjoyed my work on Gandhi. I learnt a lot and I was convinced that small communities were the right basis for a good society.

Gandhiji believed this could be founded on a decentralised socio-economic system, finding expression in village republics. He presumed that man was moral and could be morally improved. For him there was no conflict between the individual and the social progress. He was against modernity and centralisation because it created social and economic divisions and it lacked morality. He felt that the consciousness of common people was frustrated by a system of 'life corroding competition' which resulted in bondage rather than freedom. In his opinion material progress was in inverse relation to moral progress.

Gandhiji was influenced by eastern religions mainly Hinduism and Buddhism and western philosophers like Leo Tolstoy, Henry Thoreau and John Ruskin. Gandhiji was born and brought up in a Hindu family. His parents were deeply religious people who practiced religion at home. He himself read and practiced the teaching of the Gita. It was from the Gita that he derived the notion of selfless service to humanity. The Gita also taught him that a man should perform his duties without looking for any rewards or praise or recognition for his actions. In other words the Karmyog, (Action as described in the Gita) in order to serve people. He thought that he could serve other human beings by entering politics and said that he could not serve people unless he entered politics. Gandhiji was also influenced by the Buddhist philosophy of 'self-suffering' and 'non-infliction of pain' and non-violence.

For Gandhi, Ruskin was an inspiration for a simple life. Ruskin believed that the true basis of society was not wealth but it was the 'invisible gold' of human companionship. The possession of wealth and power was selfish, and perpetuated social inequities and injustice. The wealth and power should, therefore, be renounced until there was enough for everyone. This teaching went straight into Gandhi's heart. He changed his life style and started to live a simple life. He also started to work for the welfare of all.

From Thoreau, he learnt civil-disobedience. He examined the relationship between the state and its citizens. He considered that if the state worked against the interests of its citizens, they had a right to disobey the state and its laws. For Thoreau and Gandhi, freedom of the individual was paramount. If there was encroachment on the rights of individuals, the state should be disobeyed. They argued that no society could possibly be built on a denial of individual freedom. Man must follow his own conscience.

Tolstoy transmitted the notion of passive resistance and communal life to Gandhi. They both were against modernity and were critical of modern industrial civilization. Both opposed the power of the state and preached love and understanding and simple communal life. Gandhiji was called the apostle of love and peace. He believed in non- violence and non-resistance, and called his movement Satyagraha (truth-force). His non- co-operation was not a negation of action but a positive approach in order to convert an opponent and moulding him into co-operation. He maintained the view that there were times when a good cause could be supported by working with the authorities; when the work was being done for the benefit of the society.

Gandhiji knew that man was a social being. For him individual freedom was important but he also knew that individual freedom would flourish only in society. It was a freedom, based on equality and justice which sprang from the needs of society of free men with common and equal rights in the means of production. Economic independence was essential in order to accomplish freedom and justice in society. Moreover, communal individuality protected both the community and the individual.

Self- imposed laws were a better defence for freedom than an external restraint because legal authority only muddled in people's affairs. People should, therefore, solve their problems by mutual understanding and it was through mutual understanding that freedom could be maintained.

Gandhi's Sarvodaya (Welfare of all), movement, was designed for the welfare of the community as a whole. The community orientation was crucial. It was through serving the community that an individual participated in the affairs of the society. Individual participation could be possible only when people had freedom and equality in social and economic systems. Gandhi's followers started Gramdan (village ownership of land and property) and Bhoodan (transferring land from land-lords to land- less people). These movements were free from government intervention. There was, however, a limited success in the achievement of these movements.

They believed that people would work for the welfare of the community. They ignored the self-interests of individuals because people tend to work less without private incentive and personal gain. The social structure also would not work effectively because village elders and landlords would use exclusive powers. Their decision might not work for the benefit of the society and the community. It could not be called democratic because the village councillors were not normally elected on the basis of qualification but on the basis of their status. It was also possible that the welfare of close relatives and neighbours was often considered paramount. Most of the decisions, however, were geared for the welfare of the community as a whole. This was possible only when there was unity between individuality and the community.

Gandhiji was a charismatic leader and charismatic approach could not be an agent of sustained process of change. Still he visualized a unity between individuality and society. Such a society would not only be efficient and good (in moral sense) but would also meet the needs of human nature and help develop individuality and community simultaneously."

A few friends read this thesis. They liked it and suggested that it should be published and made available to others to read. I did not make any effort to get it published. However, an article was published in the GOOD SOCIETY REVIEW, in 1993, with the title "Mahatma Gandhi on Communal Individuality". Much of the material for this article was drawn from this dissertation.

During this period (1982), there was also a pressure for marking the examination scripts which I finished by the end of June. From 3rd to 8th July, I went on a Business Studies course. The purpose was to consider the curricula for vocational studies for pupils between the ages of 16 and 19 years. The course was interesting and new to me. I had to adjust a lot because thus far I had been involved in academic work. Now we were looking for practical aspects in teaching vocational courses in Business Studies. The participants on the course were good and the food was superb. I liked walking on the grass land but it was difficult to sleep at night at the new place.

When I did my Master's degree course from 1980 to 1982, by part time studies at the City of London Guildhall University (now part of London Metropolitan University), I learned many new ideas, methods and techniques especially in essay writing, learning process and dissertation. I enjoyed every aspect of the course and every minute of my time. I must pay my gratitude to my lecturers and friends and above all my family who made all this possible and facilitated my learning. The school authorities gave me half day off for two years. Without this time off, it could not have been possible to do a higher degree. I kept copies of my essays and a copy of my dissertation.

+   +

On 15th October 1982, I celebrated seventeen years of my stay in England with some friends who were with me at the Charing Cross hotel, drinking and enjoying each other's company. I looked back to the day when I landed at Heathrow airport and spent my first night in London. At that time I did not know what was going to happen and what kind of changes were to take place for me. During these seventeen years, I suffered, I sustained losses, I was discouraged from doing things, I was rebuked, looked down upon, yet I struggled on and was not ready to accept negative attitude of others. Possibly, I changed my tactics and hoped for the best. In the end, I could observe that I had been reasonably successful in all fields, be it honour, academic or socio-economic. I have a happy home and a happy family. We are not visionaries. Neither do we live an unrealistic life.

I was, however, concerned about my parents, who though, had a large number of children and grandchildren, lived in the village where there was no immediate family member to look after them. Perhaps they lived there due to the fact that they had lived in that village all their lives and they were attached to the locality and the community. They had friends and good neighbours. I had often thought of bringing them to London or to visit them quite often. They could possibly move to live in Delhi where their other children and grandchildren lived. They needed care at that stage of their lives. They wanted to remain individualistic and independent but their individualism lay in communalism and their individuality could flourish among the many. My wife and daughter went to India in December 1982. I expected them to give me a first-hand report of the situation in India especially of the family. Still, I wanted my parents to move to Delhi.

After completing my MA degree course which I enjoyed enormously, I thought of doing a research degree. I applied to the LSE (London School of Economics) and Middlesex Polytechnic. I was offered a place to read for the M Phil/PhD, at the LSE, which, I accepted. I wanted to study at the London School of Economics and political Science for many reasons. It was a part of the University of London. It was easy to reach there. It had more facilities than the Polytechnic and most important of all I had a firm offer to start in January 1983. When I looked back to the year 1982, many good things happened. I was confirmed Head of Business Studies at the school, I passed my MA degree examination and I had an offer to read for the research degree. Perhaps it was my childhood dream to become MA PhD one day. I had a peaceful environment to do my research and the peace of mind was vital in education and learning.

I started my work on the India League. I spent a few days at the British Museum Library and some time at the LSE library. Initially I was disappointed because there was not enough material on the India League and the League papers had been sent to Jawaharlal Nehru Library, New Delhi. I started digging for papers and found that there was sufficient material in England, though scattered around in various libraries and archives including Oxford and Cambridge. My enquiry at the Nehru Library was not successful. I was told that the Krishna Menon papers had been closed for Public viewing. Mrs Indira Gandhi also wrote back that she had nothing new to offer about the India League. However, she would be glad to answer a few questions. Anyway, I managed to write a few pages and sent them to my supervisor at the LSE. He made a few useful suggestions. I also did an essay on methodology.

In May 1983, I found myself at the cross roads between Mahatma Gandhi and Krishna Menon. I had always identified myself as a Gandhian and had done some research on Gandhi's Communal society based on non-violence, cottage industry and village republics. Now I was engaged on a research project on the India League, which meant Krishna Menon and his work for the Indian independence movement in Britain. I personally agreed with both these persons who contributed through their respective modes. They both were dedicated to the cause of India. But they did not seem to like each other much. Krishna Menon criticized Gandhiji for being too old fashioned and that he would be unable to solve the problems of modern India. Gandhiji criticized Krishna Menon for being too westernised, for remaining away from home for too long and possibly for his leftist leanings and that he (Krishna Menon) was not aware of the problems and prevailing trends in India. Being an intellectual he was close to the Marxist tradition.

Despite the contradictions both had many similarities. Both were vegetarians through and through. Like Gandhiji, Krishna Menon lived a simple life. He remained a bachelor all his life. He was a passionate worker for his country's freedom. He introduced the Indian question to the British people and encouraged the Indian community in Britain to unite and work for the independence of India. He worked for the welfare of the poor and the common man. He represented true India, as he was not tied to any kind of provincialism. His nationalism was not confined to India alone. His plea for freedom was for all the suppressed peoples of Asia and Africa. He was opposed to colonialism and imperialism as well as capitalism. He was, nevertheless, a modern man who wanted to live in the 20th Century with an urban and industrial civilization. The past did not appeal to him. In this he differed from Gandhiji for whom village was the best and small was great.

Where do I fit in these ideological contradictions? For me continuity was important but I was not a traditionalist. I was proud of the ancient Indian civilization which had a culture, an economic structure, where probably no one starved. Schools existed in villages and universities attracted students from foreign countries. The Indian philosophy and the concept of self-satisfaction attracted me but I was not prepared to accept that nothing else had happened in the last two thousand years. India herself had witnessed many variations and perhaps the pioneers of culture would not have tolerated stagnation. They would have initiated modifications. Every decade or possibly every year had brought alterations in the lives of the people in India and in other parts of the world. The laws of nature and society were not static. People had to move forward and make progress. In this attempt they would have to face a number of impediments and witness ups and downs. If they did not falter from their objectives, they would be able to accomplish them.

I would personally like to see economic and social equality, enough food for every one and a reasonable standard of living for all. Every one should have an opportunity to develop his/her potential and all should contribute to the progress of the society. In this I find myself one with the Gandhian concept of communal individuality as well as with the basic thinking of Krishna Menon who never imposed his will on any person. The individual development was possible only in a society but society was to facilitate the development of individuality and not to impose the will of a section of the community on others. I tried to study both-Gandhiji and Krishna Menon as an academic enquiry.

For my MA dissertation, I wrote about Gandhiji's communal individuality, his views on cottage industries and self-sufficiency in villages but for the M Phil degree, at the London School of Economics, I started to research on the India League, which functioned in the United Kingdom for India's freedom under the leadership of Krishna Menon in the 1930s and 1940s. The progress on my research was very slow but many interesting documents came to light. The most fascinating survey was found in the 'Transfer of Power'. Krishna Menon and the India League were referred many times in these volumes. I also had an interview with the writer - Marie Seton. I spent two hours talking to her about the past. She was a slim old lady but very alert. She wrote a reply to my letter on the day she received it. I took some notes of our conversation. We also discussed the present British politics. An enquiry to the journalist James Cameron was fruitless. Later I had an interview with Krishna Shelvankar. I found a great-deal of papers at the Friends House Library and decided to include the India Conciliation Group as it was a complimentary organisation to the League and had a common link in the form of Agatha Harrison who was Secretary of the India Conciliation Group and also worked for Krishna Menon and the India League. The library staff at Friends House was the best I could find.

In the summer of 1983, I was informed of my father's illness but I was also told that there was nothing to worry about. I was worried about his health as he looked very weak when I visited him in December 1980. On 4th of October, I received a telegram that my father was seriously ill and he wanted to see me. I knew that he had expressed a desire to talk to me, at length, in one of his letters. I immediately planned to go to Delhi. I cancelled all my programmes and arrangements. I phoned the family in India that I was coming and that I shall be there within the next few days. I left London on Sunday the 9th and reached Delhi early in the morning at 5am the next day. But my father passed-away on Sunday, the day I left London. His wish to see me and talk to me remained unfulfilled. I would never be able to find out what did he want to talk to me?

However, after reaching Delhi, we arranged for his cremation and the ashes were to be taken to the holy city of Haridwar. I was still a bit confused. On 15th October 1983, I wrote that my father died after a short illness. I tried to reach Delhi but found myself twenty hours too late, and I could not speak to him before his departure from this world. I stayed in Delhi for three weeks. During this period the long memories and remembrances of the past and my relationship with my father cropped into my mind. Despite the fact that I had been away in England for eighteen years and away from my parents for thirty- five years, we respected and liked each other. Suddenly, I found a gap in my life, which prompted me to look back at the life and career of my father.

My father was the only son of my grand-parents. He was born after three female children to them and possibly after long prayers. Though my grand-parents were not superstitious, they were deeply religious and followed both the religious and social customs. My father never discussed his childhood with us. Neither did my grand-parents. We, however, knew that he left school at the age of thirteen in order to help his father at the shop. Thus, he started to work at a tender age of thirteen and continued to work till his death at the age of seventy-four.

His life was not very comfortable. My grand- parents were very simple people who had no materialistic attachments. They could, therefore, give him only their love and affection. My father, being an intelligent man with an I.Q. well above average, was very ambitious and wanted to rise in social as well as financial status. He worked very hard in order to accomplish his goals. The 1930s, however, saw economic depression through out the world and our village was no exception. My parents, therefore, moved to Delhi in order to make a living. They had to leave my grand-parents in the village. Circumstances were not always favourable in Delhi either. Because of family reasons my parents returned to the village, after staying in Delhi for a couple of years.

The situations started to improve in the late 1930s and my father was in control of his destiny then. He got involved in many business activities and earned himself a good fortune. He earned money and wealth by his own efforts and hard work. He used to buy wheat and peas from the farmers in the village and sold in the town at slightly higher price. He also became the village financier and helped people to borrow money. Some times he lent his own money and charged some interest on it. He used to store goods for months and sell them later.

By the time, I was able to understand, there was no shortage of essentials in our household and we lived a comfortable life, if not a luxurious one. Having made sure of money and wealth, it was natural that he was now looking for honour and prestige. He wanted to fulfil that by educating his children. The education had become a social symbol in India in the 1950s. I was only nine when I found myself separated from parents. My father often visited me and I visited him over the weekends and also spent summer holidays in the village.

I had developed an emotional attachment with my father. I remember that once I ran for eight miles from my school to my village in order to see my parents. As late as 1980, I thought of visiting my parents and went from London to see them in India for only two days. I loved and respected my father and often remember his teachings and stories because he was a good storyteller. There were many reasons for this affection. Possibly, because we had lived apart from each other for a long time or perhaps he was disappointed with other members of the family and looked to an alternative. Some times he was unhappy with me as well but eventually he realised that I was right in the long run and that he had either hastened his decision or misunderstood the situation. He always accepted that I never answered him back or opposed him unnecessarily.

He made enormous progress and was financially well-off. He was proud of his achievements and when some of us (children) were not that successful as he was, he felt disappointed. He did not believe in a one-generation family and wanted all of us to remain united. He also desired us to start where he had left. He was a normative man and wished to see the things as they should be and not as they were. He looked to be consulted or at least informed of the events in the family. He was against changes but he never stopped others from doing whatever they did. I still recall when I decided to come to England in 1965, he was against it but when I was equally determined not to change my plan, he did not oppose and came to see me off.

When he wrote letters to me he described a few things. There were other things that he could not write. But his writings portrayed that he was not a happy man for the last few years. No reason was provided for his dejection. It was impossible to maintain his wish for a joint family as a number of units had sprung-up which had their own self interests. He passed away on 9th October 1983, at 9.20am Indian time, leaving many riddles unsolved and possibly many wishes unfulfilled. Now we could only pray for the comfort and solace of his immortal soul. We managed to take his ashes and bones to the holy city of Haridwar in order to immerse them in the River Ganga.

After the bereavement and mourning for two weeks, I thought of going out of the house. I had already decided to remain in Delhi during the whole period of my stay. I, therefore, went to Jawaharlal Memorial Museum and Library. I wanted to do some research on my project on the India League. On the first day of my visit to the library, I was not allowed to look at even the index. I had no letter of introduction from the London School of Economics, though I had written a letter to them at an early date. On the second day when the library assistant was equally unhelpful, I asked to see the Director of the library. He allowed me to use the manuscript department of the JN papers and the Congress party papers. I managed to see papers on Krishna Menon but they did not let me see the main files on the India League which I wanted to read. The workers in the library gave me contradictory statements and promises. The library staff especially one of the assistants in the manuscript department was not helpful at all. He rather hindered my work.

I could not understand why these people behaved the way they did. Perhaps, they did not know the value of time or did not understand the importance of manuscripts for research.

I received a great help in London from many libraries and archives. I was, therefore, used to a co-operative environment. The most sinister thing at the JNML was that I had to go to library to collect some photocopies which could have been done in ten minutes, I had to spend two half days in travelling from home to library. The travelling itself was an experience.

Most of the time I travelled by bus, which was always over crowded. People did not know the queue system. They all wanted to enter the bus at the same time. Delhi had made enormous progress in the last ten years but it had moved towards chaos, congestion and over crowding. It would not remain a beautiful city, if the problems continued grow.

In 1984, I continued with my research and wrote an introduction and two chapters. I also participated in writing a document on equal opportunity at the school. I attended a curriculum development course in business studies and started a vocational course called BEC (Business Education Council). Despite some problems at the outset the BEC course was a success. I did not teach on this course but I would start to teach next year. This course would, however, be short lived as it was being replaced by the CPVE (Certificate of Pre-Vocational Education).

+   +

Many problems sprang up in India in the early 1980s, which threatened the secular structure and unity of the country. It was a big country with huge problems. The communal violence and regionalism had often erupted but nothing attracted more attention than the events in the Punjab in May and June 1984. The action by the Indian army on 2nd June became headlines in the British media. The British media panicked and became paranoid. The news showed that an uncontrollable situation had arisen in India. So far I could recall, some of my friends had predicted some eighteen years ago, when they told me that the Sikhs might demand an autonomous state and the Hindu community might be threatened by physical violence. At that time, I did not believe that such a situation could ever arise because the Sikhs and the Hindus had a common culture, common names and common heritage. I had always believed that Sikhism was a part of Hinduism. The founding fathers of the Sikh religion wanted that way and the Indian constitution recognized this fact. But economic reasons and population pressure had created problems.

In the past, the Punjab had received a favourable treatment from the central government of India. Now the other states had started to demand their share of investment, development programmes and water supply. The other communities were coming up to compete for jobs. Thus some of the Sikhs (but very vocal of them) had started to think that their rights were being eroded. A number of Sikhs had become rich and they demanded a say in the central government's affairs. In the name of religion, economic and political demands were being presented violently. When the other communities and the Indian government refused to accept such demands, a section of people mainly terrorists took refuge in the golden temple at Amritsar. They had arms and the support of some foreign powers. They terrorised the common people in northern India. This posed many questions and in such surroundings the unity of the country was threatened. This could hinder economic and social progress in the country. Any communal violence was vice. In the name of religion people were encouraged to take action, which they would not take in normal circumstances. Moreover, Punjab was a border state, it was vital to maintain peace and tranquillity in the state. This also raised strategic problems and the questions of international importance.

But who encouraged this violence? The government of India had thought of American and Pakistani involvement. It could be possible. The United States was looking for an ally on the borders of the Soviet Union and China. India had refused to succumb to the US pressure. It paid the rich countries to keep the poor countries underdeveloped. India had made some progress, in economic and scientific fields, which was not liked by the West.

The Indians were not yet mature enough to understand such geo-politics. An illiterate could be easily exploited and easily swayed. India was not short of illiterates and uneducated people. It was true that Indians fought for their freedom and they were nationalists but they were also regionalists and communalists. They had not yet developed a coherent national identity. They could thus be persuaded to create chaos within their own communities on the basis of region or religion.

So far as the immediate problem was concerned, the government of India sent troops to clear the golden temple at Amritsar, which had been occupied by the terrorists for the last two months. It was difficult to say who was to be blamed. But many questions could be asked and the alternatives considered. Why did the government not take action earlier? The answers were not easy to find. Perhaps an SAS type of operation could have been possible. There were quite a few people in the temple with a great deal of arms and ammunition. It was incomprehensible to stop people taking things to the temple. Perhaps arms were passed as offerings. It was a big job, which needed an operation rather than an easy ointment on painful places. However, the Indian government could have adopted a different method than to storm the temple.

The main view was to be cautious and conscientious in order to develop an identity of nationhood in India. The present predicament would subside. The feelings would heal in course of time but long-term solution lay in selfless devotion and dedication by all. The control of population growth and an economic progress was needed. Otherwise the whole fabric of Indian society and the experiment of Indian democracy would collapse. It would lead to anarchy not only in India but in other corners of the world as well.

Early in the morning on Wednesday the 31 October 1984, I was told by my daughter Saneh that Azad had just heard on the radio that Mrs. Gandhi had been killed by her own Sikh body guard. While I was not surprised, I was shocked and dismayed because I had never thought of such a happening. I had heard of threats to the Indian Prime Minister's life but it was all-unbelievable. I had started to like Mrs. Gandhi because of her efficiency, standing and practicality. She had become an international leader in her own right and India had definitely advanced under her leadership. India had produced more food grains in 1984, than ever before. Despite corruption and bureaucratic inefficiency, people had more to eat. There was a general improvement in their standard of living.

I thought about the psychology of assassination by her own bodyguards who were sworn in to protect her even at the risk of their own lives. When I thought of this plight I felt uneasy and pale. I had not been able to find an answer. The only idea came to my mind, was, the brain washing of those guards during their stay in the Punjab. I was proved right. Religion had been misinterpreted again. Love, understanding and brotherhood of man had been replaced by hatred and violence. The British mass media, radio, television, and the newspapers gave a good coverage with a two-hour programme, on Saturday, of the cremation of Mrs Gandhi, in Delhi.

The main reason for this change was possibly an opportunity visualized by the politicians and the British government to attract Indian support and an effort to draw India towards the West. Some politicians had genuine respect for India, while the others wanted her to move towards the Western Alliance and away from the Soviet Union. Michael Foot, MP, wrote a very interesting article in the 'Sunday Observer' on this subject. The events in Britain were also suppressed though these were given more than the required coverage in the early hours of the Indian Prime Minister's death.

The events that followed in India and the killing of innocent Sikhs and the looting of their property showed anger among the masses. It was deplorable. The new Indian government, however, controlled the happenings within three days or hours after the mourning was over. It showed the strength of the government as well as maturity of the Indian democracy. The subversive forces were suppressed. There was a need to rebuild the relationship between different communities and build a national spirit. It was not difficult in India because people tend to forget things soon.

I also wrote a letter of condolence to the new Indian Prime Minister who was also Mrs. Gandhi's son. Rajiv Gandhi was chosen as the new leader of the Congress party and therefore, India's Prime Minister. He held elections in December 1984 and January 1985, and won a land slide victory and power to introduce reforms. He promised to continue with the policies of the previous government in domestic and foreign affairs. He, however, liberalised the economy and received good coverage in the Western press. He was quite popular in his country.

+   +

In Britain, the miners' strike continued for about a year and ended in March 1985. It should not be regarded as a defeat of the miners or the trade unionism. Long strikes, however, did not serve any special purpose. These should be short and sharp. The workers should make their point and then resume responsibilities. The strike, moreover, was the last weapon in industrial relations and should not be used to the extent that it lost its credibility. Alternatives should be considered. The teachers were also involved in an industrial action and non-cooperation with their employers.

There was a great unrest in Britain in the summer of 1985. Riots flared up in Handsworth, Toxteth, Brixton, and Peckham. The police were blamed for their upper hand in handling certain conditions, which led to violence. But the underlying effect was the social deprivation and unemployment. This time two Indian brothers died in Handsworth and a black woman had a heart attack in Tottenham, North London. A policeman was brutally murdered in Tottenham. These were perhaps the worst riots of 1985.

The teachers' strike continued for many months. It was probably the longest industrial dispute in the teaching profession since 1929. The government was keen to change the teachers' contract and working conditions. Only then the teachers could get a pay rise. The teachers wanted to negotiate their salary first and then negotiate the terms of the contract. They were not prepared to align the two. They sought a solution to both, the pay and working conditions separately.

On 15 October 1985 I completed twenty years in London. I had not stayed at any other place for so long. Earlier I had thought of returning to India within a decade of my landing in England. However, things had changed, circumstances had become different, ideas and observations were not the same. I still liked India where my roots lay. I suspected whether I could live there the way I would like to live. There had been a gap of twenty years between the India of 1965 and India of 1985, though I had remained in touch with many of my relatives by visiting them and by corresponding with them.

In London, I had made some friends but lost many. The new friends were reliable and they could rely on me. I was more tolerant than I was in the 1960s or 1970s. I still resented injustice and would like to live a peaceful life. London itself had changed. When I came here in 1965, I could have walked on the streets and roads at any time of day or night. By mid 1980s, it had become difficult to walk around at odd hours. Violence had increased on the streets of London. There was impersonal life in this big city. I get my comfort in looking at the past and my struggle throughout the last twenty years. I had not asked anyone for undue help. I had a good job. The neighbourhood was good. I wished it to continue like that in the future. I had been preoccupied with my work at home and at school. My contribution to the development of pre-vocational education (CPVE) was imperative. It sensed that I was needed at this ILEA School.

I however, could not visualize myself working for another ten years or so at the school. I, therefore, decided to move to teach at a college. I made three applications in October 1985. I sensed that it was easy to find a new job in the autumn term than at any other time. One of the colleges informed me that they would write to me in November. However, one morning, I received an interview letter from the South West London College where I had taught in the evenings in the past. I was not particularly attracted to the place or the job. I, however, thought of attending the interview for fun and that I shall be answering questions at the interview in a very blunt fashion. The interview took place on 31 October and the same day I was told that I had been selected for the post of a lecturer.

I was very much surprised but I showed no emotional expression and accepted the offer. I resigned my post, as the Head of Business Studies at the School, the same day. People were very astonished. There were mixed feelings in the staff room. Every one was pleased for me but they were sorry to see me leave the school. It was considered that it would not be easy to replace me because I had built up the department. I thought that I needed a change and perhaps a lecturer's post will provide me some satisfaction as I could not contribute any thing new at the school. Secondly, I had always desired to teach at a college and now I had an opportunity. I, therefore, availed it.

Some of my friends asked me whether I was excited about the new job. I had no feeling or idea about that. I did every- thing possible for a smooth transfer and helped students to prepare for their examination. I almost finished the Advanced level Economics course. The students were very co-operative. I received a great deal of kindness and co-operation from all sections of the school community. The man who told me in 1976, that I had no future at the school, asked me stay on and suggested that I should ask the Head master for scale four because I was on scale three as Head of Business Studies. I told him that money was not everything and I wanted to teach higher classes. The A level students threw a party at the time of my departure and gave me a signed card on the last day of the term in December 1985. I said goodbye to the whole school at a large gathering. It was not easy to leave a place where I had worked for more than eleven years. But there came a time when I decided to move on. I bade farewell to students and staff and wished them all success and happiness in their lives.

At the final staff meeting, the Head of Sixth Form spoke about my contribution to the Business Studies Department and in making it an important department. He spoke of the A level Economics course and the results which had been above average for the last ten years and that I had been instrumental in developing the BTEC course and co-ordinating it between two schools and a college. He spoke of a quiet revolution in the department and acknowledged and praised my contribution to the department in particular and to the school in general. I was given a present on behalf of the department and the school staff. Forty-seven members of staff signed the card. Most of them wrote comments which showed that I was close to quite a few of them. Islands of dissent remained. But life was a big phenomenon. The memories of good people would always remain with me and would be appreciated. In the New Year, I acknowledged their kindness by writing a letter of thanks to the school and another to the Head of Sixth Form

CHAPTER 3

Ladder For Advancement, 1986-95

My move to the college was positive. I enjoyed teaching, which was interesting and useful. Every one recognized that I had contributed to vocational preparation, Advanced level Economics and Law. It gave me satisfaction. It crystallized the fact that my aptitudes were suited to college teaching. My social life also improved. I gained many new friends. We became close to each other. The new Diploma in BTEC was very closely considered and three of us lecturers prepared material and held meetings every day for two weeks. I was contented at the college.

The summer of 1986, was, however, spent in libraries and archives in connection with my research. I looked through the Mountbatten files at the India Office Library and Records. Most of my time was, however, spent at the Public Record Office (PRO) where I found a treasure of files about India's membership of the Commonwealth. I found them very informative and useful. This convinced me that I should continue to work to the period-1949, as originally planned and not to finish my research project at 1947, with India's independence. If I finished my theses at August 1947, it would have left many gaps and create an impression that the Indo-British relations were based on the British rule and Indian struggle for independence.

The Indo-British relations continued and improved in future months. The India League did not play much part in these months. Krishna Menon, nevertheless, played a very significant role in the negotiations for India's membership of the Commonwealth of Nations and India as a republic was accepted as a full member of the Commonwealth headed by a monarch. Thus an organization was created of international importance and a precedent was set for other republics to join this association.

The last time, I recorded my observations was in the month of July 1986 and now it was May 1987. It indicated that I had been busy for a very long time. I could not recall a period which had witnessed such a long gap in writing my experiences and observations. The summer time was spent at the Public Record Office at the Kew. I read hundreds of files on the Commonwealth, Cabinet Papers and the Prime Minister's papers for the period 1946 to 1949. I thought of writing a chapter on India's decision to remain in the Commonwealth, when she had decided to become a republic. But most of the material was not used because it did not relate to the India League. I, therefore, had to redesign and rewrite the last chapter and the conclusion. I went back to the libraries and archives and managed to see some new files, news-papers and new documents. I wrote a chapter on the post independence period. My thesis was ready for submission.

In the abstract of my thesis I wrote,

'The mutual repugnance of Indian nationalism and British imperialism found a new expression in 1930, when the Indian National Congress proposed to establish an Independent Republic in India and to sever all connections with Britain. Such a conception, however, found no exponent in Britain. The India League and the India Conciliation Group emerged to bridge this gap. These organizations were essentially British pressure groups, which functioned within the framework of the British political system. They expounded the Indian nationalist view and lobbied people in power in order to solicit their support for India's independence. The British thought that their rule had brought peace and unity in India. On the contrary, the Indian nationalists believed that the British rule was anathema to their dignity and interests. They advanced the view that their country could be well served by self-government. The pressure groups like the India League and the India Conciliation Group also appealed to the British government to end imperialism and establish democracy in India in order to improve Indo-British relations'.

+   +

In November 1988, I got involved in a research project on good practice in colleges in work related non-advanced further education for ethnic minorities. I thought that it could increase my experience in educational research and enhance my future prospects. This project was quite good. It looked at the positive side of the courses offered for black and ethnic minority students. I was to work with two other researchers and a permanent member of the Research and Statistics branch of the ILEA (Inner London Education Authority). Previous studies on education for ethnic minorities had demonstrated that a higher percentage of ethnic minority students entered lower level further education courses. It was discovered that they were especially under-represented on work related vocational courses and it was difficult for them to find jobs in their chosen fields.

The research also revealed that little attention was given to multi-ethnic and anti-racist education. Because of these criticisms, it was realized that another research was needed to look into good practice in colleges so that others could learn from such a practice. We, therefore, started our work, prepared a questionnaire, and produced an interim report quite soon. We also interviewed quite a few people in colleges including Principals, Deputy Principals, Lecturers and Students. At the South West London College, I interviewed my Principal who provided detailed information about his commitment to fight prejudice. He argued that education was the main vehicle to combat racism and bias. He started courses for ethnic students and negotiated job placement with employers who also paid for the courses and at the end of the course, students were provided employment.

This research looked into the mainstream provision, special provision and employer sponsored courses. The TSB (Trustee Savings Bank) sponsored a course 'Access to Banking' at South West London College which proved a good example and was a success story. The course was held over a six month period. All the expenses were paid by the TSB and all students were employed by this bank at the end of the course.

We also recognized the need for multi-ethnic education co-ordinators' participation in policy making, in marketing the courses, selection of students as well as an input of multi-cultural education in curriculum content. The main emphasis, however, was on developing good practice in mainstream courses in colleges. There were some courses for ethnic minorities in work-related non-advanced further education. These were mainly Access courses leading to Diploma and Degree. These provided educational opportunities to disadvantaged students. But there was no certainty that these courses would continue in the future.

It was found that work-related NAFE (Non-Advanced-Further-Education) was considered for special initiatives. Less attention was being paid to the need for positive action to develop good practice in traditional and 'main stream courses'. There were hardly any Access courses leading to Engineering or other professional Diploma or Degree course. Most colleges did not have information on ethnic students' intake on various courses. It was, therefore recommended by our team of researchers that "senior management in colleges should take note of the tendency for good practice for ethnic minorities in work-related NAFE, to be regarded as a focus for special initiative, and consider the ways in which the various constituents of good practice evident on access- type courses could be taken up on more traditional courses." It was also thought that Academic Board and Governing Body in colleges should receive reports from teaching and administrative staff about the number of ethnic students enrolling on and progressing from these courses for higher education or employment.

The research also considered other fields of college activities which could affect ethnic minority students like the Marketing, and Publicity, link with schools and employers; Recruitment and Selection, accepting non-British qualifications, and information on fee and financial support for students. Curriculum and Resources, literacy and numeracy support, development of study skills, counselling to students, regular course reviews, extra-curricular activities, social functions for students and careers advice. The research on this theme came to an end by June 1989.

The other development was that in the early months of 1989, I led a team of lecturers at the college to develop the Diploma in Higher Education (Dip HE). We prepared syllabuses for a number of options. We held meetings every week. We had to work in our own time, often at home in the evenings and at weekends.

In July 1989, I decided to go to India on holiday and to start to build our house in Delhi. On returning from Delhi, I discovered that the London School of Economics (university of London) decided to award me an M Phil for my thesis which I accepted. Before sending the acceptance letter I asked two professors and two academics to read my thesis. They all concluded that the standard of the research was that of the Ph.D. degree. But the examiners could not agree between themselves because one was a historian and the other was a political theorist. They both were looking for different things from different perspectives. I felt gratified because I had reached the required standard and it were the examiners who had personal views and were perhaps not objective in their assessment. This could not be altered.

I also considered changing my job to suit my qualifications and interests. Besides teaching, I became interested in educational administration. I, therefore, applied to some of the new education authorities (the ILEA were disbanded in 1989) for the post of education development officer. I submitted a long statement in support of my application. This statement contained my teaching experience in many subjects, administrative experience, curriculum development, staff development and research. The interview at Wandsworth was particularly fascinating but at one stage, I had a feeling that the job was not for me. I, however, talked about curriculum related development issues, which were to be addressed by local education authorities in inner London. Obviously, there were other issues faced by them. I suggested that the borough should look at the offer of the National Council for Vocational Qualifications at all levels; trainee status, undertaking basic skills with supervision; operational level where everyday tasks could be done automatically; specialist tasks and elements of being in supervision over others; junior management level where problem solving and decision making took place. It was essential to assess skills and underpin knowledge and understanding. They should also provide access to employment via training and skills development. Adult education should be offered for leisure. This need could be fulfilled by the return to studies provision. Basic English, basic Mathematics, basic computing, community education could be offered at the Adult Education Institutes.

+   +

The year 1989, was a very busy year for me. Yet, I was relaxed most of the time. Despite the fact that I could not get access to the India League papers which had been sent to India, I finished my research on the India League and the India Conciliation Group. I was keen to publish it as a book because there was no book on this theme. I wrote to quite a few publishers but many of them found it too specialist and too academic for general reading. I, therefore, removed the theory part of it, changed the title to make it more general. Emphasis was laid on 'Indian Nationalist Movement in Britain.' Two or three publishers became interested in the book but their decision was still awaited in April 1990.

I also attended two internal interviews at the college. There was no special job specification but the questions asked related to classroom teaching, curriculum development, new initiatives and equal opportunities. I did not get the job in my Department, which mainly ran lower courses, but I was offered a job, in Higher Business Studies Department, which I immediately accepted. I would have to move to the other site in January 1990. I was told that the interview went well and the panel thought that I could do a better job for them and that they could use my qualifications, experience and initiatives in order to develop their courses. It was important to record some of the ideas, which I presented to the interviewers. I stressed that my academic qualifications, experience of teaching many subjects and the administrative experience made me the right candidate for the post.

On the question of an example of a good lesson, I wrote, that it should reflect the aims of the lesson. It should be followed by a hand out and there should be two-way communication. The students should be involved in group discussions; and role-play. They should feel that they had accomplished their objectives, which could be assessed by testing them and their work. The grading of work encouraged students to plan their studies. No single student should be allowed to dominate the discussions. All students should be involved in discussions. The student's needs and the curriculum demands should be reconciled. This sounded prescriptive but it was the method, I had often used in my teaching lessons. The efficiency could be recognized by looking at the cost per student, through examination results and the perception of students. The planning and organization of the class work should demonstrate its importance.

The marketing of the course had two sides. It was important to recognize the requirement of the community and the employers. This demand should be met. For example access to the TSB, day release courses should be offered. On the question of duties as a Course Director, I had to interview candidates, market the course, recruit students, keep records, hold meetings, register students with the examining boards, consider students' discipline. As a Tutor, I spent my time on pastoral care, attempted to understand the students' problems sympathetically, and also provided induction at the start of the course. My statement in support of my application included the pedagogic work, academic leadership of the team of staff, management and administration, curriculum development, current national and local educational initiatives, staff development courses that I attended; staff development courses that I organized; quality and effectiveness of the Department's offer, and the equal opportunities.

I must go back to the interviews; I had at the college for Senior lecturer. On both occasions I was asked about my suitability for the job and the way I perceived myself. I laid emphasis on my educational and academic qualifications and experience in many areas including administration. I thought I was a person who could take initiatives and work with others. Sociability had been my main characteristic. I also possessed team leadership qualities and could hold meetings effectively by allowing every one to participate in discussions, develop curriculum, bring original ideas, committed to succeed and keep the management informed of the developments.

I must also record here what others said and wrote about me in the past few years. Phiroz. Daji, a close friend wrote, 'he was very regular and punctual in attendance, always submitted his assignments on time, actively participated in seminars and discussions with logical arguments. As a colleague I found him loyal, trustworthy and conscientious. He had a cool and calm temperament, always willing to co-operate and give a helping hand. A man always on the move and never at rest, without achieving his objectives'. The ILEA Inspector for Business Studies wrote, 'he was a committed teacher, genuinely interested in the needs of his pupils'.

Another dear and close friend Europe Singh wrote of me 'K.C.Arora was a highly successful teacher and manager. He had an excellent record in terms of pass rates in the examinations in all the subjects he taught. His management and development of the BTEC course had been an example at the college'. He was hardworking and meticulous in his approach. His written reports on the progress of the BTEC or on in-service training events he ran, were clear and comprehensive. He continually strove in this and his teaching to attain excellence. One of his major concerns had been in counselling and recruiting students to the course best suited to their needs and abilities. In particular he had worked to improve the recruitment of ethnic minority students and to ensure their progression to employment, training or further study. Another element of his commitment to equal opportunities had been his involvement in curriculum development in the areas of business, law and economics to tackle the issue of racism, sexism and class bias'.

A testimonial also came from Ken Noble, Headmaster of my old school, in December 1985. He praised my leadership qualities which led to the development of the Economics Department into 'the most successful in the school' and Economics a popular option in the Upper School. He further stressed that 'he (KCArora) had been instrumental in setting up our BTEC course in Business Studies'. 'Mr. Arora had an excellent relationship with both the pupils and the staff'. The main reasons for being a strong candidate were 'his qualifications, competence and enthusiasm'.

At the interview in the Business Studies Department, the discussion, however, concentrated on the Diploma in Higher Education. I narrated the whole story from the very beginning, when I thought of undertaking this work. Initially, I encountered hostility from the staff. Still I decided to negotiate with the City of London Polytechnic. The fundamental reason for working with the City Poly was not that I had my education there but the nearness of the place, the transport facilities and the validation offered by the Polytechnic. Despite the fact that I faced problems, I held weekly meetings, which were very well attended. The members of staff accepted my leadership, which made progress possible in this direction.

At the end of the interview, one of the members of the panel was very complementary and praised my work at the college and the interest; I had shown in the Higher Business Studies Department. Most of the colleagues were pleased with my promotion. The Vice Principal, the Deputy Principal and the Principal congratulated me on achieving the well- deserved promotion. My students, in the General Education Department, took the news with great understanding. They were, however, worried about their own learning.

In November 1989, I felt a little disappointed and disenchanted and thought of leaving the college for any- thing that I could get. This opportunity to start afresh at a new place (the Business Studies Department at Streatham); perhaps a few new courses and new challenges would revive my interests in the college work. At the new place, I kept a low profile in order to know more about people there and the work. Soon I found myself deeply involved in many activities. I was very busy from the start. The general environment started to change with the introduction of a new course leading to the B.A. degree in Business Studies commonly known as BABS at the college. I wrote a paper on 'quality control' of the course as a part of the submission for approval of the degree course. I realised that quality control was essential in order to accomplish a high standard in teaching, to make the best use of resources and to provide the best service to students.

It, therefore, formed a very significant part of the BABS offer. Quality control was not only concerned with teaching material or delivering lecturers at high standard.

It covered all areas of the degree classes including recruitment and selection of students, the curriculum content, teaching and learning strategies, responsibilities of personal tutor, and evaluation of the course. It was suggested that the admissions tutor or a member of the BABS team would interview all candidates, before they were offered a place on the course. The candidates should normally have five passes at GCSE/A Level, of which two must be at the Advanced Level grade 'C' or above. Equivalent qualifications such as the BTEC National Diploma with distinction in four subjects, the Scottish Council for Education Higher grade, a relevant Access to Higher Education, would be acceptable. Apart from the existing academic qualifications, the candidates would have to demonstrate their ability to pursue a course for an Honours degree and show their interest and commitment to studies.

The candidates might be required to complete a college devised entrance test including an extended piece of writing relevant to Business Studies course. The students, for whom English was not the first language, would be required to take a college devised English test. In assessing the candidates' ability to benefit from the course, the Admissions Tutor would be looking for the following qualities: ability to communicate effectively- orally as well as in writing; appropriate level of numeracy; analytical skills; and evidence to study independently.

The course curriculum provided an excellent opportunity for quality control. While, the external syllabus could be followed in teaching for the Business Studies degree, efforts would be made to meet the student's needs and their interests. The staff would be involved in curriculum development through evaluation of the courses. They would also seek the advice of other academics in this area. The most important function here was to assess the quality and standard of the course. This could be accomplished by a structured programme and by setting specific objectives of units of the course. The subject lecturers would also produce their subject teaching plans which would be scrutinized by the subject teams and advice could be sought from the course team.

The aims of the course programme would include the development of level required for the award of a body of knowledge and skills appropriate to the field of study and reflect academic development in that area. The curriculum would therefore, reflect aims and objectives of the course. The curriculum structure would provide for the progression of the student from the level of knowledge and skills required at the time of admission to the level required for the award of a degree in Business Studies.

The teaching and learning strategies employed in the course would vary according to the requirement of a particular subject discipline. But emphasis would be laid on subject team teaching and double-marking of students' scripts. The subject team would not only share teaching but also hold regular meetings to discuss the content to be taught, methods of delivery and students' response to the course. Apart from set lectures, class contact time would be devoted to student centred methods such as seminars, discussions, tutorials and small group work. A continual feedback from students and staff would judge the quality of work.

The learning resource services would be involved in study support, as a great deal of learning would take place outside the class contact time. As far as possible, assessment method would reflect the teaching and learning strategies. The students might also be assessed on individual and group project-work, practical-work and practical skills. The quality of teaching would be maintained and enhanced by highly qualified and experienced staff that would have experience of teaching at degree level. Many lecturers would have research experience. The teaching would, therefore, be invigorated and informed by their active participation in research and related scholarly and professional activities. Where possible, a subject adviser from another department would act as a consultant to the subject team. It may be possible to use advisers to teach parts of subjects but their main function would be to discuss the content of work and to help decide on the expected level of attainment.

Every student would be allocated a personal tutor who would monitor students' performance and progress. Through this regular, internal process, the course team would critically appraise the operation of the course and maintain a high standard. The personal tutor would also counsel and guide students on the selection of optional subjects and encourage them to maintain their interests in the course of study. The interaction between students and personal tutors would ensure self-criticism and high academic standards. Where necessary, the personal tutor would liaise with the College Students Services Officer and advise the Examination Board of specific student's needs and also problems. He would also attempt to seek solutions to the matter of deep consideration.

The communications and Numeracy workshop would bring students and lecturers very close. The students would be given individual attention. These would provide an opportunity to eradicate any handicaps that students might have in writing good English and in the field of numeracy. Thus students' performance would improve and they would also be in a position to acquire high quality education. The language specialists and the numeracy specialists along with a study skills specialist would staff these workshops. All students would be given an opportunity to monitor and improve their study skills by a series of curriculum initiatives, whereby skills could be explicitly highlighted. The study skills programme would not only focus on skills like notes staking from textbooks and lectures, essay writing, data retrieval and interpretation, but it would also show the teaching styles so that the students could judge for themselves the appropriateness of their learning methods. In the programme, students would be encouraged to make an initial assessment of their skills and recognize the areas for improvement.

The course review and evaluation was an important method of quality control. The fundamental aim for the course review was to secure for students a high quality of education and academic experience. Its most important function was to assess the quality and standard of the course. It also stimulated curriculum development by requiring staff to evaluate their courses. This critical appraisal and self-evaluation would ensure an appropriate standard. It was also hoped that every student would undertake an evaluation of his/her progress on the course. This would provide an opportunity not only for students to gauge in the levels of performance and to have these confirmed by staff but it would also enable them to judge whether the development of various skills had taken place or whether any particular areas needed to be focused-on for improvement in the future.'

I joined the Department of Higher Business Education at Streatham in December 1989, but before starting to teach, I went away to Delhi for a few weeks. On returning from India in January 1990, I started to teach in the new Department at the College. I still continued to teach at the Tooting site on Mondays and Fridays and at the City of London Polytechnic on Tuesday. At the Streatham site, I taught on Wednesdays and Thursdays.

My teaching commitment involved the Business Environment, which included Economics, Politics and Law. I liked the syllabus and the classes. After a few weeks, I stopped teaching at Tooting but continued to take part in the development of the Diploma in Higher Education.

In April, I withdrew from the DipHE and concentrated on my work in the Department of Higher Business Studies, which decided to start its own BA in Business Studies degree franchised from the Polytechnic of East London. My involvement was deep and I wrote a paper on quality control, which has been reproduced above. We also held meetings, which were not as good as we had for the DipHE. The staff, however, became close to each other. I also started to think of working on a project on changing pattern of small businesses in Britain in the past twenty years with special reference to Asian community. This was only at the thinking stage and I would write about it in details at a later stage.

In the past few years, we have received quite a few letters from India from my relatives. The correspondence with the new relatives was quite frequent. My family members helped a lot at the time of Saneh and Azad's engagement ceremonies. There was slow progress on the house construction. The builders did not finish work on time and they prolonged the work. They argued that they were poorly paid and they did just the enough work for the money they received. This, however, hampered our programme.

We would have preferred to get the work done as soon as possible. I must, nevertheless, acknowledge that my younger brother and nephews had been of great help in buying the building material and organizing the work. They continued to talk to the contractor and contacted a carpenter to make doors for the house. I duly wrote to people concerned and thanked them for their help and co-operation. Some of the work would have been slow without their effort.

Every- thing was fine in London. The construction completed by the middle of 1990, at the house in Delhi. Both, Saneh and Azad got married in June. We started to live as a joint family in Chiswick. I was busy with some writing and also keen to publish my research as a book. I found a publisher in Delhi and left the script with him to read and review. It, however, took almost two years when my first book, 'The Indian Nationalist Movement in Britain, 1930-49' came out in August 1992. I was pleased to see this publication. The reviews in newspapers and journals were good and appreciative of the work and its content.

The new academic year brought a load of work with a great deal of teaching commitment and marking. The evening classes were particularly tiring. The college also decided to merge with the Thames Polytechnic, as there was no progress on the Dip HE and BABS. A number of meetings were held at the Polytechnic's Roehampton site. I often had to go to Woolwich to talk to Staff in the Economics Department. It continued for the whole of the academic year. But due to some problems the merger was not easy and the British government decided to disperse the staff and the students to Thames Polytechnic, the Polytechnic of South Bank and the City of London Polytechnic. I decided to go to Thames along with a few colleagues and some students though majority of my students and colleagues opted for the South Bank Polytechnic, because it was nearer to the catchments area. This transfer would be good for me. Although I would miss some of my friends and colleagues and of course the students. A new start would, nevertheless, bring a new lease of life and new ideas. I would have to travel to Woolwich and Roehampton but there was nothing wrong with that. The good aspect was that I had a good job in the area where I had been working for the last few years. New openings might introduce better prospects.

The British government saw a change in leadership. The Conservative party held a view that Margaret Thatcher had become a liability. The party, therefore, elected John Major (Chancellor of the Exchequer) their leader and Prime Minister of the country. It brought a change in the style of government but the main policies remained the same. The government decided not to hold general election, despite a pressure from the opposition. The European Federation remained a theoretical issue for the British government. It could be possible that the European Union may federate to form a United States of Europe at a future date. But many problems remained regarding taxation, parliamentary sovereignty and so on. It was unlikely that such a state could evolve before the 21st Century.

In India the Janata Dal government fell. There were disturbances on the Ayodhaya Ram temple issue and the reservation for the backward classes. Some young people started to burn themselves alive. The prices of goods were rising. There were many social and economic problems to be solved. Early in 1991, a caretaker government was formed with the support of the Congress party which withdrew its support within weeks and the Indian government decided to call an election in May 1991. It was during the election campaign that Rajeev Gandhi, the Congress party leader was blown up by a human bomb. It shocked the whole world. In the elections the Congress party won a large number of seats though not an overall majority. It formed a government with P.V.Narasimha Rao as Prime Minister of India. He was the first South Indian to become a Prime Minister. He was a very able man and had a good team.

The country was, nevertheless, faced with a number of problems. The border states of Assam, Punjab and Kashmir remained turbulent. Economic and social problems had augmented. India had become an indebted nation and would have to borrow money from abroad. My feeling was that the new government would attempt to tackle the problems. Success remained to be seen.

I wrote two articles for Hansib Publishing in early 1991. These were edited because of the length. I did not hope to make any financial gain from these articles. I thought that it could bring some prestige essential for

Polytechnic teaching. I received a few letters from Thames Polytechnic and from the PCFC (Polytechnic and College Funding Council) confirming my transfer. I was to teach at Roehampton site and one day a week at Woolwich on the combined Engineering and Management degree course. I received my timetable and started to prepare lessons. I also continued to prepare lessons as teaching went along. I enjoyed that and had an opportunity to refresh and revise the subject matter.

In September 1991, the term started well at the Polytechnic. The teaching was good. The travelling was tiring not only to Woolwich but also to Roehampton. It was time consuming despite the fact that it was only about five miles from our house. My time was spent mainly on preparing Economics lectures and tutorial questions. I had a good office at Roehampton. The staff was good and helpful. I hoped to enjoy my stay at the Thames.

In 1992, the Conservative government decided to convert all the Polytechnics into new universities because they were not only teaching institutions for the first degree for which they were originally created in the early 1970s, but they offered Masters' courses and even research degrees leading to Ph.D. The Thames Polytechnic, therefore, became the University of Greenwich because its main sites were in the London borough of Greenwich and later it bought the old Naval College in Greenwich and moved the major schools to that site. It was nice to be a Senior Lecturer at the university. It was a coincidence that I reached the University without design.

It was my desire to teach at a University. I had progressed from school to Further Education College to Higher Education College to Polytechnic and eventually to University. I suspect whether I would have become a university lecturer in India. I did not come to London to teach at a university either. I, however, fulfilled my mission and the Almighty had perhaps helped me in this accomplishment. In 1992, the teaching was good. Many students passed the examination on the BABA course and every-one on the other courses. When my commitment at Woolwich ceased, the life became a little easier. I did not write anything new in this academic year but prepared teaching notes for First year Micro and Macro Economics which became a source my book published in the year 2000.

We planned to go to India in July 1992. I aspired to relax rest and visit a few places and spend time in peace. We stayed in India for six week, visited our relatives in Madhya Pradesh, stayed overnight in Jhansi, also went to see the temple museum at Khujrao. But due to rains and lack of water and food facilities in many places, we returned to Delhi and could not see places like Gwalior, Agra and Mathura on that occasion. We rested for a few days and then went to Saharanpur, Haridwar and Rishikesh in Uttar Pradesh. We enjoyed this trip and a bath in the holy Ganga. It was not only reposing but also informative from many points of view. After that we could not go to any other place and stayed at our house in Delhi. We would have wished to go a few places in Rajasthan but because of monsoon rains we remained house bound.

In December 1992, the Ram Janam Bhumi- Babri Masjid issue flared up. Some youths destroyed the old mosque where no one had prayed for ages. But it was seen as an attack on India's secularism. The Indian government declared to rebuild the mosque and also to build the Ram temple in India's northern city of Ayodhaya. The destruction of the mosque led to disturbances and over a thousand people died in clashes. The government, however, contained the situation. The foreign governments understood the Indian position though many temples were destroyed in Pakistan and Bangladesh. There was news in the British media; many programmes were done on the BBC and Channel 4. They, however, did not highlight the problem. Many Hindu temples were attacked in Britain also. For me, however, the year passed peacefully.

The new-year 1993, started with Santosh's eye operation. Azad came back from Delhi the same day. I became busy at the University. I had to finish some courses for the February, examination and start some new courses. I enjoyed teaching Business Economics. Amar's (my eldest grandson) first birthday brought many old and new friends to our house. They all enjoyed the party. The Business School at Greenwich University published my paper on the 'Decline of Cotton Industry in 19th Century India'.

The Indian government continued with its efforts to solve its economic intricacies. On the world scene, Bosnia a province in the old Yugoslavia, dominated the news headlines for a long period.

On 5th July 1993, I was invited to serve on the jury at a Crown Court. Fifteen people were sent to a court but twelve were selected. Three of us came back to the jury assembly room and later sent to another court where I was selected and sworn in. The case started the next day. The prosecution counsel presented the case. The witnesses were sworn in and asked questions and cross-examined by the defence counsel. The defence did not bring witnesses. The case was finally summarised by the prosecution counsel and then by the defence counsel. On another day the judge gave his summary of the law and the case. The jurors were then sent to a room. It was easy to reach a verdict. Every one agreed. But on another case on a different day, there were disagreements. All the jurors returned to court but the judge sent us back to consider the case again. He said that he would accept a majority verdict. After a discussion for another hour, the majority verdict was reached which was accepted in the court. My jury service lasted ten days.

At the start of the summer holiday, I was sick for a week but did the admissions duty at the University in August. After that I left for India. At this time I was working on my books 'The Indian Civil Service, sine 1860' and 'Imperialism and the Non-Aligned Movement'. In Delhi, I interviewed T.N.Kaul the former Indian Foreign Secretary and some other people at the Jawaharlal Nehru University. I discussed Krishna Menon with T.N.Kaul and others. The conversation with all these people was very good and encouraging. Then I went to Bombay to see Dr. Mulk Raj Anand who encouraged me to write a biography of Krishna Menon. Dr. Anand and Mr. Kaul were really great men. They were polite and well informed. I could not see P N Haksar who was sick at that time. I enjoyed my stay in Delhi and Bombay. I did not visit many places in Bombay, which I would have liked. Shri Ramji (one of my dearest known person) died while I was staying in Delhi. I also had to visit another family and a very sick young man at Meerut (U.P.). That man also died later. He was not a direct relative or acquainted with me personally. On the whole this was a satisfactory working holiday in India.

The term started well at the University. There was nothing unusual in my teaching commitment or programme. It was a repetition of last year's work. I continued to teach Year 1 and year 2 courses. There was a misunderstanding about the allocation of research fund and I felt left out. The new Head of School did not realise that I was entitled to a research fund. I, therefore, had to discuss the matter with the Head of Faculty who accepted that I was entitled to money which got to be found from other sources. I, therefore, received my allocation from the internal funds for a research on cold war and non-alignment. I must state that I did not write for three months. The other development was that I had a hernia operation at Charing Cross hospital on Wednesday 15 December 1993. I went to hospital early in the morning at 7 am with Santosh and Saneh. They stayed in the hospital during my operation and I was allowed to go home at 1 pm the same day. I had to stay at home for four weeks or more.

During Christmas break I took complete rest. There was no complication in the operation. In the early days of 1994, I started to write the introduction of the biography of Krishna Menon. I had collected a great deal of information from archives and interviews which I conducted in India as well as in London. I used to write a little and read a little while recuperating from the operation. I read Krishna Menon's speeches at the United Nations in 1957 and in 1962.

My research money was used to pay for my visit to Bombay and Edinburgh and also to pay for a tutor who took four of my tutorials a week. I started to work on the biography of Krishna Menon, The Non-Aligned Movement and the Indian Civil Service at the same time. I was busy but enjoyed it. I wanted to complete three books in three years. I used to go to libraries for research. I joined the University of London library, the SOAS library and the British library. I made some progress on the work. In June 1994, I went to Edinburgh to attend a conference on India, which was organized by the SOAS (School of Oriental and African Studies) librarian Ramesh Dogra who became a friend.

I wrote to the Indian archives, requesting if I could be permitted to see old documents. I also wanted to interview some people in India. I received a good response and decided to go to India for a month. I went to Delhi in August and worked at the Indian archives, the Sapru House library and the Indian Foreign Office library. People were really helpful this time. I interviewed A K Damodaran at his house in South Delhi, M S Rajan at JawaharLal Nehru University. Some politicians and Civil servants were not helpful. It was, nevertheless, a useful trip. Apart from research-work, we visited relatives at Meerut, Saharanpur and Baraut.in Uttar Pradesh. It was a busy schedule.

On returning to London, I found that my timetable was slack. I was asked to teach one- day week at the Roehampton site, one day a week for four weeks at Churchill House in Woolwich. This was a teaching programme on India in Politics Department. I taught about colonialism and Indian nationalism. Many students wrote good essays, which I marked and enjoyed reading. By the end of 1994, I completed my book on the Indian Civil Service and sent a copy of the script each to Vikas publications, Inter-India Publications and the Sanchar Publishing House. The Sanchar Publishing House published the book in 1996. On the cover page, I wrote, 'the Business administration refers to the demands and choice of consumers while public administration attends to externalities and welfare of individuals and society. Both were concerned with the use of resources. The success of these objectives depended on the organization and its employees. There had been much criticism of the Indian administration stigmatising it for corruption and inefficiency. The Indian administration lacked consultation and understanding with the public".

"The gap was, however, as wide today as it was during the British Raj. Nevertheless, it provided continuity from an empire to the republic whereby democracy had survived in India. It had contained the growth of provincialism and provided leadership in times of need. Still it was essential to change the attitudes of administrators and democratise the system in order to reflect the public sentiment. It was possible only if the people of right calibre, moral courage, perceptibility and integrity were appointed and provided with proper training. Efficiency could also be improved by accountability, management and delegation of responsibility. The recent years had witnessed, that gifted young men and women had moved away from the public services, towards business management, due to attractive financial rewards. It was vitally important to recruit and retain personnel of high competence and intellectual capacity to administrative services. Experienced people from other fields like the academia and the business could be seconded to government departments and public services".

I further wrote, 'a good administrator required enterprise, strength of character, energy and vigour. There had been a decline of these traits in India. There was, therefore, a need for character uplift. It was vital to develop administrative democracy. Despite all sorts of shortcomings and inefficiency the government of India was rated among a dozen or so most advanced governments in the world. India did not lack skilled workers or intelligent people. Many Indians were the backbone of the United Nations, Britain, the United States and many other countries. The pan-Indian characteristic and loyalty to India rather than to any particular state had contributed to national integrity and unity. The top civil servants provided their service to the district or the state, yet remained steadfast to the centre and did not forget their responsibility in implementing the laws of the land and following the basic principles of the constitution. It was still essential to make improvements in order to win the hearts and minds of common people. They should identify themselves with their countrymen and with the values of social change. They should form a partnership with the public and its political representatives'.

………...   ….

The Economics Division of the Greenwich University held a meeting in Kent about the reorganisation of the subject and its role within the school of social sciences. It was decided that we should all stay together. On 20 December 1994, we had a grandson who brought happiness in our lives and brightened the home environment. I also managed to do some writing on Menon's biography and read some documents on non-alignment. I sent an article on Krishna Menon: A St. Pancras councillor, for publication to the New Society Review. This article came out of my research on this subject and a paper I read at the Society of Afro-Caribbean and Asian Associations on 29 October at Leicester. The visit to Leicester was refreshing. We turned it into a family outing.

CHAPTER 4

Golden Period, 1995-2000

In May 1995, I read a paper on Indian nationalism at the Humanities School, University of Greenwich and in October, I presented a seminar at the School of the Commonwealth Studies. This year was good for academic work. Through-out the year I continued to work on the biography of Krishna Menon and the Non-aligned Movement. During the summer time, I managed to interview Dr. L M Singhvi, the Indian High Commissioner in London and Tony Benn MP. Dr. Singhvi gave me a lot of original information and some photographs taken at the India High Commission a few years earlier. We did not go on holiday this year and I continued to work on the books. I sent a copy of the script to Dr. Anand in Bombay who liked it very much and also wrote an afterword because he wanted the readers to read my work first and judge for them-selves, the justice done to the subject.

I spent the month of July on research at the Public Record Office, Kew, London. The months of August and September were spent on word processing the Biography. On 20th September, Amar and Sangeeta started to attend a nursery school in Chiswick. They did not resent, though they were not very happy at the beginning. We received very few letters from India. I did not write many either. My nephew Vijay Kumar was angry at one stage with the situation in India –politically and socially. He expressed his discontent in a long letter to me.

I completed Krishna Menon's Biography by the end of September. After reading a couple of times, I sent a copy of the script to Orient Longman at Hyderabad. They acknowledged the receipt of the script but I did not hear anything after that.

On 2ⁿᵈ December, Azad went to India on holiday. On the 13ᵗʰ, he phoned to say that our dearest mother passed away that day at 3pm Indian time (9.30am London time). She had been ill since August but we did not expect her death at that time. She lived a good life of 85 years. She always walked straight and reasonably well. The news obviously disturbed me and I was prepared to go to Delhi but Azad told me that the cremation was to take place the next day on 14ᵗʰ December 1995. I could not have reached there on time. He felt that there was no need for me to be there. He phoned me again on 15ᵗʰ that the ashes of my mother were taken to Haridwar by my younger brother and one of the nephews. Azad promised to keep me informed.

I had some recollections of my mother bearing in mind that I had lived in England for over thirty years and even before that I lived away from her since August 1948, when I left my family and went away to study at Khurja. She did not visit us in London or Chirawa where I lived and worked in early 1960s. Once or twice she came to Khurja, when I was young and a couple of times to Delhi in 1964/5, before I came to England. My mother was a strong woman. She had her own personality. She hardly ever accepted her weaknesses. We used to meet quite often, when I started to go to Delhi after building our house in 1990. My first recollection of my mother goes back to the 1940s, when we started to go to visit her brothers in Delhi. I occasionally visited her in the 1950s and 1960s and then came to live in England.

She was more accommodating in her later years, though as firm as in the past. Since we built our house we had gone to Delhi every year except in 1991 and 1995. My mother used to talk a lot but had become hard of hearing in her old age. She remembered her past, her parents, her brothers and others but she never talked about her childhood. She talked of the hardships of the early 1930s and how my father and grand-parents worked hard. She narrated a few incidents of her eldest brother's behaviour towards their parents. My mother did not talk of her other brothers much, though they were all in Delhi. My uncle and my mother did not see each other even at festivals. Her nephews and niece sometimes came to visit her in Delhi and they wanted her to visit them at their houses but she never went to see them.

She always liked my sisters and their children and all the grand-children. She had become fond of her grandchildren. She expected a little more from her sons that they should take her around to holy places and pilgrimage. She fell ill in the summer of 1995 and perhaps she never recovered. I was not informed of this illness. I could not see her in the last year and the last days of her life. The last time I saw her in September 1994, when she came to see us off, at mid-night. I looked at her for the last time. She had a pale gaze at me in despair as if she was saying to me 'Keshava, take me with you to London, do not leave me at this place because I am not happy here any more'. I had hoped to see her again but I could not go to India in the summer of 1995. I will miss her when I go to Delhi next time.

Despite the fact that we had not lived together for forty-seven years, I had a genuine liking of my mother. We had different ways of thinking because of our diverse experiences but the natural bond was there and she appreciated that I never answered her back even when she told me-off. I wanted to treasure this as the good memories, her devotion to the family, and her hard work in the early years of the family life. A life of eighty-five years was good from any standards. She used to rejoice in happiness and took part in weddings, which she enjoyed most. If she remembered others or was to compare with the deeds of the past, she said, 'my mother-in-law' used to say that or used to do that (hamari Ammaji kehti thi). She often remembered my grand-mother but never talked of her own life with my father or her own parents.

I must also write that in 1989, when we started to build our house, I stayed with her. She was very happy and wanted me to return to India for good. In 1990, when Saneh and Azad got married, we stayed in Delhi for more than two months. She actively participated in their weddings and made suggestions. She was not afraid of saying or asking for any thing. She liked both the new members of the family. She used to visit us at the house when we were there. She was sometimes critical of some relatives. She did not force any one to do anything. She would be remembered for her strong views, good memory, curiosity and search for good family life.

+   +

The year 1996, dawned quite well. Sanchar decided to publish the Biography of Krishna Menon. They published "The Steel Frame-Indian Civil Service Since 1860." Some good reviews came out in journals and newspapers. This book aimed to examine the roots of corruption and inefficiency in Indian administration. It was essential to look into the historical background of the Indian Civil Service, social and economic reasons and the type of service needed and provided at different times in India. Gandhiji found the British-Indian administration too expensive and too bureaucratic, which had nothing in common with the aspirations and needs of the common man in India. He wanted the British administration in India to work for the benefit of India and for the welfare of Indians. He differed with Pandit Nehru who wanted the British to leave but the British system to remain in India.

Many British administrators had misbehaved and looked down upon Indians. They had also opposed the nationalists and nationalism in India. It was mainly because of Mountbatten that the British Officers, who had worked in India, received a good deal from the independent Indian government. They were given pensions and severance pay from the Indian Treasury for the work they did for British imperialism. The Indianisation process of the Indian Civil Service (though belated) provided Indians an experience of running the affairs of the state and when freedom was accomplished, the Indian Civil Servants were ready to take over the reins of administration. This continuity served the Indian democracy well. Of course certain changes in the administrative system were inevitable to suit the needs and requirements of new India.

+   +   +   +

In May 1996, I found the relations between India and the United States of some relevance. The Indians had always perceived that they were not supported by the United States in their struggle for independence, despite the fact that the US became free and united many years ago. The British government ensured that the Congress party did not propagate or attempt to influence the US public opinion and administration. During the Second World War, President Roosevelt could not obtain any concessions, for India, from Churchill. After freedom, Nehru's visit to the United States in 1949, started with wrong impressions.

The Indians were on their high moral plateau and the Americans were proud of their financial riches and economic strength. India's decision to remain away from the power blocs also created misgivings and the US efforts to show superiority, and not to recognize India's efforts for the world peace were antagonistic. In the 1960s, the US did not come out immediately to assist India against the Chinese aggression. Their insistence on the removal of Krishna Menon from the Indian Cabinet and solving the Kashmir problem was paramount in order to obtain military and financial assistance.

In the 1970s, the US support for military dictators of Pakistan and their criticism of Indian Prime Minister Indira Gandhi was not positive for Indo-US relations. During the 1980s, however, the US administration encouraged almost one million Indians, mainly doctors, scientists, technologists and shopkeepers to settle in America. Nevertheless, it did not bring the two administrations any closer. The 1990s, dawned with the US criticism of the Indian government action in the Punjab and Kashmir and the human rights issue as seen by the Americans. The Indians, however, had their own way of doing things and still considered them- selves as the moral leader of the world. They reminded the Americans of their actions in Vietnam and their behaviour with their own people where human rights had been taken away and equality distorted.

In 1991, the Indian government had liberalised the economy and opened its gates for foreign investment. But the move had been slow. The foreign businesses criticized Indian bureaucracy and political and administrative corruption, which hindered investment. Some businesses were, however, encouraged to develop trade relations with a democratic and stable country. The Indian scientists, technologists and other professionals were determined to make India self-sufficient in defence. The Indian missile programme was being undermined by the West. The United States feared that the Indian missiles might attack the US fleet in the Pacific and the Atlantic. India would never do that. Firstly, India's efforts were defensive. They wanted to provide defence to the country. Secondly, India had never attacked any country in the past. It had fought many battles on its own soil and often lost due to lack of modernisation and preparedness of the defence system.

Thirdly, India could never envisage an attack on a powerful country like the United States with which it was trying to develop friendship and understanding.

The United States had developed fear because of the Japanese attack on Pearl Harbour during the Second World War. Any good relations could not be founded on fear. There was a need to enunciate trust and understanding between the two nations. After all both the countries were democratic. The resident Indians in the United States played a crucial role in bridging this gap. The education, good communication, extension of Indian culture in the United States improved Indo-US relations. The United States of America was promoting its education system and culture in India.

In June 1996, I fell ill. The blood tests showed that I had a glandular fever and could be sick for weeks or even for months because there was no cure for this fever. I was advised to take rest. Still I continued to go University. I used to get tired. My work suffered.

The most disappointing thing was that any reputable publisher in Britain did not accept my biography of Krishna Menon. The Oxford University Press, New Delhi set on it for six months. When I sent a reminder they simply replied that their assessors had not reported yet. I decided to get it published by Sanchar who were keen to publish and they had published many books related to Krishna Menon including his speeches at the United

Nations. Dr. MulkRaj Anand found the book of a high standard. He felt it deserved a D.Litt (Doctor of Letters) award.

While waiting for the book to be published, I managed to publish an article, on Krishna Menon's birthday 3rd May 1996, in the India Weekly. Another article was published in the New Society Review. I became involved in the Humanities department and prepared a course outline on the Third World Politics and the Non-alignment for the MA degree. In 1997, I started to research for a new book on India's economic history from 1765 to 1947, and wanted to publish a book in order to celebrate India's fifty years of freedom. I decided to use the existing material from my paper on Colonialism and the Decline of the Cotton Industry in the 19th Century India; the Fight for India's Freedom and some other researched material, especially on political parties, the coming of railways and the improvement in irrigation system. An extensive research was needed for this book.

In India, the Congress was no more a major ruling party. It had lost prestige and a national base, which was built by Gandhiji and nurtured by Nehru. The Congress started to disintegrate in the 1960s, especially after Nehru's death. The personality cult took over the policies. The political heavy weights started to influence the selection of Parliamentary candidates. The interests of the nation were side lined. The leader (Indira Gandhi) was not consulted in many decisions. In 1967, the party was divided into two groups- The Indian National Congress (I) led by Indira Gandhi and the Indian National Congress led by Morarji Desai. The Congress (I) continued to rule through out the 1960s and early 1970s. In 1975, there was a great opposition to Indira Gandhi and the Congress (I) and the old guards formed an alliance of various parties and called themselves the Janta Dal.

In the 1977 election, the Janta Dal received more seats than the Congress. It, therefore, formed a government under the Prime Minister ship of Morarji Desai who was an old Congressman and had been Chief Minister of Bombay in the 1950s; Finance Minister in the central government in the late 1950s and early 1960s. He was also Indira Gandhi's Deputy from 1966 to 1967. But there were ideological differences between him and Mrs.

Gandhi. However, he did not last long as India's Prime Minister and the Janta Dal was defeated in the 1979 election.

The Indian electorate started to show maturity. They had rejected Indira Gandhi in 1977. After two years they rejected the new party and brought the Congress back to power with a substantial majority. The Congress party had, however, lost its ideological base and it had started to appeal to special constituencies. It was still popular among the Muslims of India. They saw it as a secular democratic party. The suppressed classes and the low castes supported it. They saw it as a better alternative to other parties. The people of India were being divided into rich and poor, rural and urban, young and old. The urban population did not get a better deal from the Congress. The taxes were high; housing and education problems remained unsolved. The reservation for the scheduled castes did not help any body but kept the aspiring middle classes out of government schools and government jobs. They sought and found an alternative in private schools and foreign universities. They moved away from government employment to private sector where remuneration was high.

Politically, they started to move to the right centre and voted for the BJP (Bhartiya Janta party), which was originally established as the Jan Sangh in the 1950s. It had no representation at the centre or at the state level at that time though it had local councillors in Delhi and other places. It appealed for common elements of citizenship and the law. The BJP argued for no favouritism, no reservation for any class or group of people. It was, nevertheless, identified with the middle class urban Hindu community. In the 1984, elections it had only two MPs, but in 1991 it had 80 MPs and in 1996 it had about 190
MPs and formed a government for eleven days under the Prime-Minister ship of Attal Bihari Bajpai who had been India's Foreign Minister from 1977 to 1979 in the Janta Dal government under Morarji Desai.

The 1990s saw a minority government of the Congress party under PM Narasimha Rao. This government started on the economic reforms and opened up Indian industry and commerce for foreign investment. This government, however, became identified with inefficiency and corruption.

The civil servants refused to perform their duties properly without bribery. The political corruption was rife, as new projects needed cabinet approval. Foreign businesses bribed politicians, which was quite common in the developing countries. The people of India felt cheated and they voted the Congress out in the 1996 election.

The electorate had become disenchanted with politicians. Yet Indians generally remained very political in their outlook and discussions. They did not easily trust any group of people. No national alternative had emerged to the Congress party and the Congress party had lost its national base. Consequently regional parties emerged to bridge the gap. They had the same objectives, i.e. removal of poverty, provide employment, improve education and health. All the political parties had accepted economic reforms and foreign investment in order to accomplish economic growth. Secularism and democracy had been adopted as political objectives and non-alignment as a part of foreign policy. The Hindus made up 86% of the population and it was they who had decided to keep India secular and showed respect for all religions.

After the defeat of the BJP (Bhartiya Janta Party) government in 1996, the Centre-Right National Front was asked to form a government at the centre. It had the support of the Congress party with its 130 MPs. There was no change in policies. Educated middle class had withdrawn from politics. Lower ranks, who even had criminal records, took charge and formed their own political parties. Politics had taken a different shape in India. It was not confined to ideology and administration. Its aim was to acquire power in order to use it for personal purposes rather than for the welfare of the people.

The people of India should themselves decide what form of politics they wanted, which political party they needed to support. If the Indian electorate had acquired maturity in considering the welfare of the country and its people, they would be able to judge the good of the nation and elect leaders, who could achieve economic progress, social welfare, high culture and good education along with national unity and integrity. The electorate would themselves produce these leaders who would take active part in politics. They should not have a negative attitude and simply reject leaders and parties.

In August 1996, Dr Mulk Raj Anand visited England and Scotland. I went to see him in North-London on a Sunday. He enquired about my book on Krishna Menon. I told him that I had written to a number of publishers in England and in India. Perhaps one of my old publishers in Delhi would publish it. He said that an obscure publisher should not publish such a good book. He gave me a letter for Vision publishers in New Delhi. I posted that letter immediately. Santosh and I went to Delhi on 16th August 1996. We went to Vision publishers on Friday in the week we reached Delhi. We saw their Manager who said that he would like to read the script before taking a decision. I went to see him again after a week when he told me that he enjoyed reading the script and would publish it. I handed him the disk, which had the latest draft. He promised to read the entire script and would point out the areas for clarification before we returned to London. He never responded and did not publish the book. He was angry and questioned, why was Dr. Mulk Raj Anand's letter sent to his brother who only ran the distribution department. But the letter was forwarded from his office because it was addressed to his brother. There should have been some problems between these brothers.

In the mean time we went on a holiday to Dehradun, Mussorie, Rishikesh and Haridwar. It was a nice break though the journey was very hectic and uncomfortable. The buses were dirty, the roads had pit-holes. The visit to hills and valleys was pleasant. On our return to Delhi we became very busy. A large number of people came to visit us. The next day we came back to London and I became occupied at the University.

In May 1997, election was held in Britain and the New Labour party won with a substantial majority. In 1979, the Labour party was defeated for two reasons. It had lost touch with people. The Trade Unions, which were a major part of the Labour party, had lost sympathy among the masses. There were strikes in almost every public sector which led to winter of discontent when the dustbin men refused to collect rubbish, the grave diggers refused to bury the dead and the train drivers refused to drive the trains. The government lost in the House of Commons on the question of devolution of power to Scotland and Wales.

The conservatives had a charismatic leader in Mrs Margaret Thatcher who appealed to the masses and brought a new vision and promised new policies. The consensus politics of the 1950s, 1960s and 1970s, was abandoned. The conservatives offered home ownership and a share-owning society. They privatised the British Telecommunications, British Steel, British Gas and almost one hundred companies. In later years they were to privatise the public utilities, like the water boards and finally the British Rail. It was not the selling of the house silver because these companies had become inefficient and burden on the Treasury. The British Steel alone was taking 2 million pounds a day in subsidies. Nine billion pounds investment in the Coal industry remained ineffective. The privatised sector became efficient. The government introduced new technology and investment.

The people of Britain witnessed an improvement in their standards of living. They voted for the Conservatives four time and the Tories ruled for eighteen years. But things started to get sour in 1993. Unemployment was rising, people became homeless, the burden on social services increased. The standards in education and health services declined and discontentment returned to Britain. There was bickering and infighting in the Conservative party. They had lost the will to govern, despite the fact that the economy was improving. The rate of inflation was around three percent. The interest rates were 6%.

The Labour party had modernised itself. It changed its rules. The power of the Unions was reduced, the Clause 4 was dropped. They promised to keep the Tory employment laws. But it did not have a charismatic leader. In 1992, John Smith emerged as the new leader and took the party forward into the city of London and businesses. He developed contacts with businessmen and recruited them into the Labour party, making it a broad church and not only a mouthpiece of the organised labour. His untimely death, however, plunged the party into some uncertainty. After a couple of months a young Tony Blair was elected as the leader of the Labour party. Because of his background, he introduced further changes and appealed to the masses. His Deputy, John Prescott was committed to increasing membership and changes in the organisation. In this, I also supported the New Labour and the new leadership though I had always admired Michael Foot, Tony Benn and Barbara Castle.

I had been against the strikes and power of the unions. I had believed that there should be other methods, apart from strikes, in order to solve the industrial problems and look after the interests of the workers who were more educated today than one hundred years ago. Britain was, moreover, not only an industrial country it was also moving towards a postindustrial era. The education had increased. Some 30% of 18 year old were now in FE/HE institutions. There were more professionals today than ever before. I agreed with almost all the new policies, which were adopted democratically through consultation.

In March 1997, Prime Minister John Major declared an election and six weeks of electioneering. The differences among the conservatives surfaced and the sleaze (corruption) in politics became visible. The Labour party on the other hand remained united and their appeal was heeded by the electorate. Astonishingly the media also supported the Labour party this time. There was a mood for change in the country. People looked to new ideas and new personalities. I also made my contribution at the election time. Apart from the financial contribution for the election, I attended local Labour party meetings, distributed leaflets and pamphlets and on the election day, I did a four hour duty at the election booth. The turn out was quite good. The Labour party won the election with a majority of 179 and returned to power after 18 years in wilderness.

Tony Blair became the youngest Prime Minister in the 20th Century. He, however, kept his gentleness and humility and still remained a man of principles. When he went to 10 Down Street (Prime Minister's residence), he shook hands with a large number of people who had lined up to greet him and showed their appreciation. On Sunday, he went to his local church like an ordinary citizen. He also decided not to take the increased salary of the Prime Minister and accepted the Cabinet Minister's pay. He started the use of first names at Cabinet meetings.

It was just over a month since the new government took office. It had not been criticized by the media or the public, despite the fact it had taken some tough decisions. It was determined to implement the election manifesto in its entirety. The Scotland and Wales devolution bills had taken shape. The referendum bill (to remain in the European Union) had already been passed by the House of Commons. The Environment and Transport department was determined to improve both the environment and the transport system. The budget was due on 2 July when the public utilities would be required to pay tax worth three to five billion pounds in order to provide jobs to long term unemployed.

The education reforms and measures to improve the school standards were being considered. People were less afraid today of losing their jobs now, than they were a few months earlier. They were hoping for the return of the old culture of stable and permanent jobs. There was a great talk of welfare reforms and to encourage young mothers with children to return to work rather than to live on social security and dependent on the state. The welfare system had been misused by some in this country.

In July 1997, we went to India not only for holiday but also to get some work done at the house in Delhi, because a burglary had taken place in October 1996. We had iron bars erected at the front of the house to make it safe. We also raised the walls all around. We managed to do all that within the first two weeks. We postponed the other work regarding the electricity connection and the sewage system.

I fell sick and was unwell for a week, with high temperature which reached 103F. One day, I had to consult a doctor. I liked the local doctor who was young and intelligent and prescribed the right medicine. He knew his job well. Because of my back pain, I stayed at home lying down in bed most of the time. I could only sit for about twenty minutes and needed to be in bed again. I avoided travelling because I felt uncomfortable in going out. However, after three weeks, we decided to go to Jaipur in Rajasthan. The pink city had changed enormously since my last visit in October 1962. It was not that beautiful as it had been thirty five years earlier. The pollution had increased. The day coach tour was fine. We liked a few things, also did some shopping. We went to a restaurant on the mountain where there use to be the Amber. We also saw two films in Jaipur. On the third day when we were due to return to Delhi, I fell ill again. Still we returned to Delhi by coach and reached Delhi early in the morning at about 6am. I then relaxed. On 15 August 1997, there were great rejoicings in Delhi because it was India's 50th Independence Day. We went to Pashchim Vihar and watched the proceedings on television.

It was a common knowledge that corruption had increased in India over the years. The Prime Minister spoke on this subject and pledged to eradicate it. He asked people not to take bribe or give bribe because if you would not give how could someone take bribe. But people were used to the system and it was difficult to get any work done without a bribe. The people would suffer, their work would remain undone. I also noticed that people lied about their finances and property. It was said that there were two hundred million middle class people in India who had durable goods but only a small percentage of population paid the taxes. The house owners and residents in cities and villages did not want to pay house-tax or the income-tax, even when they could afford it. The government was aware of this problem but politicians themselves avoided tax and did not pay their bills on time.

We returned to London on 18th August 1997. I had pain in the lower back and could not sit for long. Though I could watch TV, walk straight and sleep well. I had a prostrate operation on 16th February 1998. I took some time off from the University but returned to teach after four weeks. I did not want my students to miss out on their learning. We had good results in Business Economics and Industrial Economics. There was an increased number of A and B grades in both the subjects. We received excellent comments from the external examiner.

The British foreign policy seemed to follow the American foreign policy. Prime Minister, Blair even supported Clinton on his personal matter when a scandal was revealed. Britain supported the American bombing in Afghanistan and the Sudan. The British economy had suffered this year, despite the decline in the number of unemployed. The interest rates remained high. The industrial decline and factory closures continued. The crime rates had gone up. In September, the British government decided to build more houses and to demolish the big towers, which looked ugly.

In May 1998, India experimented her nuclear device. It had its repercussions on her relations with the West, especially the United States. Pakistan also exploded her devices in retaliation to India's. There were articles in the newspapers about the nuclear tests, effects on India's economy and the question of her security. Some political parties in India started to play the western tune but most parties recognized the need for these weapons. The scientists and the Army Generals accepted the need for such weapons and thus experiments. Public supported the government policy on the security of the nation. India was a big country and could not rely on other nations for defences. Moreover, India had been invaded and ruled by foreigners for a long time. It was vital for her to be militarily and economically strong and self-sufficient.

In July 1998, we went to India on holiday. The temperature was high, 43C in the day time and 30C during the night. It was humid. We did not go out of Delhi which had now become a crowded city. It was not easy to travel there. Still it was a refreshing and comforting holiday for me. I rested, read newspapers, listened to the radio and the music. I stayed away from television and telephone or even serious reading and writing. I spent my time observing the Indian politics, society, social and other changes. Often, I discussed these subjects with other members of the family who used to visit me in the evening. The Indian society was going through a transition. The joint family system was being challenged. Some still clung to this system. But there was a friction in the families because younger generation wanted their freedom and wanted to live on their own as they wished.

More people were in employment rather than in family businesses. They earned their income which they wanted to spend on themselves and not on the extended family. In the past salary or income was given to the head of the family who decided how and on which items to spend the money. Now people were moving towards a nucleus family. They did not want to live with the oldies. There had been examples of misbehaving with the elderly parents-who were regarded as burden and interfering.

In a family, people looked for personal needs rather than the joint needs of all. They spent money on themselves or saved for themselves. Joint families were scarce in Indian cities and towns. It was believed that India was moving towards the Western system of small families. However, unless India had western type of education, social services, National Health Service and the welfare system, there could be problems for the elderly, the young, the unemployed and the poor. Without the taxes, the public services, good roads, houses and hospitals could not be provided. India's problems lay in half-baked Westernisation.

Delhi's population had increased by half a million every year in the past decade. The Delhi government had not been able to provide even the primary education for its children. Consequently, small schools had sprung up in the neighbourhoods to fill in this gap. The parents were keen to educate their children. They were ready to spend money for this purpose. They sent their children to small schools, run in one and two rooms of a house by half educated and untrained teachers. There was no way the standard could be maintained or uniformity achieved.

The children had no place to play sports or do PE. Parks were non-existence in many localities. In Secondary schools, there was no opportunity to learn sciences, though commerce, typing and computing could be taught. The influence of education on society was not constructive. The students become self centred, secluded and lonely. They found it difficult to face the larger community. They lacked social identity. In the past and still in some places, education was provided in large institutions where students reacted with each other, which was not possible in small schools.

The crime rate had increased in India generally and in Delhi in particular. There were many robberies in Delhi while we were there. The buses were looted, houses were burglared, shops and factories were robbed. People had become selfish. They wanted to have the things for themselves without working for them. The gap between the rich and the poor had widened.

It was not essentially the poor who robbed the rich. The criminals carried out such acts.

On the international scene the south-east-Asian countries witnessed financial and economic chaos in 1997/8. Indonesia's President Suharto was deposed. It was, nevertheless, a peaceful period for me. I published two books in 1998, and managed to complete the third one, which was being considered by Hamilton Publications Ltd.

In 1999, my teaching was fine. I enjoyed teaching political economy. The students were often quiet but sometimes participated in seminars. The standard of their work was good. The Business Economics students were excellent. They contributed in seminars. Even the first year BABA students were nice. I cannot recall, a year when all my students were good, keen to learn and able to contribute. However, I still had problems with sitting for a long time. I, therefore, found travelling to University tiring. I had a local injection in the bone but it did not improve my condition.

At the end of March the same year, the United States of America and its NATO allies started to bomb the Serbian province of Kosovo and later the rest of Serbia and Yugoslavia. There had been an ethnic problem in that country. Many Albanians moved to live in Kosovo in Serbia because it bordered the state of Albania. In course of time they formed 80% of the population. They started to demand independence from Serbia and formed their own KLA (the Kosovo Liberation Army) in order to fight the Serbian police and army. The West had hoped that Yugoslavia would join the NATO and the Western bloc after Tito. It had been the policy of the USA and the European Union to form a big bloc. But Yugoslavia wanted to remain non-aligned. Moreover, Serbs were a Slavic race and belonged to the Orthodox Church. Thus they were closer to Russia. They had no closeness to the West culturally, politically or religiously. In the Western game plan, however, they should have been with them. Firstly, Yugoslavia was fragmented and Croatia, Bosnia, and Macedonia were separated from the federation. Then the West wanted to fragment the rest of the Yugoslavia.

The Serbs were a strong race. In the past they fought the Austro-Hungarians, the Germans under Hitler and refused to follow the Stalin's approach to communism. Despite the bombardment for more than three weeks, the NATO was not been able to accomplish its objective. It had dropped bombs worth six billion dollars. The President of the USA asked the Congress to sanction another four billion dollars to continue the war activities in Yugoslavia.

The bombing of Yugoslavia, however, created a refugee problem when thousand people left the war torn Kosovo. The NATO did not consider this problem in its war plan. A large number of civilians died in attacks and many became homeless. It became a disaster of human creation. Twenty-one rich and strong countries continued to bombard a small non-aligned nation. It was tragic. It looked as if no morals were left in the world.

On 17 April 1999, India's Prime Minister Attal Bihari Bajpai resigned because his coalition lost support in the Lok Sabha (the Lower House of Indian Parliament). He was leading a coalition of many parties. In a democracy like India's, coalition was not always successful. In politics ideology was also important. If parties came together for their self- interest, it was not good for the nation. The leader of the All India Dravid Munetra Kargam (ALDMK) party withdrew from the coalition. She demanded sacking of the Defence Minister, George Fernandez. The Prime Minister refused to remove him from his portfolio. It was the Prime Minister's prerogative to appoint a minister or to remove him. No one else could force him to appoint or remove his ministers.

George Fernandez had been an effective Defence Minister. He brought some essential changes in his department. He sent civilians to see the army in action on the borders. He was perhaps the best Defence Minister for a long time. Fernandez had been interested in the defence and security of the country since his youth. He had written on this subject and was out spoken about India's enemies. For the first time, he made it clear that both China and Pakistan were India's enemies because they had attacked India on many occasions. There was a pressure from those countries to remove him from his position as India's Defence Minister.

I recalled when Krishna Menon was appointed Defence Minister in the 1950s, there were calls for his removal and people did not rest until he had gone in 1962. The same tactics were applied to remove George Fernandez. Jayalalita Jaya Ram did the dirty work for foreign powers. She handicapped the improvement of India's defences. She also created a political conundrum. It was very easy to create problems but it was not easy to find their solutions. There was no clear alternative to the present government because no other single party had a majority in the Lok Sabha.

When a new government would be formed, it could be a coalition again with interest groups showing their power. The Congress party was not able to form a government. It did not have many good leaders either. The country was in chaos. Murders, kidnapping and disturbances took place in Bihar. Delhi was not peaceful either. The Delhi government had not been successful in stopping the killings, kidnappings and other crimes. It had failed to provide housing, water, electricity and schools to many of its citizens.

+   +   +

In 1998, the Greenwich University started the Ph D by publication. Under this system lecturers, who were research active and had published books and articles, were encouraged to submit their work to the Research Committee to be assessed for the Ph D degree. Alan Foster of Humanities School encouraged me to apply and submit my work. In order to consider this matter Ron Ayres, Alan Foster and I met on Friday 23rd April 1999 at Woolwich. Alan had read my biography of Krishna Menon and he understood what was new in it. He also gave me a copy of the University regulations. But Ron was still confused. He said that it was essential to identify the problem which had not been made clear in the book and that it should come out in the submission. He was, however, very supportive of the system of PhD by publication at the University of Greenwich. Alan wrote a report, which Ron accepted as perfect. He did not alter or add any thing. He typed it and signed it. Later Mike Kelly and Alan Foster signed and I submitted my application with my published book to the Research Committee on 30th April.

On 5th May 1999, I had a staff appraisal meeting with Mike Kelly (Head of Social Sciences). He asked me about my health, my publications and teaching. If I had any traveling difficulties. He enquired, if I was researching on another topic. I told him that I was planning to write an economic history of British India and I had written a textbook for the First Year degree course, which was being published by Hamilton & Co. He said that he would like to have a copy of that book. He also asked about my submission for the Ph D and that I would have a full year to complete and that we would have to get a registration. On the appraisal form, however, I wrote,

1. The closure of the Roehampton site transferred all my teaching to Woolwich and Avery Hill sites. I continued to teach Principles of Economics, Economics for Business and Industrial Economics in the Business School and took seminars in Political Economy on the BA Economics course at Avery Hill. I also provided personal tutorial support at Avery Hill. The number of students taking the second year courses had increased within a couple years of starting teaching. The results in both subjects were 100% passes. The external examiner found the students' examination answers of high standard and consistency in marking.

2. After some hiccups, I was provided a room at Avery Hill and I was able to read my e-mail more regularly, attend more subject group and school meetings than in the past.

3. I designed two new courses in 'Non-Aligned Movement and the Third World politics' for the MA degree in the Humanities School and the 'North-South Economic Relations' for the BA Economics course. Both courses were on offer and I hoped to teach these courses next year.

4. In 1998, I published two books 'Imperialism and the Non-Aligned Movement' and 'VK Krishna Menon-A Biography'. I was working on these books since 1993.

5. In the near future I hoped to attend a workshop on the use of the Internet.

In the column on the year ahead I wrote,

(I)   Next year, most of my teaching would be in the Business School, where I would continue to teach Principles of Economics, Economics for Business as well as Industrials Economics

(II)   I would continue to provide personal tutorial support at Avery Hill.

(III) I hope to continue my research interests by deepening the study of North-South as a part of the Economics Department offer.

Mike Kelly wrote a very good comment on this form before sending it to the Personnel. He wrote 'it was nice to have KC as a colleague in the School of Social Sciences. He had been an asset in the Economics Division and made enormous contribution. He (KC) has set a high standard and I would like it continued.' This comment reflected Kelly's feelings and I was delighted to know that my work and contribution was appreciated. It was good to have a good report and support from the Head of School. It gave me pleasure and satisfaction.

The summer months of 1999, were spent in marking the examination scripts and working on my submission in support of my theses. Although, I was to submit my published book, I still had to do some literary review and write a justification for the award of the Ph D and to write three articles based on my book. It was to be supplemented with the up dated research.

In this part of Chiswick, where we lived, there were very few Afro-Asian families. However, we had a neighbour who was born in Guyana. We had hardly talked to each other for almost twenty years. In 1998, we started to exchange greetings and meet on the pavement or in the park. In June 1999, he bought my book on the Non-Alignment and invited me for a talk with him on this subject at his house. We talked for an hour. Our memories went back to the 1960s when we arrived in this country. The local people used to ask us why we came to England. How long were we to stay in this country? The same types of questions were asked of all of us and everywhere.

If we applied for a grant to study or wanted to study while working full time, they used to ask how we found out about these facilities. Who told you that? Why do you want to take advantage of our system? They showed that we were unwelcome in offices, public places, pubs and libraries. There were hindrances to get suitable jobs and promotion. We both laughed at that because despite all the hindrances, we made progress through hard work. There were some good people who understood us, recognized our skills, talents and qualifications and made the progress possible.

I recalled a few cultural shocks. When we walked to catch a tube train, I saw people running to the railway station attempting to catch a train as if it was the last train like the one at India's small stations. The tube trains were always over crowded. People used to stand in the middle of the compartment, near the door. Some one would attempt to open the windows while others would try to shut them. Some were holding to each other and young people kissing in these public places. They talked very slowly. Some passengers hid their faces with newspapers. It was not possible to judge whether they were reading it or just looking at the paper. Some times they dropped papers on the floor.

There were some young men who had long hair and they dropped their hair on their faces. Some one thought that he/she was a girl. It was amazing and embarrassing. But it was the system in those days. Things were different in the 1960s and 1970s, than they were today. We both talked of that. The global warming had affected England. There was more pollution, more congestion and the weather was warmer today than in the 1970s. It was, however, difficult to determine whether the people had changed or not. Since 1980, no one had asked me whether I was returning to India or not? The government was also committed to racial equality. Though there had been racial attacks in Brick Lane and Brixton.

We did not go on holiday in 1999. We went on day outings twice- once to Hampton Court and then to Brighton. We stayed in London most of the time, despite our desire to go out. The weather was also not good. It rained almost every day in July and August. I was busy with the project. I read two new books published in 1997, did some literature review and word-processed the interviews, which were carried out many years ago. At the University, we held meetings every Wednesday. Thus the year passed peacefully.

I was busy in the months of April and May. At the University we were involved in revalidation of the First-degree courses. I had to prepare course outlines for Business Economics, Industrial Economics and International Economics. Then there were examinations and exam script marking to do. I was also unwell for two weeks in May. As I stated earlier the University of Greenwich had started the Ph D by publication for the academic staff and ex-students who had substantial qualifications and were research active and had published books and articles. I wrote a letter to the Research Committee and sent my CV along with a synopsis of my book V K Krishna Menon – A Biography. Professor Mike Kelly and Professor Mick Ryan read this proposal. They both suggested that there was a prima-facie case and I should formally apply justifying that this book had contributed to new knowledge and added to scholarship. I filled in form RS11 with details of my existing qualifications. I decided to submit only one book though I had published extensively on a variety of themes.

About the book V K Krishna Menon- Biography, I stated,

'The first half of the Twentieth Century witnessed the emergence of nationalism in Asia, more particularly in India which challenged the legitimacy of British rule in India. Apart from the islands of dissent, the Indian nationalism progressed within the legal framework. It was rare in history that an overseas empire was ended through negotiations rather than an act of revolt or revolution. It was in India that the British authority was withdrawn through negotiations between the rulers and the ruled and it was followed by an Act of Parliament. In this the anti-imperialist pressure groups like the India League and the India Conciliation Group played a vital role. Apart from my M Phil thesis at the London School of Economics in 1989, on 'The India League and the India Conciliation Group as Factors in Indo-British Relations' and my book 'The Indian Nationalist Movement in Britain, 1930-49' published in 1992, this area remained unexplored.'

'It was through the efforts of indefatigable Krishna Menon, who told the British politicians and policy makers of the futility of the British rule in India, that an environment was created whereby the Labour party committed itself at its 1944 annual conference to establish self-government in India, which became a reality in 1947. Krishna Menon also contributed to improving the Indo-British relations, India's modernisation and the formation of her foreign policy. The trend of international decolonisation continued and most of the colonies were peacefully freed in the 1950s and 1960s, though the Algerians had to fight against the French; the Indonesians against the Dutch; the Angolans and the Mozambiquians against the Portuguese; and indeed the Indians fought a short bloodless war in Goa against the Portuguese, in order to accomplish their objective of independence.'

'The termination of British Empire in India was, however, an extra ordinary achievement in history which should be given due credit and debated as has been argued by many politicians and academics.' 'The lack of significant acknowledgement of Krishna Menon's contribution to many issues of international importance convinced me of the remaining gap, which I attempted to bridge in this political biography of this international statesman who challenged the superiority of the Western leaders and asserted the Third World Unity. V K Krishna Menon- A Biography, drew the underlying themes and areas where Krishna Menon's contribution was paramount.'

'The objectives of V.K.Krishna Menon – Biography, were to examine the questions of independence struggle for India, the end of colonialism, advocacy of peaceful co- existence, to remain non-aligned at the time of bloc rivalry and the continued reasoning for disarmament. It also contributed to an academic debate and opened up a vista for further research. It had itself attempted to bridge a historical gap that remained in the understanding of the above themes and areas of knowledge. In many ways it took up the theme touched upon in my earlier study of the India League and of the key role played by Krishna Menon in that organisation.'

I also provided a list of interviewees with dates when I interviewed them, and also the archives and libraries where I saw the government and private papers related to my area of study. In support of this application my colleague and friend who was also my supervisor, Alan Foster of International History and politics Department wrote,

"K.C.Arora's book V.K.Krishna Menon –A Biography had its origins in the author's earlier study of the India League, The Indian Nationalist Movement in Britain, 1930-49, in that Menon played the leading role in that organization. Mr. Arora's study of the League proved original in both senses i.e. it explored primary documents in the first place and secondly it became on publication and remains the first and only study of that influential anti-imperialist pressure group."

"He had now followed this earlier study with a full political biography of Menon, which tracked his subject's career through the early years of India's independence. During these years Menon was to establish himself as an international statesman and subsequently, became India's most controversial Defence Minister. In this period, scholars generally agreed Krishna Menon's influence over India's foreign policy was second only to Pandit Nehru himself. Surprisingly, hither to no serious English language biography of Menon had been published since his death. K.C.Arora's study, therefore, filled an important gap in the existing scholarship for all students of India's foreign policy in the years when India played a leading role, in the creation of the Non-Aligned Movement, based as it was on much original research in both India and Britain".

The Research Committee accepted these proposals in June 1999. I then started the literature review and read the books published on Krishna Menon and the areas he was interested in. I read a few new books published in 1997 and 1998. I found that all other books were still inadequate and I was right in publishing this biography.

I had to make a submission of ten thousand words arguing a case for the award of the Ph D degree. It was to be read along with the published book by the examiners. I divided this submission into an Introduction, Methodological Issues Raised by the research, Literature Review, three articles on important subjects related to Krishna Menon and a Conclusion. I further provided a short bibliography. In the Introduction I wrote,

'This was a submission for the Ph D by published work at the University of Greenwich. Only one book "V K Krishna Menon –A Biography" published in 1998, was being submitted. The introduction and literature review that followed provided a framework through which the publication could be understood and contexualised. The introduction outlined the background to the work, the purpose and scope of the book. The literature review showed where the book was located in the broader literature on Krishna Menon and assessed its originality and contribution to the study of Krishna Menon and his activities in many fields, particularly his role in the Indian independence movement, formulation of the Indian foreign policy and world disarmament debates. It was followed by an appraisal of the contribution to the research on Krishna Menon and the above areas. The conclusion examined the accomplishments and progress made in areas where Krishna Menon was most active.

In identifying the necessity of writing the book, V K Krishna Menon- A Biography, it was perceived that the study of Krishna Menon remained undervalued and unacknowledged by historians and academics because of his estrangement in Indian politics and India's defeat by China in a short war in October 1962, when he was India's Defence Minister. Many academics identified him as a defeated man. However, the question was whether the responsibility for a national disaster could be pinned to a single person when the Indian government and Parliament had collective responsibility for the defence of the country.

It was the failure of diplomacy and the government's neglect of India's defence needs and the developments in China itself, which caused the Indo-China conflict in 1962. The Gandhian approach to non-violence further discouraged modernisation of the army and its material requirements.

Menon did a great deal to revitalise the armed forces, procure weapons and other materials. A period of five years (1957-62) when he was Minister for Defence was, however, not sufficient to bring the Indian defence system up to the Chinese standards and to fight in the difficult mountain terrain.

Menon's contribution to India's domestic, foreign and defence policies along with his efforts in solving international problems in the 1950s and 1960s, therefore, needed to be assessed. Krishna Menon was a great Indian patriot and a great internationalist. Because of his deep philosophical conviction, he was keen to see a New World Order established in a democratic fashion through peace, progress and mutual respect. He appealed to European powers to end imperialism, colonialism and repression.

In exploring the life and functions of Krishna Menon, this book had aimed to investigate some of the major issues, events and processes of historical importance. Apart from decolonisation, these included disarmament, apartheid in South Africa, regional problems of Korea, Indo-China and the Suez crisis in the 1950s, the Non-Aligned Movement and the Third World Unity. It added new knowledge in these areas and attempted to bridge a historical gap, which remained in the understanding of the above themes.'

'The end of cold war and the emergence of a unipolar world had led to an academic debate on the achievements and continued relevance of the Non-Aligned Movement when countries and continents had become interdependent, could self-reliance be sufficient in order to improve the living conditions of people in the developing nations? The problems, which Menon attempted to solve, still remained unresolved. Nations still continued to interfere in the internal affairs of other states and the disarmament problem had not been fully addressed'.

'An opportunity to write a full biography of Krishna Menon became feasible when original documents became available in the 1980s and 1990s. Some of the associates of Menon, who had witnessed the making of history, were also prepared to provide me information necessary to present the political work carried out by Menon in the United Kingdom as well as in India. The interviews became a source of oral history, providing an insight into his character and personality. It was vital to analyse and explore the contribution of Krishna Menon to the 20th Century Indian politics in order to counter some of the myths and misunderstandings. V K Krishna Menon –A Biography attempted to fill an important gap in the existing scholarship for all students of the Indian foreign policy during the period when India played a leading role in world affairs."

Under the sub-heading Methodological Issues Raised by the Research, I wrote,

"In this research, semi-structured interviews as a method of oral history had been used. Questions were prepared to ascertain a balanced view on the necessity of the India League and Krishna Menon's role in pursuing the phenomenon of Indian foreign policy, world disarmament, nuclear disarmament and apartheid in South Africa. Both Indian and British interviewees were selected. Some of these interviewees had been members of the India League, members of British or Indian Parliament or had served in the Indian Ministry of External Affairs. Efforts were made to engross an objective opinion on Krishna Menon and his accomplishments. Still their objectivity could be questioned. Their closeness to Krishna Menon and their participation in the India League and other organisations might suggest their pre-determined views. However, all interviewees accepted his dedication and commitment to India and humanity. Some of them were critical of his acid tongue and openness."

"Besides interviews, primary source material had been examined along with material from secondary sources of books and periodicals. The primary source material was made up of a large reservoir of unpublished government papers consisting of the Indian Ministry of External Affairs files at the National Archives, New Delhi, the British Prime Minister's files at the Public Record Office, the Foreign Office papers at the Public Record Office and the private papers of the India League at the British Library, London, the India Conciliation Group papers at the Friends House, Euston, London, the Linlithgow papers at the British Library Oriental Section, London, The Sorensen papers at the House of Lords Record Office; the Middleton papers at the Labour party archives and the

Stafford Cripps papers at the Public Record Office, London. Pamphlets written by Krishna Menon in the 1930s and 1940s were available at the British Library, London. The House of Commons Debates were examined as were the Lok Sabha Reports, which provided an insight into the opinion of British and Indian politicians about Krishna Menon and the issues that interested him."

By the end of 1999, I completed the writing of justification of my work and reason why my book deserved a Ph D award. There was a need for an internal examiner and an external examiner. Alan Foster of the school of Humanities agreed to be the internal examiner and we looked for an external examiner who should be proficient in Indian studies. After the retirement of Bhiku Pareekh, Professor Guru Harpal Singh was appointed Head of South Asian Studies at Hull University. I corresponded with him and he agreed to become my external examiner on condition that Viva (oral examination) took place in May 2000, because he was very busy until then. I passed on his note to our Research Committee who arranged for a copy of my book and my submission of ten thousand words to be sent to him in February. Professor Singh had ample opportunity to read the material. Lewis Johnman was to be the other external examiner. He was at Westminster University at that time but he had been our colleague at the Greenwich University in the past.

We had a viva on Wednesday 24th May 2000, under the Chairmanship of Roger Fox of the School of Social Sciences. Lewis Johnman, Alan Foster and Ron Ayres also came along with Professor Guru Harpal Singh. They all asked me all sorts of questions for over an hour. Professor Singh expressed that he enjoyed reading the book and new things came to light of which he was not aware. Eventually after a discussion they unanimously decided that I should be awarded the Ph D degree, which had been my vision for a long time. On that day I became a Doctor of Philosophy and added another degree to my academic accomplishment. They all congratulated me and then we all went for a lunch at Woolwich. It was arranged by Roger Fox.

Apart from my wife, I did not tell my family and friends about this project. On 24th May, I circulated a note to the family members regarding my Ph D award and on Saturday we had a small party. I showed them a copy of my submission. My colleagues at the University were delighted with this award. I also told Joseph Okoroji and Ram Sankar. Both of them were delighted and Joe sent me a card of congratulations. He was happy for me that I had eventually done it. It was better to get late than never. I was glad that I full- filled my own dream and ambition because of the good wishes, of Dr. Mulk Raj Anand and Ramesh Kaushik who knew that I had the ability and knowledge of a Doctor of Philosophy. I received congratulations and congratulation cards from many colleagues and friends. They were very joyful at my achievement. One letter came from the Research Committee, another from the Pro-Vice-chancellor. Jan Drucker, of Business School, also sent me a note. It showed that she had respect for my work. I appreciated it all very much. It gave me pleasure. I completed my effort in order to attain my objective.

The remaining days of May and the whole of June were very busy. I was overwhelmed with work, marking examination scripts, examination invigilation and the examiners meetings. On 3rd of June Santosh fell very ill. We had to call an ambulance to take her to hospital. Later we discovered she had a stroke. She stayed in hospital for a week. We then decided to go to India on holiday. We cut short our stay there and returned to London on 27 July after staying in Delhi for 25 days only. Still it was very relaxing for me. In the first week I felt switched off and forgot all the hassle of London or traveling to University. While in Delhi, we visited an astrologer who lived near our house. He read my birth chart and said that I had struggled all my life but have obtained substantially by my own efforts. A few days after our returning to London my younger brother Ramesh passed away in Delhi. I moaned his death by remembering our early days at the village and at Khurja. Santosh continued to go to hospital almost every week. It was found that she had blood vessel disorder. She was treated with warfarin for that. She could not walk for long and used to get tired.

The University Semester started in mid September. We had quite a few meetings on quality control and assessment procedures. My teaching programme was fine. This year, I taught a new course in Economics for the M Sc in International Business and Finance. Most of the students were foreign. It was a large class. It took us a couple of weeks to organize tutorials. There was hardly any tutorial discussion. The students were there to receive and not to contribute. A large number of students bought my text book "A Short Introduction to Principles of Economics". They found it easy to understand because it was written for non-economics courses and it stayed away from complicated jargon. It still had the necessary diagram and explanations. But the simple and lucid language made it easy to follow, especially by foreign students whose first language was not English.

We still studied Micro and Macro aspects of Economics. Micro Economics attempted to understand how firms decided to produce (supply), individuals decided what to purchase (demand), and how their individual choices were brought into consistency with each other through the price mechanism or market mechanism. The economy could be considered for the whole nation rather than for individual firms. This was the area of Macro Economics. It focussed on public policy issues such as inflation, unemployment, the balance of payments, economic growth and the impact of government policy on the national economy. However, there was an overlap between these two branches and could not be studied in complete isolation of each other.

This year (2000), I also taught an MA course, 'Non-Alignment and the Third World Politics' in the History and Politics Department. My friend and colleague Alan Foster was impressed by my book "Imperialism and the Non-Aligned Movement" He asked me to design a course which could include the study of non-alignment. We, therefore, offered it at Master's level and included the Third World Politics as well. In this course we studied nationalism in the 20th Century in Asia and Africa. We examined the biographies of leaders like Nehru, Nkrumah, Marshall Tito and Sukarno of Indonesia along with Nasser of Egypt. They were the leaders who founded the non-aligned movement in Bandung in 1956. The leaders of this movement held meetings to look at the problems of the developing countries and to impress the rich countries to help them in developing their resources and improve trade with them. The developing countries were faced with a number of problems including unemployment.

There was a need for economic co-operation between the capitalist countries of the North and the advancing countries of the South. In 1951, President Truman of the United States proposed to wage a war against man's ancient enemies-poverty, disease, hunger and illiteracy. Such an aim could remove all causes of differences between nations and it would also bring the industrialized and the developing countries closer to each other. The non-aligned nations had argued for economic progress and removal of poverty. However, the gap between the haves and have-nots widened within nations as well as between the nations. There was a need for constructive efforts to eliminate the economic disparity.

The industrialized countries had, however, not been co-operative. They had mostly looked to a good rate of return on their investment in the developing countries in order to sustain their own welfare system and research and development (R&D) in the field of defence and medicine. They had ignored the effect of such policies on the socio- economic environment of the poor nations. There were enormous natural resources in the world which could be used for the benefit of all. An alternative organization system was required. It was essential for the non-aligned and other developing countries to take initiative and plan for their uplift by uniting among themselves. There was, nevertheless, a need to increase trade between the developed and the developing nations.

In the 1980s, the Brandt Commission was set up in order to look into North-South economic and trade relations. It criticized the protectionist policies of the industrialized nations and maintained that protection threatened the future of the world economy and was inimical to the long term interests of developing and the developed countries alike. It suggested that protectionism by the industrialized countries against the exports of the developing countries should be rolled back. This should be facilitated by improved institutional machinery and new trading rules and principles. Such recommendations were, however, not heeded or implemented by the rich countries of the North. Despite the sustained economic prosperity in the North was not possible in the absence of stability and continued growth in the South.

The economic growth depended on investment, resources- both natural and human, technology and training. There was a necessity to transfer technology and financial resources from the North to the South. Environmentally sound technology was required for the developing counties. It was also vital to develop international trade in order to reap the advantages of specialization and availability of resources in order to achieve economic growth. The Conference of Non-Aligned countries in 1992, in Jakarta, Indonesia, stressed that only a free, open, rule based and non-discriminatory international trading system could provide an effective and viable basis for the promotion of the equitable development and economic prosperity of all countries of the world.

In the absence of progress in investment and marketing facilities from the rich to the poor nations, it was important that a developing country should develop self- reliance which could maintain its freedom and economic growth. However, the developing nations themselves should co-operate and engage in trade between them-selves. They were mostly at the same stage of development and could use their technology which was mostly at the intermediate level. They could also specialize in producing certain goods and exchange among themselves. This could enhance trade. This was indeed happening among some nations. The South East Asian countries were providing men power to develop the countries of the middle- east. China had started to invest in African countries and was helping in developing their natural resources, infrastructure and some industries.

There was a need for a New World Economic Order essentially founded on fair and just distribution of international wealth and income and to enjoy sovereignty over their natural resources, which had thus far been exploited for the benefit of the rich countries. North had, therefore, continued to prosper at the expense of the under-developed countries. It was essential to change the trading and financial systems in order to provide opportunities for the countries of Asia and Africa. There was also a need for economic nationalism and patriotism among the people of the South.

X   X   X

129

In England the weather had changed by the end of the 20th Century. It rained almost every day. There was flooding in various parts of the country. The train service was bad. Driving to University was problematic. But I continued to travel to University every working day. I could not do any writing and did very little reading. The journey on the Jubilee line, the Docklands-Light-Railway and bus service from North Greenwich station was hectic. Some-times, I attempted to change routes but there was no advantage.

The home front was quiet. Azad immigrated to Canada on 28 December. I was a little concerned about the children, though they were excited at the time of departure. Amar was never happy with the dry, cold or hot, climate. Education was also a matter for consideration. Azad continued to phone every week in the New Year. We also talked more often with relatives in India than ever before. Ashish did not settle down easily in Canada. He was ill quite often and once he was very emotional and asked his grandma to come to Canada and collect him to take back to England. We miss Amar and Ashish and Azad very much. He had never lived away from home. He was quite successful in London and could have done better. Hopefully he will settle down in Canada with a good job.

CHAPTER 5

Winding Towards Retirement, 2001-07

In March 2001, the British media was hysteric again. They were after Keith Vaz a Labour MP of Indian origin and the first Asian to be a minister in the British government. The right wing politicians were astonished why and how an Asian had access to the British establishment and how an Indian could be a part of that institution. The Indians had progressed in England and made contribution to British economy and society. There was some jealousy but the British media increased the heat and attempted to bring racial issues before the general election, which might take place this year.

The Easter holiday, were spent at home. In April 2001, my eldest sister Angoori Devi passed away, after a short illness. I phoned Vijay Kumar and wrote a letter to my nephews Vijay Kumar and Sudhir Kumar. We had been away for far too long but in the last decade, it had become our habit to meet during holiday in Delhi. Once, my sister came back from Bulandshahr (UP) in July because she knew that I would be in Delhi at that time. It was very emotional. Last year we met only twice but my sister reminded me how our father had worked hard when we were young and he did so much for us that he did not have a life for himself. He built houses for the youngest brother in Delhi and for my elder brother at Kakore. Both had sold parts of their properties because it was not the fruit of their own efforts. My sister was very disappointed with these incidents. She wanted to see all of us progressing and acquiring properties as our father had done. I would miss her on my next visit to Delhi this year.

In the month of May, I travelled to University only a few times. I did all my marking at home. This year's students were polite and kind. They also produced some good answers in examinations. The British government decided that the general elections were to take place in June 2001. The parties geared their efforts to win votes. The Health services, education, the law and order situation and transport were main issues this time. There was some mud-slinging by the parties at each other. It was common in this country to do so at the time of election. The conservatives did not provide any alternative polices. The Labour party was always in lead at the poll surveys. The Labour party did really win the election with a substantial majority and Blair continued his Prime Minister ship.

Before we went to India, I had an opportunity to visit a family in Isleworth and discussed a few things with a young man. I liked his attitude to life. We started to make preparations to go to India for holiday and stayed in India for about seven weeks in July and August. I also had an opportunity to talk to a few old friends who had retired by this time. I went to Barelly in UP to visit a distance relative. It was a busy schedule, a crowded bus and a city in Uttar Pradesh, with various problems. But overall we enjoyed ourselves in Delhi.

On returning to London we followed the same routine. The University teaching started a little early in September. We had full thirteen weeks term before Christmas. My teaching was on Tuesdays and Fridays only. I attended a few meetings on Wednesdays. I used to go to University by tube through the Canary-Wharf and the DLR

On 11th September, terrorists attacked the World Trade Centre. They crashed aeroplanes into the Twin-Towers in New York and the Pentagon building in Washington. Many thousand people died. It was a surprised and horrible aggression. Nineteen terrorists thrust the world's most powerful nation. President George W. Bush declared war on terrorism. Osama Bin Laden and the A'L Qaida Organisation were identified as terrorists who were being supported by the Taliban of Afghanistan. The Americans, therefore, attacked that country and after two months of bombardment the Taliban was defeated and a new government was set up in Afghanistan. On 13th December the terrorists attacked the Indian Parliament in New Delhi. It was thought that Pakistani agents were involved in this assault. It was predicted by a terrorist caught in October 2001, that the Indian Parliament would be attacked in November or December. There was also a thrust on J&K (Jammu & Kashmir) Assembly in Srinagar. Quite a few people died in both the incidents.

When I reviewed this year (2001), I realized that this was a normal year for me though lots of things happened around the world. We were only two of us most of the time. Sangeeta and Akash stayed with us after school hours and slept at our place over the weekends. Arun and Saneh moved to live in Brentford in September. Arun also received his PhD in June, and they all went on holiday to India in December. We received weekly calls from Azad. I sent e-mails to Amar, Ashish and Azad. Santosh often dreamt that Azad, Amar or Ashish was knocking at the door at night. Even after a year she had this nightmare, which showed that she was missing them enormously. I am sure Azad is happy in Canada.

The year 2002, dawned quietly. We received the same goodwill cards as last year. We phoned our relatives in India. Saneh and children returned from holiday. They enjoyed their stay there. Azad continued to phone on Sundays and sent e-mails on newspaper articles. He did not write anything about his experience in Canada in the past year. The weather in England was wet and cold.

The University work had been easy for the time being. My teaching was divided between Avery Hill and Greenwich. The teaching load was not too heavy. I travelled by Tube to Greenwich and by car to Avery Hill. On the last teaching day in May, some of the International Economics students gave me a thank you card and a bottle of whisky. During this Semester in 2002, I was also asked to retire but I decided not to take a retirement. The package was not attractive. I would retire in 2003. In England, the queen mother died in March 2002. Various TV, programmes, took place about her life. She lived a good life of 101 years. The Queen's Golden Jubilee also took place that year but there was not much enthusiasm in the country. The TV programmes, however, showed that the Monarchy was still popular in Britain. There was a decline of racism in Britain. The minorities were improving their standard of living. There was, however, anti-Muslim feeling because of the terrorist aggression.

On the international scene, there was some quietness in Afghanistan with the change in government. It emerged that Pakistan was involved in creating Muzahiddin in Kashmir and Taliban in Afghanistan. Benazir Bhutto once expressed that Pakistani army thought of sending commandoes to attack the Kashmiri government in Srinagar in the 1990s. They did really invade the assembly in Srinagar and Parliament in New Delhi. India demanded the return of twenty terrorists but Pakistan refused to do so. It was believed that Pakistan was supporting terrorism and sending terrorists across the border. Tension grew between the two countries. Both countries massed troops on Kashmir border and shooting took place on the line of control.

India and Pakistan both had learnt nothing in the past fifty years or so and have not been able to improve their relations. Pakistan had been waging a proxy war since 1990, and militancy had increased. The Indian government was determined to take action against the ruffians but did not pursue them into Pakistan. Pakistan threatened to use nuclear weapons against India. The Western nations got nervous and asked their nationals to return from India and Pakistan. India declared that it would not strike first but it would certainly retaliate if attacked. This posturing continued for the whole month of May 2002. The Americans sent their missionaries to calm down the situation on the sub-continent. President George W. Bush spoke to the leaders of both India and Pakistan and asked them to reduce tension.

Pakistan temporarily stopped terrorists from crossing the border. The fear of war had, therefore, receded. It was difficult to judge whether any permanent solution would be found or Pakistan would return to its old tricks. It was an unreliable nation with a set of attitudes of the middle ages. It still believed that Muslims should be the real rulers of India and that

India was too soft a nation and could be easily bullied. India had never shown any strength either. It was too cultured and believed in international laws.

I had myself given some thought to this problem and I had written in some detail about the Kashmir problem in my book V.K.Krishna Menon – A Biography. My feeling was that Kashmir would remain divided. India would not be able to claim the part of Kashmir occupied by Pakistan but would not allow any further land to Pakistan. Pakistan should have been happy with what she got. The problem could not be solved by fighting now.

People had different thinking. They could move from one country to another country for social, political or economic reasons. Goods and services could be sold across the borders. No one could acquire land by force. It was a new kind of nationalism and internationalism. People did not have to occupy land in order to acquire raw material, goods or services as happened in the 15th, 18th and 19th centuries and earlier invasions in India. She had perhaps learned its lesson and was ready to take action and defend its land. It was not an emotional outcry but a rational view.

Something vital emerged in the first week of June 2002. The United States, despite its drawbacks, behaved responsibly as a Superpower. People did not care about the United Nations or any other country any more. They listened to the United States. It had also decided to end terrorism and had championed democracy. In the tension between India and Pakistan, the US did not immediately side with Pakistan as it had done in the past, at the United Nations, in the 1971 War for the creation of Bangladesh. This time the US was sympathetic towards India because of horrible assault on Indian Parliament.

The Indians refused any mediation, which was offered by the Russians, the British and the United States. They did not want to internationalise the Kashmir issue and wanted to solve it bi-laterally with Pakistan. However, this complex problem, point could not be solved until Pakistan had created an environment of trust and spoke the language of peace. Some Pakistani politicians had started to speak that language but they should create democracy in their country as well as reduce the power of the army and put an end to intimidation and siding with militants.

Because of the tension between India and Pakistan and a possible mistake by Pakistan and retaliation by India in the use of nuclear weapons, one of my colleagues suggested that I should not go to India at that time. But I knew that there had been some rhetoric in the past. These countries were not foolish enough to destroy each other. The Indians always love Pakistan and many in Pakistan had respect for Indian secularism and democracy. As the clouds of war receded we decided to go to India for six weeks. We stayed mostly in Delhi and relaxed. We had lots of visitors that year and sometimes they stayed with us at night. We returned to London on 7th August and informed our relatives of our safe arrival.

India also suffered communal violence in Gujarat. Muslims burnt fifty-eight Hindu pilgrims alive in a train which was returning from Ajodhya a city in Uttar Pradesh. Violence flared up as some people resorted to retaliation and hundreds of Hindus and Muslims died in various cities in Gujarat. But the situation was controlled soon and peace returned to this economically advanced state. A great deal of economic growth had been achieved in Gujarat. It stood on top of all other states. Uttar Pradesh and Bihar with Orissa remained under developed. These states were under the grip of social and political turmoil. Crime had increased in many parts of UP and Bihar. People with privileges were not ready to face the reality and were keeping the backward classes suppressed. There was a lack of real democracy and equality of opportunity in many areas of India, despite efforts since independence in August 1947. This backwardness and suppression was more visible in villages than in big cities, which had become overcrowded, as people had moved to live there from villages because of violence and unemployment.

I went to University to do my summer rota. I was later told that the Head of School of Social Sciences wanted me to retire at the end of March, as I shall be sixty-five then. The Head of Social Sciences was a weak and unsociable person. I never met him while I worked with him. I simply said that, it was impossible to leave in the middle of the session because of my teaching commitment. I also corresponded with the Union and they advised me that as long as I had teaching commitment during the Second Semester, I would have to complete my lectures, complete my assessment and then I would be entitled for research time and summer holiday. It would take me to the end of August. Moreover, colleagues, in other schools were to retire in August. The University could not have two policies in two different schools. I was, therefore, informed that my retirement would commence on 31 August 2003.

In September 2002, we did floor tiling in the extension. It took us three weeks to complete the work. But it looks clean now. We had two weeks induction at Greenwich. I had a heavy timetable in the first semester of 2002-3. The students were different this year. Some of them were good and behaved as University students while the others behaved like school kids. The other thing I noticed that students started to sit at the back as they arrived rather than starting from the front as they entered the room. The front seats were left for late-comers. It showed that either they were not keen students or wanted to avoid serious listening and participation. It gave me an impression that they were being forced to be there. Some good students sat at the front rows. There was also an increase in the number of Asian students. I had taught British Asians but for the first time I saw students from Delhi and other parts of India on First as well as Second year Business Administration courses. They did their First year in India, then completed their Second and Third years of the degree in England.

At the University, I maintained my standard. I used the same lecture notes as in the previous years. Some students enjoyed the lectures and they participated in seminars and tutorials. I used to get tired after teaching and traveling. Every thing else had been fine. At the end of September, we decided to get an Asian T V channel and we chose, Zee TV. This gave us Indian programmes, news from India and of course Indian films. We could not fully understand and appreciate the Hindi serials because we were not used to them. For thirty-seven years we watched the English and American programmes. We had watched Hindi films for many years on a video player. In November 2002, we started to watch the Ramayana produced by B.R.Chopra the maker of the Mahabharata. There were many good stories in the Mahabharata and the Ramayana. In the third week of November a strike took place in England organised by the lecturers' unions and the Fire Fighters Union. I wished it did not turn out to be winter of discontent.

On the international scene, the Al-Quida bombed, a club in Bali- Indonesia, killing two hundred people. There was also a fear of chemical attack on the London underground. The British government was very vigilant. The secret services foiled the attack. The Americans were keen to attack Iraq though the United Nations had started their search for weapons of mass destruction in Baghdad. India remained peaceful at that time. The Indian economy had made some stride. It had a long way to go. Simply producing more Information Technology Engineers and exporting them to the West was not sufficient. Social and other changes were essential and vital for a progressive society.

The first Semester, in 2002, was rather long. It lasted thirteen weeks because we had meetings before Induction. The teaching started in the second week of the term for the continuing students and in the third week for new students. New students came in year 2 and year 3 also and not only in year One. For the First year, we started a new subject called Business Environment, which included Economics and Law. I taught such a course in the 1990s at South West London College. There were two large groups. One Group started Economics for six weeks and the other Group started Law. Then we swapped over. This subject was taught on Monday and Thursday. Business Economics continued as in previous years. I found that the HND group was not keen to learn or committed to learn as in the previous year. The attendance was appalling. Even during revision weeks the students were writing notes rather than contributing to discussions. The answers to questions were 'I do not know'. These were simple questions on the taught topics.

The most astonishing thing was the First Year degree class sat at the back in the room. I got the impression that they were challenging me as a lecturer and telling me 'look we do not want to learn. We have been put in front of you. Now come on and teach us'? There was a comprehensive school attitude of non-academic behaviour. Perhaps they came from large comprehensive schools. They told to me that they wanted to read but they did not have books, nor did they intend to purchase any. Reading books, acquiring knowledge and participating in class discussions were not their objectives. Some foreign students were good and keen to learn. They paid a fee of over six thousand pounds a year. They had left their families and countries in order to study in England.

The Business Environment course for the HND (Higher National Diploma in Business and Finance) went quite well. Even for the BABA it was fine. We covered most of the ground despite the lack of time. My travelling to and from the University was not comfortable this year. The trains were full and it was not easy to find a seat. I was unhappy and annoyed with the situation. People had compared traveling by tube in the morning and evening rush hours with cattle trains, milling each other. It would, however, be unfair to compare the London Underground service with cattle trains. It could reduce human beings to the level of animals. The fellow travellers were all nice people. They travelled to their work in the city of London, West End or Canary Wharf. My own opinion was that there could be more trains, which could run more frequently.

I had sleepless nights because of tiresomeness. It was not the journey that I regretted, it was the teaching which posed questions about my continuation at the University because I did not enjoy teaching this year and should perhaps have taken an early retirement. I could not force students to study. They were not keen to learn. They did not show any inclination towards studies. Perhaps there was a generation gap. My expectations were high. I wanted to pass on my knowledge and skills to students. I would have preferred to discuss topics, write on the board, watching the student's progress and contribute in seminars. They did not do that because they did not want to acquire knowledge or skills. They felt that the University was an extension of school. They lacked a sense of responsibility and maturity for University life. I had a different experience this year than that of the previous years of my teaching career.

My winter holiday in December 2002, was spent in relaxing and doing nothing apart from watching Hindi Movies and Soaps on Zee net work. I read a few Hindi and English novels. We kept in touch with the children in Canada. I often thought that if Amar and Ashish were here now, I could have guided them in their development and spent more time with them as I had more time in the last year of my teaching career. I reconciled with the fact that I was retiring at the end of the academic year on 31 August 2003. I had prepared my-self psychologically for this reality. At the beginning of the year 2002, I was not ready to retire and I resented to a suggestion to do so. But now I was looking forward to my freedom pass and state pension within the next few months. I, however, did not know what was I going to do after leaving the university, except that I would like to divide my time between India, England and some time on visiting places.

Early in 2003, I received a letter from the Personnel Department of Greenwich University that I shall leave on 31 August and then I shall break all relations with the University. I would like to keep in touch with some of the colleagues. At the beginning of the year, I marked 500 scripts in all the subjects taught by me. I was very busy in the month of January. During this Semester, I used to go to University only on Friday. Santosh remained unwell. She had Hypo a number of times. We also had to go to hospital many times in the early months of 2003, mainly for blood tests, eye test and diabetes clinic. I myself had a test for diabetes. My blood sugar was not too high though I have put up some weight because of lack of exercise. I watch too much television.

I reviewed a Business Economics book by Begg and Ward. It was an interesting exercise. In January, Vivek had an assignment in Surrey. He stayed in Denton with his colleagues. I went to collect him for the first time on Friday and took him to his BB (Bed & Break-fast) on Sunday. He came to visit us four times. He liked England and its culture but found it very expensive to live. He did not want to live in London. He was getting married on 21 July. We had been invited but could not attend his wedding in India. I asked Azad whether he would like to go to India for a week and stay with us for two weeks in London. Amar and Ashish could stay with us. They did not have to go to India. It was very hot there in July. He found it a good idea but it was impracticable.

On the world scene the Americans were keen on military action against Iraq and showed their military might. They could not get the UN resolution. Yet they started the war along with the British and some other allies. The British still thought that they had a role to play in the world. But the United States had taken over that role and Britain had become a camp follower of the US. The US had so much firepower. The other powerful nations simply opposed the US action but did not do any thing. There were demonstrations around the world against the Iraq war but to no avail.

After twenty days of fierce bombardment the American forces reached Baghdad and the British controlled Basra in the South. It was a military adventure. They had no plans for peace. The Iraqi people suffered in death and destruction. The Americans and the British government argued that the Iraqis will govern Iraq. Only for a short period the Americans would take over the administration of the country. It looked like a return of imperialism. Perhaps the West wanted to ensure the supply of oil from the Middle East. It would be the return of the 19th Century European imperialism in the guise of Americans in order to dominate the weaker nations and to destroy the diverse cultures of the world.

People still showed their discontentment against the war. The Indian Parliament came out against the US action and passed a resolution asking the US to stop bombardment and withdraw from Iraq. But nothing was done to stop the destruction in Baghdad, Basra and other cities. There was no UN meeting. The British TV showed some rejoicing on the streets of Baghdad where the destruction was serious and enormous.

The debate on Iraq war lingered on. The politicians in Britain did not find it easy to justify. Claire Short and Robin Cook resigned from the Blair Cabinet. It was argued that the British Prime Minister misinformed the public and the European Union members who were still angry. A Parliamentary Committee investigated the reasons and the conduct of the Iraq war and whether the war was justified or it could have been avoided. This was a democratic system to investigate and setting up of Committees and Enquiries.

I finished my teaching at Greenwich in early May. Then there were examinations and marking of scripts. I attended only three meetings this year. I went to Avery Hill a few times to check my post. On 26th June, we celebrated Jack's and my retirement at India Club at the Strand in Central London. We had good quality food though the service was slow. We bought our own wine at the club bar. The restaurant did not serve wine. I enjoyed the company of the colleagues from Economics and Politics Departments. A couple of old colleagues also came along. Ron Ayres gave me a card signed by twenty- five people. Jack brought a separate card for me. I gave him a card and a copy of the biography of Krishna Menon. It was an enjoyable event. I also went to the Business School party at Greenwich. I found my self very busy in the months of May and June.

I did not do much reading or writing over the summer. Azad decided to come to England during the summer holiday in July/ August. The Children were excited that they were coming to London for the first time since they immigrated to Canada in December 2000. We were excited because we had not seen them for over two years, though we used to talk every week. It would be good to see them, talk to them and take them around London and other places. We were almost cut-off from our brothers and other relatives in India.

Azad and children came to London in July for three weeks. They hardly stayed at home or relaxed. They went out of the house on many occasions. They did some shopping and found a few things cheaper in London compared to Edmonton (Canada). Perhaps they did not have time over there for shopping. We went to Brighton, South End on Sea and the Blue Water Shopping Centre. The trip to Blue Water was a waste. It was a hot day and nothing attracted us. We went to Woolwich for a lunch. We also went to cinema in Southall. Azad went to visit his old colleagues and friends. There was no time for us to catch up or make plans for the future. He seemed to be happy in Canada and liked his job. He had almost forgotten his life in London though he had lived in Canada only for two and a half years. He lived in London for almost thirty-three years. He always talked about dollars though it was only worth about 40 pence.

Certain things were cheaper in London while other things were cheaper in Canada.

Amar and Ashish looked very weak as if they had not grown tall. Their diet was very limited and they did not eat much. Ashish was often sick. He could not digest food. He did not drink milk. The Indian food was not being accepted by their bodies. It also looked that the Canadian Education standard was not of high standard. I would have liked Amar and Ashish to have studied in England where standard of education was high. But they were very young. It would not be wise to separate them from their parents. They were both very clever but needed a little guidance. Ashish had grown more angry and irritating. He wanted everyone to agree with him. In case of disagreement he used to get angry and leave the room. He was still a lonely person and did not mix with other children very often. He, though, called Akash many times and asked him to come over to Chiswick. He himself slept in Brentford once. He enjoyed his stay in London. So did Amar. We went to local- park a few times and also played tennis in Southfield park. I was glad to see them here. We did a prayer at the house on Tuesday 7th August. My friend and colleague Ram Sankar conducted it. It was a thanks giving on my retirement, that there was no major problem during my forty three years in employment. Ashish gave me a garland. We were busy during these three weeks but enjoyed each other's company.

Now I get tired soon and could not do more than one thing in a day. If I went out of the house, I could not go to other places. If I read, I could not write as well. The weather was hot in July and August. Temperature reached 37C or 100 F in London. On many occasions we slept with a fan on and had sleepless nights because of humidity. One day we took Sangeeta and Akash to the Tennis club. Then we went to Southall. Our car broke down near Windmill Lane in Norwood Green. We had to walk one full hour in the scorching heat to collect Sangeeta and Akash.

Arun and Saneh discovered that Brentford was not a place for them to live. They wanted to move out of there. First, they rushed to buy a house nearer to Chiswick without thinking of the locality and other intricacies, like schools for children and shopping facilities. Akash never liked that place. The immediate neighbours were good but in that street some people were uncultured and rude. They stole Arun's motorbike within a few days of their moving to that house. Arun had to call the police a couple of times.

We decided to go to Delhi on 8ᵗʰ September and spend about three months there because I had just retired and I needed a little change in my routine. We went to Delhi by British Airways. It was a direct flight. We reached, the Indira Gandhi Airport at 10.30 pm Delhi time. It took us more than an hour to come out of the controlled area. We, therefore, decided to stay in the waiting room. We stayed awake and saw people coming from all over the world. Brides came to collect their husbands or future husbands, mothers and fathers came to collect their sons and daughters. A few families came to see their loved ones. All sorts of people, Indians, foreigners, businessmen and tourists came to Delhi not necessarily to stay there. Some were in transit to the Punjab and other parts of India. We spent time in the waiting room observing their behaviour and moods. Many were excited. Some cried in happiness. Others smiled at each other.

At about 4 am, we came out of the waiting room and hired a pre-paid taxi. The taxi driver was fine. He was a quiet man. He concentrated on his driving. We reached home at 5.30 am. Anil and Ajay came to our house at 6 am. After a while we went to Krishna Nagar to find a cleaner. He was a young adult man who cleaned the house but moaned at lot. Our sweeper also helped him to clean the garage. He cleaned the house but not the roof terrace. He also washed the floor. I asked him to come back the next day but he did not turn up. I cleaned the doors and windows over the next few days rather than in one day. We wanted some work to be done at the house. We asked the plumbers to put a water tank in the small room on the first floor, to install toilets and sistern and also to replace the taps. They did a good job and finished their work in three days.

We also hired a builder to build a room for the tank, to put tiles. He did a few other odd jobs. We also decided to get electricity connection to the house. It was contracted out. He promised to get the connection within two weeks but he took two months. He annoyed me a great deal. Then the carpenter came. He told us that he will buy the wood and dry it himself. So he would take fifty days. At the end, he did an excellent job. Every one praised his work. We now had doors and windows in the front room.

We celebrated a few festivals in Delhi. Our Diwali in Delhi was the first in forty years. I enjoyed it. We decorated the outside of the house with lighting. We put flower garlands on the doors. We exchanged fruits and sweets. We had visits from many relatives from all sides. On bhaidoj, Rameshawar Dayal, Ashok, Rakesh, and Bobby came to see us. Bhushanlal came a few days later. Santosh fell ill and she was sick for almost a month. Her diabetes was out of control. She had hypo many times. Her blood sugar was high most of the time. She used to drink water everywhere and did not control her food intake either. She lost weight. My nephew Vijay Kumar also fell seriously ill in November. He developed a liver bug. He went to a local doctor, stayed at his nursing home. The charges were extortionate from the Indian point of view. I then talked to Dr. Vijay and Dr. Amit who prescribed medicine and also removed abscess from his liver. Vijay Kumar had to have ultrasound many times. I used to take him to doctors. He started to make progress.

We could not go outside of Delhi because of Santosh's illness and a lot of work had to be done at the house, which was also redecorated just before the Diwali festival. But we enjoyed our stay in our house at Delhi. I used to go to bring milk in the morning. We went shopping a couple of times. We bought food supplies locally. We kept in touch with Saneh in London and Azad in Canada. There was a break of fifteen days when Azad did not phone us because he was staying in the basement of his brother-in-law's house. He had sold his house a few months earlier but his new house was not yet ready to move in. I was annoyed because my grandsons were made to live in a small place in basement when we had twelve rooms in our houses in London and Delhi. I often thought and some- times told a few friends that I had worked for forty-three years and accomplished so much and had been blessed with everything, yet my grandsons were living uncomfortably.

We also attended a wedding in the family. It was good and well organized. We had an opportunity to meet many relatives. Bhushanlal's family was very good to us. They helped us in many ways. Dr. Vijay visited Santosh. Dr. Amit operated on my nephew Vijay. We enjoyed their company. We came back to London on 27th November. We used to go to sleep at any time and in front of the television. I had not watched TV for months. I checked my post. One of the letters was from Charles Clark the Education Secretary. He thanked me for my work in Education and wished me a long and happy retirement. I had posted a few Christmas cards and received some from friends in the UK.

I also got in touch with Jack and Ron. We decided to have a lunch at the India club on 15th December.

We recovered from the journey fatigue and attended appointments at hospitals. We returned to our routine, walking at Chiswick High Road and Acton High Street, going to Southall, Hounslow and Hammersmith. The weather was not good in January 2004. It was very cold and it rained quite often. We also had a visit from the Ealing Environment Officer because the neighbour had complained that they were getting water from our roof. The Environment Officer told us there was no way that water could have gone to the neighbour's roof from our side. He asked me to get in touch with him if the neighbours troubled me on this issue. We celebrated Christmas and the New Year in London. We again started to talk to Azad every Sunday. He moved to live in to his new house before the end of the year. He sustained some losses of jewelry in the process. Some one stole his property from the packed goods before his move to the new house.

We were very busy in London since our return from India at the end of November 2003. We had to cancel many appointments and outings. Early in 2004, Saneh decided to move out of Brentford where they had had many problems. They did not like the area. They saw a few houses in East Hounslow but these were sold before they could sell their property in Brentford. They were keen to move back to Chiswick, because Akash would attend Chiswick Community School for his secondary education. In March, Santosh was given a clean chit of health. She had no problem with heart, lung or kidney. She will continue her medication. The same month, I had a serious pain in the stomach. My doctor referred me to Hammersmith hospital. On the 30th, I saw a doctor at the hospital. I was told that I must undergo colonscopy because I had colitis. This was to take place on 19th May. I shall be allowed to return home the same day.

Azad and children went to Calgary during Easter break but they did not enjoy it. The museums were shut because of the holiday. Amar was making good progress but Ashish was at a loss and was not enjoying himself. He would have preferred to come back to London. Amar would also like to stay in England.

I went to the University on 27 April. Ron Ayres wanted me to do some teaching in the new academic year when I was in London. I did not have to change my programme to visit India and spend some time there. I also did some invigilation in May. On 29th April, when I was returning from Brentford after showing the house to an agent, my car was damaged by a big van at Chiswick High Road near the Kew bridge station. We could not trace the van, despite the fact that I complained to the police. The Insurance Company decided not to get the car repaired because the cost of repair would be greater than the value of the car at that time. I used my car for eleven years. It served me well but eventually I had to it go and decided not to buy another car but to travel by public transport.

In India the general elections took place in India. The BJP coalition lost its majority. Prime Minister Bajpai tendered his resignation. The Congress party received more seats than the BJP, and formed a government with the help of the left parties. Manmohan Singh became Prime Minister. Sonia Gandhi and Rahul Gandhi were elected as MPs. The Nehru- Gandhi name was still a vote catcher. People flocked to them. India was gaining respect in the world but people did not vote for foreign policy. They might take some interest in foreign affairs. It was the booming economy, which had divided the nation. The rich had become very rich. They could afford to send their children to study abroad. The poor especially in the villages had not made much economic and social headway.

The BJP was considered as the party of the urban educated middleclass. The Congress and the other regional parties appealed to the masses in villages. Secularism and Hindu nationalism had nothing to do with this election. It was the economic disparity and lack of social services, which made an impact. The BJP led coalition worked hard to improve roads, housing and education. Some Indians had progressed from peasantry to high technology, while others had remained static and backward.

In Britain, Prime Minister, Tony Blair had become unpopular because of the Iraq war. He was also not sure about the European Union and Britain's role there. The conservatives under Michael Howard made some headway among the electorate. The real test would come in June when the European and local elections were to take place. I was not happy with the prevailing Labour policies. Taxes had increased, cost of education and housing had increased. There was hardly any improvement in public sector services. I thought of resigning from the Labour party but I kept my membership.

In the United States, the leadership was strong but their policy on Iraq had failed due to treatment of the detainees in prisons. Pictures of maltreatment were printed in newspapers and shown on Television. It degraded the US image in the world. The US administration did not hide these facts and set up a Commission in order to enquire about the treatment of Iraqi in prisoners and under the care of the US military. It was a good democratic system. But the question was whether democracy could be planted in to Iraq. The Western powers wanted to pass on the administration of Iraq to a democratic government and the people of Iraq. In June 2004, the United States did really pass on the sovereignty to the new Iraqi government,

We had been planning to go to Canada to visit children and to see how they were coping with the cold climate and the other environmental problems. I made enquiries at travel agencies for air tickets and decided to go to Edmonton on the 19th of July by Continental Airways via Houston, Texas, United States. Akash and Sangeeta decided to come with us and Saneh would join us a week later. We made some preparations but we wanted to travel light. On Monday 19th July we went to Gatwick airport via Turnham Green and Victoria stations. I had never been to Gatwick airport. It was an experience. We booked our luggage and cleared the security check and immigration. Saneh and Arun came to see us off. We did not do any shopping at the airport but waited for an hour before boarding the plane. The flight was about half an hour late. The service was not good. The food was not tasty. Sangeeta and Akash did not eat at all. The flight was also long. It took us ten hours from Gatwick to Houston. It was tiring as well. Any way we reached Houston and collected our luggage. It was a huge airport. It took us time to collect our things and clear immigration.

We had to redeposit our luggage bound to Edmonton. There was nothing exciting at the airport. We exchanged some money and bought potato fries. We had to stay at Houston airport for four hours. We then boarded a small plane for Edmonton, Canada. It was a four-hour journey again. We were not served any food on the plane. We had some soft drinks and peanuts. The children fell asleep but I could not sleep. We reached Edmonton at 12.05 midnight. We had to go through immigration again. We collected our luggage and came out of the airport. We were met by Azad, Meenakshi, Amar, Ashish, Mr. Manchanda and Akhilesh. Akhilesh took our luggage and we went home in Azad's van.

It was our first visit to Canada. The roads were wide but mostly empty. The design of roads was the same as in other countries. They avoided round about and preferred straight roads and high ways. People drove on the right side in Canada. The airport was out of the town. We did not see any residential localities for miles. It took us more than half-an- hour to reach home. Azad's house was in a residential area which was still developing. We did not see any solitary houses as we expected. Communities had grown with Avenues, Roads and Crescents. There were detached houses with space in between the houses with front garden and back garden. Most houses had garages for two or three cars. People mostly parked their cars in garages though some parked on the drive way or on the road and used their garages for keepings things.

We stayed in Edmonton for four weeks and I kept a diary of our visits. After his visit to England, Azad moved to this house in November 2003. It was a three-bed room house but it had a large basement and two reception rooms over two floors. It had three washrooms and two baths. He claimed that it was built east facing and was set according to Vastu-Kala. He had trees and statues of elephants at the house. He kept the house clean. People had to remove their shoes on one side at the entry before going into the rooms. Any way, we went to sleep at about 2 0'Clock and woke up at 8am on Tuesday. On this day we went for a local walk and visited Akhilesh's house, which was next door. We saw Meenakshi's parents. For another two days, we visited local areas and local shops. The nearest local shops were about two kilometers from the house. On Friday we hired a video and a DVD. We went to the nearest mall called Millwood- Mall and saw all sorts of shops including food shops, cloth shops. This mall was not different from the London malls except that some shops were larger and it had a huge car park.

On Saturday we went for an outing in Central Edmonton, which was about thirty kilometers from the house. This place was developed one hundred years ago. There was a river nearby. The city was built on the hills. It indicated that settlement took place near water supply but higher than the flood plains. It was also argued that the original settlers found gold there which attracted people to the area. And then timber brought more people to Edmonton. The State Parliament and the ministries were in that central part of Edmonton where original settlement took place. Some private sector offices were also located there.

We went inside the Parliament building. It was a round arch building and the main debating hall had green chairs, which represented grass because in olden days the people's representatives used to sit on grass in order to discuss local issues. Now they sat on green chairs to discuss the state's affairs. The State of Alberta had 83 MLAs. We also saw the portrait gallery with portraits of all the state governors since the formation of the state. Outside the Parliament there was a water-flow and a park. The children played in water. We sat on the benches. It was a good day's outing.

The same evening we went to visit a family in Edmonton. It was argued that the Indian population in Alberta was not much. They, therefore, introduced each other and visited their houses to spend some time together and feel homely. They were a nice family. They talked mostly in Punjabi language. I understood what they were talking about but the content of their conversation did not relate to me. I was mostly quiet except when they enquired about something or I made enquiries about their life in Canada. Some of them had visited London but they seem to like the easy life in Edmonton.

On Sunday we went to a fair. The children went on rides. It was a one-ticket fare, which we bought at the entry, and children could have as many rides as they liked or could manage. The fair had its own features. I had not seen a few things in the past. For example the children could go round in monkey type bowl. We also went into a big hall where we saw a circus performed by East Europeans. The performances were fine, on the rope and through the metal circles. Next day, we stayed mostly at home and watched DVD. We went for a local walk. On Wednesday we went for a holiday in the mountains. It was a long drive of about three hundred kilometers. We saw the mountain city of Jasper and went to mount Canyon in a trolley. The mountain was about 8,500 feet high. We walked on the mountain and also sat on the stones. The children went further up the mountain. There was a valley underneath which was breath-taking. We relaxed for an hour or so and then returned to Jasper where we stayed overnight.

On 29 July, we drove through the mountains and the valleys. The road was not straight. Some times we reached quite high and then came down into the valley. The route was also zigzag. We stopped almost every hour and then for two hours at Lake Louise named after Princess Alberta's daughter and Queen Victoria's grand daughter. Once we strayed into British Columbia for a few kilometers but came back to the main high way to Calgary. We reached Calgary in the evening after driving for more than three hundred kilometers. We stayed at a hotel in the city center. Azad had stayed there on many occasions for office work. We had dinner at an Indian restaurant. We walked around the city center but did not visit any shops or supermarkets. Next morning we visited many shops including Indian shops. We bought a dozen Hindi DVDs. In the evening we left Calgary and drove through the valleys and mount Canyon and reached Edmonton at night.

On Sunday- 1st August, we went to the heritage fare on the out skirts of Edmonton. Canada was still a new country and people from many countries had come to live there. They were allowed to maintain their cultures. Though English and French were the main languages, people were not discouraged from speaking their own languages and keep their own customs. The fair represented cultures of many countries. We watched Greek dance; Indian dances-the Bhangra and the Kathakali. We had Indian food at an Indian stall and rested on the grass. We listened to Arabic songs and a saw Peruvian dance.

The local area, where Azad lived in Edmonton was called the Millcreek Meadows. It was a small town but it was not self-sufficient. There were no local shops or local work places. Though there was a bus service which was not frequent. People had to visit malls in order to purchase goods. These were about two kilometers away. We visited most of the malls and supermarkets. This place was entirely different from what we had in London.

While we were in Edmonton, we went to Drum Heller on 6th August. It was three hundred kilometers from Edmonton. It had a museum, which combined the geological museum, Dinosaur museum, the natural history museum, the science museum and the botanical garden. It had the largest dinosaur in the world. The geological and scientific history of Alberta was shown in these museums. It had very detailed information about rocks and oil in the state. We enjoyed our stay there. It started to rain, which dampened our pleasure a little. We also visited the Mud Mountains. It was suggested that there was a sea at that place and it had dried up leaving Mud Mountains and valleys. The valleys, lakes and the mountains represented and reflected the natural beauty of the area. We returned to Edmonton in the evening. On our way back we stopped at a town called Camerose.

For the next couple of days we did some shopping and visited shopping centres. We also watched a movie called the 'Helen of Troy' in a theatre in Millwood Meadows. We enjoyed the family atmosphere and the company of each other. I suggested to Azad and Meenakkshi, that if they were not happy there or it was too cold in Canada, they should come back to

England. Just before returning to London, we went to local malls and shops though we did not buy anything there. We left for London before dawn on 16th August.

Azad, Meenakshi, Amar, Ashish, Akhilesh and Asha came to see us off at the airport.

We deposited our luggage, had the security check and immigration clearance. We first took a flight to Houston and from there to London Gatwick. The flight was not pleasant at all. There was no recreation and the food was not good either. However, we reached Gatwick in the morning at 6.30 am on Tuesday 17th August. We took a train to London, which was packed and crowded because of office commuters who were going to their work places. Still we managed to get in and get out of the compartment. We changed to another train and reached home at 10 am.

It took us more than a week to fully recover from the journey fatigue. We used to go to sleep at any time. After a week or so I went to University. Ron asked me if I could teach a First Year class on five Thursdays in September/ October and in January, Second Year Business Economics; because he had found someone to teach in the First Semester. I agreed to teach both the classes. I attended an induction and also did a lecture on 30th September 2004. I enjoyed teaching and perhaps I was helpful to students. Whenever I felt tired, I could not sleep well. However, I wanted to continue at Greenwich that year. Then I would review the situation. People had different views. Some were happy to see me there while others felt that I should enjoy my retirement. I took five tutorials on Thursdays and one small group on Mondays. I also delivered a lecture on Thursdays to almost three hundred students. I did enjoy the tutorials. Some students were good. But the lecture was wearisome. Many students wanted to listen and take notes while there were some students who could not hear in that large lecture theatre. They, therefore, became noisy. I did not know how I survived for five weeks. If I had a choice, I would not like to repeat it.

We also planned to go to India on 29th October. After teaching on Thursday we were to leave at mid night on Friday. We were misled in this by the travel agent. We booked our ticket through a travel agency who did not fully explain that we did not have to reach at Heathrow just after midnight. We reached at Heathrow at 3.30 am but the counter did not open until 5 am. The passengers were annoyed at this inefficient arrangement. There were no benches or place to sit and relax. We had to stand with our luggage. Surprisingly, the plane left on time and we reached Milan Airport on the scheduled time. We changed to another plane but had to go through the security check again. We waited for about an hour before the plane took off for Delhi. We reached Delhi at 10 pm Indian time. It took us another hour to come out. We, therefore, decided to stay in the lounge. Despite our wish to go home immediately after coming out of the airport we could not do that. It was after 11 pm. We stayed awake all-night and left for home at 5 am on 30th October.

We reached home at 6 am. The house was very dirty because of rain and summer dust. It had remained shut for almost ten months. We opened all the doors. At the beginning, the house looked a little strange. We were used to a different setting. It took our eyes to adjust with a different outlook. After a while we went to look for a cleaner. We found a young man who came with us and did the cleaning all day. We were happy with his work. We asked him to come back the next day to clean the roof terrace and the doors and windows. He came the next day to complete the work. The house started to look clean and fine within the next few days.

We stayed in Delhi for two months. It was a quiet life. We did not go outside of Delhi except for a visit to Baraut and once to Paschim Vihar. This time we did not go to New Delhi. We went to Chandni- Chowk, old Delhi a few times. There were two reasons for this. After about a week, I developed pain at my bottom and found it difficult and uneasy to sit. I consulted a local doctor who diagnosed abscess and gave me some medicine. But there was no improvement in my condition. I, therefore, consulted Dr. Vijay who advised me to speak to Dr. Amit Rangan. Dr. Amit asked me to come to his hospital immediately. We went to his hospital in Yamuna Vihar. He checked and also diagnosed that it was abscess, which was not old and had developed recently because of sitting for long hours.

A part of the bottom had become hard because of the abscess which would need to be drained. After waiting for two hours, he operated on me. Dr. Vijay and Bhushanlal also arrived at the hospital. Dr. Amit and his colleagues carried out the operation and removed the abscess. I stayed in the recuperation room for about an hour. Dr. Vijay then drove us to our house but he did not stay at the house. It was already late at night. I, nevertheless, had to stay in bed for three weeks. I used to sit in a tub bath. I was asked to repeat it three times a day but I hardly repeated the process and sat in the tub only once a day. My wound started to heal and after two weeks of the operation, I started to walk to get milk in the morning. I was fully well within a month.

We attended a wedding ceremony in November. After dinner at Rohini on 26th November Santosh became ill. There after we were cautious about our food and eating. My nephew Vijay Kumar had informed us that his daughter Neetu was getting married on 6th December 2004. He consulted us on many matters and we supported him all the way. Santosh wanted to give Neetu a tangible thing as a wedding present. But we told Vijay not to tell anyone about our gift. Perhaps he was the only one who knew about this. Our relatives and people in the neighbourhood asked about our present to Neetu but we did not make it open to any one. It remained a secret. We, however, told them that we gave Neetu a gift of a watch set, which we brought from Canada and some clothes for her husband Vikrant. We gave these things on their first visit to our house. We all enjoyed the ceremony, which lasted a few days. Vijay's house was small, so he used our house for the rituals of saat-farey (seven rounds around veneration fire). Some sixty people gathered together. Many of them fell asleep. We stayed awake all night. After the departure ceremony of the wedding guests, we slept for many hours, the next day.

We did some shopping in Old Delhi and decided to return to London on 28th December. We informed of this decision to our relatives a few days before our departure. It also started to get a little colder in Delhi in the last days of the year. But we enjoyed our stay in Delhi. We had kept in touch with Azad and children in Canada. Ashish phoned at mid-night on 24th December, which was his grandmother's birthday. It was a sweet thought on his part for a family commitment. Other members of the family phoned the next morning.

We returned to London via Milan (Italy) where we stopped for four hours. It was boring and exacting. We slept in the plane this time and felt sleepy for many days at home. On 31 December, we all got together on the New-Year's-Eve. Azad phoned us exactly at mid night. We had a simple celebration of soft drinks.

In the year 2004, I considered writing about Outsourcing which had become popular in the United Kingdom and the United States. As the cost of running services had increased in these countries, they decided to transfer some of the back office functions to India and other low- wage nations. Outsourcing was another part of international trade, i.e. to reap the gains of comparative advantages. It was a new phenomenon of this Century. It had been in existence for many years and in many fields. It had become a part of free trade and globalization. India's Information Technology based knowledge, use of English language and abundant supply of skilled and qualified manpower had become profitable for cost savings and efficiency for the British and other Western firms.

In the 1990s, many British banks and insurance companies decided to transfer some of their call-centre jobs to India in the cost cutting exercise and to achieve savings for their customers. It was considered that call-center would be created in India in the coming years especially to assist the British financial institutions. As the cost of financial services increased in Britain, the employers in the banking and insurance sectors decided to transfer their operations to India. With the use of English language as a medium of education and in the daily use in the Indian middle class families, the British employers in financial sector found a ready market for the supply of manpower for their call-centers, which had become common in Britain in order to deal with customer services and customer enquiries.

Security questions were widely considered. Many questions had, however, been posed regarding the validity and reasonableness for transfer of call-center jobs to India in particular and to the other developing countries in general. The memories of the decline of the UK manufacturing sector were still fresh in the minds of the British people. 60% of British people were against outsourcing. The trade unions felt socially responsible in order to stop the flight of call-center jobs which might have dire consequences on employment and local economies in North-West England and Northern Ireland where most call-centers were located. This was a problem for macro-economic policy makers and manpower planners.

Besides the private sector, the British government departments and local authorities were offshoring some of their functions to India and other low wage nations in order to make savings as the Blair government had to reduce government expenditure. It was considered that the Indian call-center workers could work for only 10% to 15% wages what was to be paid to British workers. Taking into account the infrastructure costs, it could still lead to 40% savings. Besides financial savings, the level of work force was also considered as there was a shortage of office workers in the 1990s and early 21st Century. The number of civil service workers dramatically declined. Even the Tax departments considered transferring some of their functions to India.

The fundamental argument about outsourcing by businesses was customer satisfaction. They should feel comfortable and happy in dealing with foreign call-center employees. It was strange to find that half a million jobs were transferred abroad by Britain. However, this did not have any impact on employment in the United Kingdom as was feared by some unions. In India some of the large cities like Delhi, Mumbai, Bangalore, Hyderabad, Chennai and Kolkata became the hubs of offshoring. Apart from the United Kingdom, the United States and Germany also transferred jobs to India. The General Motors created 100 research jobs in Bangalore in order to develop lightweight material and conduct crash tests. Some of the large corporations like the General Electrics, Dell, HSBC preferred to set up their operations in India through their subsidiaries. This allowed them to impose their own corporate ethos and management.

Outsourcing of Information Technology (IT) jobs, health care and financial administration as well as using Indian hospitals, was beneficial for Britain. India was to gain 23,000 crore rupees for offering back office health service. Medical image processing and diagnostics were also being outsourced to India because it had a large number of trained and internationally recognized professionals in this field. Besides qualified personnel, India provided time zone advantage. The ECG, and Pathology slide images, sent at the end of the day from the US and the UK could be returned with interpretations, reports and diagnosis by next morning. A neighbour of mine who worked with an investment bank at Canary Wharf, London, told me that he emailed work to Bangalore at the end of the day and the analysis would be returned to him before he reached office the next morning.

The criticism of Indian call-centers was, however, growing. It was suggested that poorly qualified staff was being recruited due to increased demand from the West. British customers complained that the British way of life was not appreciated and Indian call- center workers did not have knowledge of the British society. Still India remained the top destination for the UK outsourcing.

The outsourcing across the world had become so popular that it was being suggested that between 3 and 13 Million jobs could be created for call-center workers, mainly in India. The United States was planning to transfer half a million legal profession jobs by 2015. Call center jobs were, nevertheless, repetitive and often boring and exhausting. It kept every day work and decision making separate and promotion prospects for workers were minimal except for a supervisory position to look after the new entrants. In Britain some ex-miners joined call centers in North-East England. They found their new jobs more industrious than their old work in mines. Moreover, it was exploitation of people in the developing countries. The call center would have negative effect on social life of these workers. They had to work at night. Many had been attacked on their way home or going to work. The salaries were poor by any standards. Young people worked in these centers due to high unemployment in their countries. Yet the Indian call centers earned 30 billion dollars in 2007.

x   x   x

On 5ᵗʰ January 2005, I went to University to collect the First Year course work. I marked it over the next few days. This Semester, I started to teach Business Economics to Second Year BABA. I took this class on Friday after noon. We hardly ever had full class. Some students turned up only for one or two lectures or tutorials. Only three students attended all lessons regularly. I enjoyed teaching this group. I also took a few weeks of tutorials and lectures for Economic Frame work for Business for year one, of BA Business Administration. The curriculum for this subject was the same one, we taught in the previous years. It studied Micro and Macro Economic theories at introductory level. It was a slim class this time. Some students had left. Others were busy with their course work and did not attend Economics lessons. There was no noise or disruption in lectures. Those who attended, they co-operated in every way. The course work done by students was of good standard. One student scored over eighty percent marks. No one failed. I also marked the Second year course work. It was of high standard. Yet two students failed and some received low marks. Those who attended lessons scored high marks. It showed a co-relation between attending lectures and the course work result.

There was a natural disaster in Asia following an earthquake and tsunami in that part of the world. It affected the Andaman Nicobar Islands, the Tamil Nadu and some other southern parts of India. It also affected Sri Lanka, Thailand and Indonesia. Fifteen thousand people died in Indian Territories and some 155,000 people died in other parts of South East Asia. People all over the world donated money for the victims. We did our bit. Things started to settle down but the community life did not return to these lands. The villages and schools were destroyed along with livelihood of many people.

I continued to enjoy my retirement, watched Hindi movies and serials. I also read a number of Hindi novels. In April 2005, the British Prime Minister decided for a general election. The economy had been strong. The interest rates were low. Still the house prices were rising and consumer demand was increasing. The election debate revolved around the National Health Service (NHS), crime, immigration and asylum. The Council Tax also became an issue because it was very high in all areas. The Liberal

Democrats wanted to abolish the Council Tax altogether and substitute it by a local tax. There was a need to change the local tax system, which was unfair at that time because it hurt the old and the poor most.

We went to Acton, Hammersmith, Hounslow and Southall many times. The physical and social face of these towns had changed enormously. Most of the old shops and electricity and gas showrooms had disappeared from Acton High Street. There were more vegetable and fruit shop to day than they were ten or twenty years ago. The ownership has also changed. There were Somali and Arab traders now when there were none in the past. The NatWest Bank was still there. Some more banks have emerged on the High Street.

I had seen the changing face of Southall. On the Broadway and High Street, there were many travel agents and mobile shops. There was no big store or food shop. But there were many restaurants, mainly owned by the Asians. The British population was replaced by Indian immigrants in the 1960s and 1970s, but now they were also moving out. Afghanistanis, Somalis, and Pakistani had come to live there in large numbers. Only 17.9% percent population was old British. The bus service was, however, good. The sweet shops and cloth shops though small out lets were quite good. The Ealing Council had put many benches on the pavement. People could sit and relax.

Hounslow High Street had become paved for customers to walk. There were benches to sit on. There were food shops, many good cloth shops and stores. The traffic had been diverted from the High Street. The shopping Mall was also good with all sorts of shops and a public library. Hammersmith had a one-way traffic system. A large area had been paved for sitting and walking. Quite a few coffee houses had emerged there. It still had a few stores and a good shopping area in this part of London. Chiswick High Road has seen a great change. Today it was more European than British. Open space coffee shops with seating arrangement on pavement. It had lost shops and stores. People had to go to other areas in West End, Hammersmith and Hounslow for all sorts of shopping whether shoes, clothes or even food.

On 19th April, as I returned from Brentford at 6 pm, I heard our telephone ringing. I quickly opened the door and attended the phone from Delhi. I was told that my elder brother, Gopi Chand, had passed away at Kakore. Some members of the family had gone there. I phoned the next day and found out further details. I discovered that my brother died on the 18th at 3 pm. It was Ram Navmi according to Vikram Samvat. It was the same day when my eldest sister died a few years earlier. I was very sad to hear the demise of my brother. I felt bad all day on the 20th.

After composing myself and accepting the fact, I wrote, My Recollections of my elder brother. I liked my brother. We never quarreled and there was never any misunderstanding between the two of us. I never blamed him for any thing. He was a kind man and an innocent soul who had been a victim of his own gentleness all his life. He had lost stamina to fight with the situations and circumstances. He often succumbed rather than to face them. He had a weak will- power because of lack of education and to some extent lack of experience in life. He was controlled and dominated by certain members of his immediate family and relatives. He never questioned their actions or decisions. He listened to them and obeyed their instructions even when they were wrong. He had been ill for some time. Yet we did not expect him to die.

My brother was four years older to me and I had memories of our early years. We hardly corresponded in the past forty years, I had been in England. Surprisingly, I wrote my last letter to him in March 2005, about a month before he died. He did not reply because of illness. My grandfather always said that he was his favourite grandson. In the early years of his life he used to stay at the village shop with grandpa, especially when father had gone to town to buy goods for the shop. He used to skip school in order to work at the shop. One day our father returned early from Khurja (the town from where he used to buy articles for the shop). He asked him why he did not go to school. GC simply replied that grandpa asked him to stay at the shop. It was a routine. Whenever our father was away, brother would stay at the shop. This disrupted his education and it was quite late at the age of almost fourteen when he completed his primary education.

He lost interest in his studies. Our father wanted all of us to have proper education and perhaps a degree. My elder brother was sent to study at town. My eldest brother and I were already there. I was in Seventh standard by that time and my elder brother would have been admitted to class sixth as it was the first year of the Secondary Education in those days. However, he questioned how he could be junior to me at school when I was much younger to him. He was hoping to skip a couple of years and study in class VIII. I spoke to my Form Tutor Manohar Lal Sharma that my elder brother wanted to join the school but in a higher class.

The teacher suggested that he could join the same class as me but it was not possible for him to be admitted into a higher class, as he would be unable to cope with the subjects. English language was a major problem for him as he could not pick up any English during the summer holiday. He then decided to give up formal education altogether and learn Munimai (rudimentary bookkeeping for simple balance sheet). He waited for a few weeks but was not happy with the city life. He, therefore, returned to the village to work at the shop. After a couple of years he started a milk dairy at the village. He bought milk from farmers, took the cream out and sent the skimmed milk to Delhi to be sold. This continued for a few months but he had to give it up because of lack of support from his workers who often cheated him and took advantage of his gentleness.

In 1954, he got married at the age of nineteen. It was difficult to say whether he was happy in his married life. He never discussed it with any body. In 1958, he decided to leave the village. He thought of opening a shop in a town. He looked for places in Uttar Pradesh but settled for Krishna Nagar in Delhi. I was with him for about a month and found that sale was good though he did not like when the customers demanded credit facility or home delivery. Anyhow, he stayed at Krishna Nagar for about ten months. Then he gave up the shop and again thought of starting a shop in U P. It was difficult for one man to run a shop in Delhi. He wasted almost one year. Our mother asked him to return to the village. Our father bought some land at Kakore (a town in U P) and built two shops with two rooms on first floor for residence. My elder brother ran this shop for a few years. Then he obtained electricity connection and started a flourmill. Later he added a cotton-spinning machine, a mustard oil mill. It was a small factory. He employed six workers who were hard working and faithful.

My elder brother, GC, did not have any children. Our parents suggested that he could adopt one of the nephews. It did not happen. My youngest brother went to Kakore to study but he was sent back to the village after a few months. He, therefore, got cut- off from the family. He was lonely and sometimes sad. His wife's sister sent one of her daughters to live with them at Kakore. When this girl was about eighteen, it became vitally important to arrange a marriage of this girl. My brother had to sell all his belongings and the machines for that. After that he became a poor man and never recovered from his poverty. He also became sick of tuberculosis, Asthma, bronchitis and lung problem. He was ill and poor for the last twenty-five years of his life. Other members of the family tried to help him but he always returned to his relatives who often exploited him.

I saw my brother in December 2004, for the last time when he came to Delhi, to organize a marriage for his wife's sister's granddaughter. Like her mother this girl lived with him from childhood. For this marriage he sold my younger brother's house at Kakore for over one hundred thousand rupees and gave twenty five thousand rupees to his family. The rest was used for the wedding of that girl. He did not spend a penny on himself or for his medicine. He never showed it, but he was a broken man and a destitute for many years. He tried his level best but those close to him cheated him and deceived him. In the death of GC, I lost a dear brother who could have lived a better life if the circumstances had been different. He could have talked to right people.

In the last five years from year 2000 to 2005, I lost three siblings. Three gentle faces had gone. I loved them all very dearly. I mourn their death in great sorrow and I will miss them on my next visits to India.

I hardly had anything to do in the summer of 2005, yet I felt busy. I went out many times, for no good purpose. Life had been at ease for me in London. On 7th July, we heard in the news that London had faced a terrorist attack in the central part of the city. Three bombs went off simultaneously on the tube and one on the bus. These were suicide bombs. Fifty- six people were killed and many hundred injured. The emergency services went into action. I was shocked and very perturbed. We heard that some Muslim youths were involved. Though there were not open disturbances, many Asians were attacked by the whites. The police and the government tried to calm people down. It was also the time for the G8 summit and for the first time the Indian Prime Minister took part at this summit. There was condemnation of the London bombings throughout the world.

We received phone calls from Azad, Ashok and Vivek to express their sympathy and horror and to find out our well being. Astonishingly, I was not too far from the attacks in London that day. I had an appointment at the Hammersmith Hospital. I could not get a bus to hospital. I walked all the way and afterwards I roamed around East Acton and walked back home. I kept my mobile switched on and enquired whether there was a message at home for me. I was told that we had a few phone calls. I called all of them on returning to the house.

Two weeks later on 21st July, four more bombs were planted – three on the tube and one on the bus. This was done at midday. The bombs did not explode and there was no injury. The police raided many houses and arrested a number of people. The police found out the names of the July 7 bombers who had come from Leeds in Yorkshire and also the names of the 21st July bombers who mostly came from London. One of them travelled to Rome by the Euro train but was later caught. The fear of bombing had not subsided in London and other parts of the country though people were putting brave face and had not stopped their daily routine. On 4th August 2005, some six thousand police guarded London transport. After the bombing, the number of people using London transport, declined in the immediate months. Tourism also went down in London and other parts of the UK.

It was surprising that even the moderate Muslims did not find it wrong to put bombs in London despite the fact that they would not like to kill innocent people. But in this indiscriminate bombing innocent people were bound to be killed. Some Muslims wanted to set up a Muslim state and control the world. They did not want to know about other cultures or religions.

On 15th October 2005, I completed forty years of my living in England. I had never lived for so long at one place as in West London. I have lived in Chiswick for over 28 years. I had been happy there, and had observed many changes in this area and other parts of London. The weather had changed in the past forty years. The month of October had become milder. Day light was still visible at 7 pm. Forty years ago it was a cold and dark night when I was to start a new life in a new land which was strange to me. A few hours earlier on the same day, I was with my family in Delhi but left them and the country to come to England. After forty years, I was with my family including my grand children. At that time, I had small children of my own whom I had left in India. Now I had four grandchildren.

What had been the cost-benefit-analysis of these forty years? I had gained in some areas, while I had lost in other areas. It was difficult to judge what would I have done or become if I stayed on in India. But before coming to England I found myself in strange circumstances when I was unable to control my own destiny. Though I would have provided food to my family, I was in no position to meet all their requirements and see them through a good life. Here we worked very hard but managed to attain most things needed for a happy living. Of course, I had made progress in India in some fields and hoped for better things as well. England had, however, given me a great deal more than I expected or desired for. These forty years had been fulfilling. I must, nevertheless, confess that during these forty years, I lost my father, mother, elder sister, elder brother, and a younger brother. Many members of my wife's family passed away during this period. I miss them all whenever I visit India. I, nevertheless, still preserve their memories.

In London, we have had many benefits. I obtained five qualifications, wrote books and articles, taught at schools, colleges, polytechnics and eventually retired at the Greenwich University. It provided me enormous experience in educational and social fields. When I arrived in London forty years ago I was a young man of twenty six, now I was a retired man and a grand-dad. My son and two intelligent grandsons moved to live in Canada in the year 2000. They started a new life in a new country across many seas. London afforded me facilities to study and obtain education. It provided me employment and residence. My life had been reasonably comfortable and at ease. I had taken advantages of many facilities in this beautiful city. I was a Londoner, perhaps a West Londoner. I was happy and reposeful here. I mostly travelled by public transport but also owned a car for eleven years. My forty years here had been effective and fulfilling. I enjoyed the company of my friends, colleagues and the family. Amar and Ashish continue to speak to us every week and send emails. Sangeeta and Akash visit us every day and some times stay with us in the evening.

There had been some set backs from time to time but there had never been any arduous problems which I had not been able to solve. I had kept in touch with my family in India and maintained good relations with almost every one. The family relationship was like an infrastructure. It got to be maintained and kept steady all the time. Otherwise like a road without maintenance, could not be used at the time of need. After my retirement in August 2003, I started to go to Delhi, every year and celebrated Diwali in 2003 and 2004. My relatives in India wanted us to celebrate Diwali in Delhi this year (2005) as well. However, this year we wanted to celebrate Diwali in London with our daughter and grandchildren. Moreover I had a commitment at the University and some appointments for medical check-up. When I came to England I had no physical problem. Now I had knee pain, prostrate problem and diabetes. I was getting treatment for all these ailments, and I take 5 tablets a day.

London had changed since I came to live here. The city of London had changed and had seen many new buildings with new architecture. The Canary Wharf had revitalized East London. West London was being influenced by the European culture. Forty years ago, there was hardly any Indian restaurant in the UK but now there were 16,000 Indian restaurants in this country. Indian films were shown in theatres. Quite a few Indian films were made in different locations in England and Scotland. The scenes of London and its buildings did appear in many Hindi films. Southall, in Middlesex a suburb of London, had become an Indian town with a large

Indian population, Indian shops, restaurants, sweet houses, temples and Gurudwaras. I enjoy visiting Southall. It was from there, I bought my supplies of rice, flour, lentils and vegetables. Wembley and Harrow were also Indian hubs but not that popular.

The Indians themselves had made enormous progress. There were only a few Indian shops in England to supply Indian food material for the Indian population. Now, 60% of retail trade was in the hands of Indians. There was hardly any business that was not run by Indians. They work in education, health, civil service, local government, banking, estate agents, travel agents, accountants and solicitors. They were home owners, property developers and ordinary workers. There were Indian Councilors, Members of Parliament, and Members of the House of Lords but not many judges. Perhaps because of various accomplishments and breakthrough in many fields, I had been happy in London where I followed the best of Indian and Western cultures and had enjoyed a mixture of both. It had been advantageous for me. I had written books about India but in English.

I believed, that man was a product of his environment and when I look back to my own experiences and observations, I come to the conclusion that I was also influenced by the social environment. I was brought up in an humble family. Our house in India, was situated near people of all castes and creeds. When I went to school, I mixed with students of all backgrounds. I had Muslim friends, Hindu friends, Jain friends. The city people and the village folks were close to me. I had a few friends from scheduled castes and backward communities. There were very few students from backward communities in those days. This, nevertheless, made me a sociable person and I did not develop any complexes. When I came to England, I lived in a house which had a multicultural environment. The workplace, the schools I taught in, the college and the University had students and staff from diverse social backgrounds. I could not imagine myself living in a ghetto situation where only Indians or Asians lived. This made it possible for me to enjoy the company of people of good nature irrespective of their ethnicity and background.

After quietly celebrating my forty years in London, I continued with my routine. During October 2005, I did some teaching at the Greenwich University. I offered to do only tutorials and refused to take large lectures. The lectures had become overwhelming and noisy when I delivered some in October 2004. Moreover, it was not worth it. Financially there was no incentive. I was paid the same amount for teaching 250 students in a big room as I was paid for a small tutorial group in a small room. After finishing teaching for a few weeks, we went to Delhi on 6th November 2005. It was a strange experience this time. When we reached Delhi International Airport, it was midnight and we decided to stay at the airport and went to the house in the morning.

We stayed in Delhi for seven weeks, visited old Delhi on many occasions and Connaught Place a couple of times. We went to Paschim Vihar to visit Ashok's family only once. Apart from that we did not go any where. It was a quiet holiday at the house. I practiced yoga exercises in the morning, collected milk, read newspapers and sat at the roof terrace at mid day. It helped my knee pain to ease. We used to get a few visitors every day and I used to go around visiting the extended family in the neighbourhood. We decided to return to London on 29th December. Before returning to London, I went to Kakore with my eldest brother and two nephews. My brother, Gopi Chand, used to live there, before his death in April. The visit was considered essential for social formalities. The family house had been divided into units. Some parts had been occupied by my brother's brother-in-law and his family. In a small part my sister-in-law lived. The rooms on the first floor were vacant. The house had not been repaired for a long time. It was difficult to judge whether my sister-in-law was happy or not. Though she claimed that her nephews looked after her and she had no conundrum. She had always liked that family. She did not attempt to be a part of our family.

This visit to Kakore was, nevertheless, an experience. We used the road to travel. The roads to the immediate vicinity of Delhi were fine but when we crossed into the Uttar Pradesh (UP) the roads were in a bad state with pit-holes. They were made with mud and pebbles and had never been repaired. I had not experienced such a situation before. The journey from Sikandrabad (a town in UP) was really absorbing. Kakore was only seventeen Kilometers from there but it took us more than an hour to reach and about one and a half hours to return from Kakore. On our journey back to Delhi, our car broke down at Dadri (another town in Western UP) not too far from Delhi. We enquired for a mechanic. A welder directed us to a repair shop where a group of young ignorant boys tried to repair the car.

They did not know what was wrong with the car but managed to put an old belt on the engine. They told us that the car was not in a good shape for driving and it would break- down at any time. We would be unable to reach Delhi in that car. However, once the car started we left that place and reached Delhi within an hour. I was under the impression that we would return home in the after noon. We, however, returned home at ten o'clock at night because it took us three hours to reach Kakore and more than five hours to return to Delhi. Despite the troubles and distressing journey, we enjoyed each other's company. We were not bored at all. There was always some thing to talk about or to discuss.

There was another experience when we reached London. After landing at the Heathrow airport we collected our baggage and put the luggage in the car. On reaching Chiswick we discovered that we left a bag on the trolley in the car park though it was collected at the airport. We put our things in side the house and dashed to the airport. We reached there within half an hour and spotted that a security guard had the bag and was looking at my passport. It was at the same spot where we had left on the third floor of terminal four at Heathrow where we left the trolley. The trolley had been collected by some one but they did not take the bag.

The security man asked me my name and address and returned the bag to me. He asked me to check the items because he found the bag on the floor. I told him that there was a file and few other items in the bag. After checking the things, I told him that nothing was missing. I thanked him for his kindness and thanked God that we found our bag safe and secure. On returning to Chiswick we spoke to Azad, Arun and Vivek who were pleased to hear that everything was fine. After that we became a little lazy and slept for many hours each day for almost a week. I used to doze off watching TV.

It had been a little cold in the winter of 2006. We hardly went out. I continued my Yoga exercises. I also returned to University in the second week of January and started to teach Business Economics. The class was good this year. The students were keen to learn and they were co-operative. There had been a change this year. The Group Presentation became a part of assessment. The lecture would be for an hour a week as usual and the tutorial time would be used for presentation. My life was at ease at home and at the University. I had some physiotherapy lessons at Hammersmith hospital and Santosh at the Doctor's surgery. We had both developed arthritis. We felt a little better after these exercises. Azad continued to phone on Sundays. We spoke to Amar and Ashish as well. They were planning to visit India towards the end of this year. We would plan to go to India when they had decided some dates so we could make preparations for their visit and make it a rewarding change. They should enjoy their visit and our company.

I did not do much reading except for newspapers and some Hindi novels. We watched TV mainly on the Zee channels, Hindi films and Soaps. South Asia News was good on Zee. Yoga exercises on Astha channel were fine but I still had to see some effects of Yoga in getting rid of my illnesses. The reporting in camps (gatherings) was encouraging. I have read all the Yoga books, I brought from Delhi. 19th July 2006, was the hottest day of the year and the hottest day in July since 1911. It was in that year when the temperature reached 36C or 37C. It was 37 Centigrade on this day after ninety five years. Vivek's wife (Diviya) gave birth to a baby girl on 3rd May at St. George's hospital, Tooting, in South London. Santosh and I were in hospital at that time. Mainly to support Neelamji (Vivek's mother) who had come from India because of the child's birth and to look after Diviya in her pregnancy and in the early days of the baby in this world. We went to hospital for Vivek and Diviya as well.

We would have been there any way for them and to support them under any circumstances. It was a long wait and we felt a little tired afterwards.

Vivek's mother stayed in England for about two and a half months. We went to Surbitton three times during this period and they visited us in Chiswick once. Neelimaji formed an impression of places in London based on whatever she was told by Vivek. In her opinion England was a nice country. On her return she phoned us twice in a week. We were not able to visit Vivek after that because of hot weather but we used to talk on phone many times a week. The baby was making good progress.

I visited, the University, a couple of times and told the new Head of International Business and Economics that we would like to be in Delhi at Diwali time in October. I would, therefore, not be able to teach in October. I, however, had no objection to teaching Intermediate Economics for Business (a new name for Business Economics) in January. I could also do some tutorials for the Framework for Economic Institutions, which I did on returning from India in January 2007.

On 11 July 2006, a terrorist attack took place on suburban trains in Mumbai. A total of seven bombs exploded within minutes in different trains and at different stations. These bombs ripped apart the doors and roofs of some compartments. Some 200 people died and more than seven hundred were injured in these blasts. The Indian authorities blamed the militants and those who trained them. It was a reasonable argument. But the Indian government agencies, the Home Office, the secret services, the police and the Maharastra administration should have taken responsibilities to protect the citizens and the commuters. It was not good to blame others and do nothing. They should have taken precautions to defeat the ruffians. Mumbai had been attacked many times in the last thirteen years since 1993, when hundreds of people died in the Bombay blasts.

In India, the authorities become active for a few weeks then they forget. In the meantime the dread organized themselves and when they felt safe, they attacked the civilians again. India still behaved in an immature way. Despite economic progress, there was no political leadership and no plans to protect the citizens. It was a phenomenon of the 21st Century. The rowdy would attempt to attack soft targets and the economy of the country. It was, however, the responsibility of the state to guard against intimidation and violent attacks. The United States had not been attacked after the 2001, blasts and the destruction of the twin towers. London was still safe after the July 2005 attacks. We went around without fear. The state was taking precautions rather than feel angry and sorry after the blasts. The Indian administration was corrupt and inefficient and some politicians looked to vote banks which lead to consternation. Some new dreadful organizations had sprung up in India of which we knew nothing, only a few years ago. They carried out the terrorist attacks.

It rained a great deal in England in the months of July and August. It was an indication of climate change. I did not have much to do except marking Business Economics scripts and the re-sit examination papers. I went to the University three times during these months. On 9th August the British authorities raided some houses in Walthamstow, East London, High Wycombe and Birmingham. They smashed a plot to highjack ten US- bound aero-planes and to bomb them over the Atlantic Ocean or over some densely populated cities. The British airports witnessed chaos for about a week. The security checking became intense. Passengers were not allowed to take hand baggage apart from their passports and wallets. People did not moan much. They regarded it, for their own safety and security.

There was a great debate of the Muslim distance. The multiculturalism in Britain was also questioned because all suspected terrorists were Muslims mainly of Pakistani origin. Their parents and grandparents came to Britain to improve their standards of living. These young people, however, were brain washed in the name of religion. They became anti-West especially against Britain and the United States. I could not believe this development because most of my friends from day one in England had been Muslims from Pakistani. I always got on well with them. But the segregation and non-coherence, their demand for Muslim schools, halal meat, their own food and eating habits, even dress and growing beard by some to show to society that they were different, made it impossible to mix with others including Asians. Their affinity was towards Islam rather than towards neighbours, schoolmates and fellow workers. They sometimes stayed away from the main stream British way of life. Some of them did not pick up the language and insisted on speaking Asian and their own languages rather than to become bi-lingual.

When I looked back, to my own stay in London and making a reasonable progress, I found that perhaps I was right in adopting some of the customs and habits of the British way of living. I started to read English news papers and books. I ate bread butter, beans, biscuit and other local food rather than insisting on Indian vegetarian food. I always worked mostly with British people whether it was in an office, school, college or university. I did not have any complex in accepting the local systems. Of course, as an immigrant and perhaps as an Indian in the 1960s, in Britain, I faced many conundrums in the early years of my living in London. Had multiculturalism failed in Britain? For me multi-culturalism meant many cultures functioning side by side and to show respect to people of all backgrounds without prejudice. Every country, however, had its own traditions and legal frame-work and people had to make progress within those parameters.

Many foreigners had demanded the use of their language, food of their choice in schools. It was a fair demand. But home grown consternation, to change policies of a country, was not good for any one. Most of the Asian restaurants were run by Pakistanis and Bangladeshis and yet they demanded halal meat in schools. They wanted others to eat their food but they themselves did not want to eat British food. They refused to read British news-papers or English books or to learn about other religions. How could they make progress in the British society without mixing with the British people? They had created ghettos in some cities where they remained backward, underemployed or unemployed.

Britain had a system to express discontent and opposition to policies and behaviour. People could demonstrate against unjust policies, influence politicians, write articles in newspapers and write pamphlets. Participation in pressure groups, political parties, trade unions and other organizations in order to influence policies. But to create their own religious organizations and to bring co-religionists together, not to pray but to influence government policies through violence, was rather an odd way of expressing one's views and opinions. It was being argued that the Muslim terrorism was taking place due the British government policies on Iraq and Afghanistan. But quite a few people from these countries now lived in Britain. They were not involved in barbarian acts. They found themselves safe here in Britain. I had not seen many demonstrations against the war in Iraq or a demand to get the British forces back home. There were demonstrations in the 1960s and 1970s against the Vietnam War. This led to policy change in the United States. The current consternation without ideology, however, could not accomplish much.

It was good that the British authorities stopped the August, aero- plane attacks which were designed to kill many thousand people. The police had taken an approach in investigation, collection of evidence, taking the suspects in custody and then to courts. This was a civilized method of tackling the intricacy. Some people had been inconvenienced but majority were made safe. A big dreadful attack with dire consequences had been averted.

From 13th to 18th August, I attended a yoga camp at Harrow, Middlesex. It was organized by the Indian community there and they invited Ram Dev, a yoga teacher from Haridwar, India. I had become interested in Yoga in October 2005. I read about it on the internet and borrowed a book of Acton library. I started to practice a few yoga pranayams (breathing exercises) and physical exercises for my knee pain. When I was in Delhi in December, I bought three books and a CD. I sent the CD to Canada. I also started to watch yoga on a TV channel. It was presented by Swami Ram Dev. We followed and practiced a few pranayams (breathing exercises) and yoga- asans in the evening from 5pm to 7.30pm. It was advertised that Ram Dev was coming to England. His first camp was held at Hainault, Ilford. Prior to the camp we went to see this place. We, however, found this place too far from West London and difficult to reach. We concluded that it would be difficult to travel for five days and take part in the yoga exercises.

It was later advertised that another camp in Greater London was to take place at Harrow View. I went to visit this place one day but could not reach there. I, therefore, phoned one of the organizers who provided me some guidance about the place. We went again on a Saturday to see this place. It was accessible by bus from Raynors Lane. I bought a ticket at Quality Stores, Southall, in order to attend the camp, from 13th August. I had to take my own sheet to sit on. I travelled by District line to Acton Town and by Piccadilly line to Raynors Lane and then by bus to Harrow View. I used to leave at 3.30 pm in order to reach there just before 5pm. The proceedings started on time with a shanty path (peace prayers).

There were demonstrations and explanations of pranayams and asanas. We used to practice for two and half hours. I used to leave the camp at 7.30 pm in order to avoid the crowd at the exit. Many thousand people attended this camp. Some-times, I was given a lift to the station. On one occasion a gentleman told me that millions of pounds were collected at the Harrow camp. It was more than at any other place in India or in Britain. This money was collected to build a Yoga and Ayurveda University at Haridwar. I used to reach home at about 9 pm. These yoga camps were also held at Leicester and Bolton (Manchester).

It was difficult to suggest whether there was any improvement in my physical condition. I felt less pain in my knee. But it could be due to warm weather in July and August. I still had the diabetes and the frequency of urine had not receded. I continued my yoga exercises in the morning but did not do any more exercises in the evenings.

The month of September, was quiet. We made preparations to go to India. Azad also made a plan to go to India from Canada. He kept us informed of his plans and finally decided that they would come over to Delhi for about three weeks in December. We left for Delhi on 3rd October in the evening and reached there early in the morning on the 4th. We had the house cleaned on 4th and 5th. On 6th October, we went to visit Subhash and his family in Noida. Vivek's daughter's hair cutting ceremony also took place on this day. I had an opportunity to talk to Subhash's children's in-laws. They were well informed about us. We discussed many things including life in England in the 1960s. They were very complimentary for our assistance during Vivek's daughter's birth at the hospital. They found our presence at St. Georges, very helpful. It was good to hear all the admiration. It was during this conversation, I said that by default, I became an Englishman and a successful person, having taught and retired at a university and had an opportunity to live in Bedford Park area of Chiwick, a middleclass inner city suburb. However, we returned to Delhi, with Rakesh and Mahendra Singh, the same evening.

We relaxed for a few days. Then we started to prepare for the children's visit from Canada. We bought some new furniture, had our washrooms and flooring updated. We also had the whole house redecorated. Initially we planned to decorate the roof terrace walls and a few rooms. We found a good painter who was very efficient and knew what to do. We had all the rooms and walls painted. We designed the outer side of the main gate which looked nice after painting. We celebrated Diwali at home. After visiting some relatives, my wife and I both fell ill. We recovered within a week. Though, some weakness persisted.

During the months of October and November we visited old Delhi many times. We bought clothes and other things from Chandni Chawk, Fatehpuri and sadar Bazar. We used to get up early in the morning at 6 am in order to bring fresh milk from local dairy. The Delhi businesses were suffering from sealing. Many residential houses had been converted into shops and for other business activities. Many business men had extended their shops on to pavements and even roads. The Delhi government and Delhi Municipal Corporation decided to take action against these illegal extensions. They obtained orders from the High Court against these businesses and sent their officials to seal their business premises. It first started in South-Delhi which was later extended to cover the entire Delhi State. The businessmen did not like it. Many of them closed their shops and went on strike against the government action. It was repeated many times during our stay in Delhi. The shops would be closed for three days and then opened again. And then after a few days they would close the shops.

There was some progress on sealing but no permanent solution was provided. No alternative businesses were offered by the government. The

Delhi government argued that they were taking action against illegal premises and were closing and sealing buildings which were built for residential purposes but had been converted into business places. It was not proper to convert them into commercial property. The businesses argued that they had been there for fifty years or more and no guidelines had been afforded regarding the use of these shops as commercial property. There was, therefore, a stalemate on this question of sealing.

Another change that had taken place in Delhi was the rise of shopping malls It was argued that shops should move under one roof. It was, however, not possible to change the Indian business culture. Malls were a part of the American business system because of the climatic conditions and to provide all types of shops at one place. Even in the United Kingdom and Europe, there had been a slow progress. In India most of the businesses were family owned and run by family members. People had often inherited shops or converted part of their residential houses into shops because they could not afford to pay rent for commercial shops. Even the educated people started their own shops at small level and mostly in their own houses as they did not have an employment opportunity in the corporate sector or in government offices. But they worked long hours as they did not have to travel to work. The introduction of malls had not helped.

I visited a few malls around North East Delhi. The goods were costly compared to traditional shops. They were not near residential areas. People had to travel to these malls. Some middle class people who had cars visited them. Still there was one advantage at these malls. People could buy all sorts of goods in a supermarket- from food and vegetables to electrical goods. They also had amusement arcades, clean washrooms and ice-cream parlours. The malls were, however, not for the working class who still earned just around one hundred rupees a day. It looked that the Delhi government and some businesses were moving towards the Western business culture. It was not easy to change old habits. Delhi had a substantial number of people coming from villages in order to look for jobs. They could not afford to purchase goods at high costs. The prices in malls were high because of high rents for shops as well as other expenses on security and facilities. The success of the malls was still to be seen.

Returning to the problem of sealing of shops, it continued for three months while we were in Delhi. Now the central government had brought a master plan, which sought to clean up the capital and turn it into a beautiful city. The master plan, however, allowed residential areas and businesses to exist side by side. Still, it was not clear whether the existing businesses would be allowed to persist or some alterations and changes would be demanded of these businesses or they would all be forced to close down. The master plan would be applicable to the new developments and new areas.

Azad and children arrived in Delhi on 14th December. After resting for a day, they went shopping to old Delhi. We also decided to celebrate Ashish's birthday by doing a Havan Pooja (veneration) on the 20th and to have a party on the roof terrace at midday. It was a winter day. It was, therefore, not difficult to organize the function. We decided to get our own food prepared by sweet vendors and to put a tent on the terrace. We invited only close relatives. Some one hundred and twenty people came to the party. Ashish was pleased with the Pooja (veneration) and the party. Every thing was finished by 5pm. We had a lot of food left which we distributed in the neighbourhood. Vinod and Shiv Kumar helped in organizing this party. Vinod also had a CD made of the function. Everyone was reposeful. One or two people could not come during the day and wanted to come in the evening. We were blunt and told them that they were invited for lunch. If they could not make it at that time, there was nothing we could do.

Amar and Ashish stayed with us quite often when Azad and Meenakshi went out. We enjoyed their company and they were delightful to be with us. Sometimes we went to other parts of old Delhi which they liked. They would have preferred to spend more time with us. One thing was good that no one fell sick during December.

We visited parts of old Delhi and New Delhi and we also went to Jaipur. This journey was made by train. We travelled to Sarai Rohilla, Indian Railway station by Metro from Shahdara. We also had to take Rickshaw from the Metro station to Indian Railway station. We reached before the scheduled time but the train was late. The journey was reasonably good. We had reserved our seats. We saw some other parts of Delhi, which we had not seen before. There was no difference. The city houses and huts (Jhuggies) existed side by side. It showed the disparity in Delhi in particular and in India in general. Despite the enormous economic progress by some middle class people, poverty had not decreased. It had become worse. People did not have houses to live. They, therefore, put their own tents and converted parts of footpath into shanty-towns. We also saw villages in Haryana and Rajasthan states, the green fields and the deserts.

We reached Jaipur just after mid day. The station was crowded. An agent followed us and he asked, if we wanted a hotel to stay. I told him that we were waiting for a relative and later we would look for a hotel to stay. We came out of the station and we saw three- wheelers. The drivers ran towards us to get our custom. One of them said that he would take us to many hotels from which we could choose and he would charge only twenty rupees. We decided to use his services. He took us to a number of hotels. They were either not clean, were noisy or were under construction. We did not like any one of them.

We asked him to take us to Jawahar Nagar but he said that it was too far from the main visiting places. He took us outside of the center of Jaipur. There were a few hotels. We stayed at Anand lodge. It was fine but did not have many facilities. After leaving our luggage in rooms, we went out to the market. We visited a few malls and shops and had our evening dinner at a restaurant.

A cinema hall was a visiting place in its own right because of its architecture. We also decided to watch a Hindi movie there. It finished at midnight. We hired a three- wheeler to return to the hotel. We lost our way and it took us almost an hour to find the Anand Lodge. We went to sleep at about 2 am. In the morning we had our tea at the hotel and decided to go to visit the famous places in Jaipur. It included the Hawa-mahal (air palace) and the old Amber- palace on the hills which was being repaired. Ashish wanted to have an elephant- ride. We thought, we would avail this opportunity at Jaipur but the Rajasthan tourist board had stopped elephant ride. In the previous months an elephant got angry. It dropped its rider and killed a passerby. For us, however, the trip was good. We could have enjoyed a little more if we had more time and some one with local knowledge.

We returned to Delhi by coach after staying one full- day and one night at Jaipur. The coach journey was at night and it took us many hours to reach Delhi. We stopped for a break near Rewari. We had some food there. It was not very crowded on the roads. We reached Patalia House in New Delhi at about 1 am and reached home at 2 am. After staying for a few more days, Azad and children returned to Canada on the night of 3rd January 2007. We stayed in Delhi for three more days and returned to London on the 7th. I had a class on Monday the 8th. Our return journey to London was good.

The University Semester started with the same routine. I had classes on Monday and Friday afternoon. There was no problem except that attendance was poor this Semester. I organized the 2nd year, Intermediate Economics presentations which went well. Most of the students turned up to do their presentations. They did not attend the tutorials all the time. The lectures were well attended but some students disappeared in order to prepare for presentations or to finish course-work in other subjects. We continued to talk to Azad, Amar and Ashish every week mostly on Sunday but sometimes on Saturday, if they had a busy programme on Sunday. Azad had to go to Calgary many times during 2007.

I started to cough in February, which persisted for many weeks. It was dry cough and did not last more than a few seconds at a time but it gave me enormous trouble. The University Semester ended on Friday, 27th April. I faced no challenges at all. I was rather pleased with my visits to Greenwich. The journey was fine using underground services and the DLR (Docklands-Light-Railway), I had an opportunity to meet some of the colleagues and talk to them. It also provided me an opportunity to leave West London and had some experience of other parts of London including the South- England. To teach only for a term was good in a sense. I did not have a commitment for the whole year. I shared teaching with other colleagues who utilized my experience. It worked well for me.

After finishing teaching at Greenwich by the end of April and marking examination papers, I did not have much to do except reading Hindi novels and some history books. We used to go for a walk at Chiswick High Road or Acton High Street. I noticed that Santosh used to get tired and did not generally enjoy walking. She insisted on taking a bus even for a short distance. In May (2007), she even stopped going over the bridge to Sainsbury's and preferred a long route. On 19th May, we went to Southall and came back at noon. She again wanted to go to Chiswick High Road to buy fruits. I did not go with her as I was watching soccer match between Chelsea and Manchester United. She went on her own and did not come back for over an hour.

When she arrived at 5.15 pm, she was tired and said that she started to sweat and sat down in the park and ate chocolate. She thought that her blood sugar had gone down. At home she lay with a chest pain complaint. When she continued to press her chest for a while, I phoned NHS direct and made enquiries as to what could we do? She was breathless and complained of chest pain and headache. The NHS direct decided that she should go to hospital. They arranged for an ambulance. A paramedic arrived within 15 minutes. He started to take ECG and blood pressure. He thought it could be a minor heart attack. Within the next five minutes the ambulance arrived. They took her to Hammersmith hospital where she had been under treatment for diabetes and other problems.

We reached Hammersmith hospital at 7pm. She was first attended by nurses. At, 9pm, a doctor arrived and checked her and concluded that it could be a heart problem or breathing problem. She should stay in hospital. They would do a blood test twelve hours after the attack. Santosh was moved to a ward. Her file was brought from the repository. On Monday, she had endoscopy and further ECG. Two days later she had scanning and the doctors discovered that she had the same problem as in the year 2000. A young doctor came to see her and said that a case conference had taken place under Dr. Shovlin, Santosh's consultant who also visited her in the ward. On Thursday, I was present at the hospital when Dr. Shovlin and other doctors arrived at 4pm. They diagnosed that Santosh had thrombosis of the lung. Her veins had blood clot. Her blood did not circulate properly.

She, therefore, had chest pain and other pains. The blood was not reaching regularly to the heart and the heart was not pumping blood to mind.

They decided to give her warfarin injections for a few days and then they would put her on warfarin. She would have to undergo another scanning on Friday and that she should stay in hospital for three more days. She was also advised to see a heart specialist. This time Santosh was worse than in 2000. Saneh, Sangeeta and Akash continued to visit her in hospital everyday and I kept Azad informed of the developments of her condition. Vivek was in Surbitton for a short visit because of some office work. He enquired about Santosh. I told him the truth about her that she was in hospital. Subhashji and Azad phoned us while we were in hospital on Monday 21st May.

The last three days had been humid and hot. Santosh came back home on Saturday but we had to go back to hospital for warfarin injections for the next three days. After that she returned to her normal dose of warfarin and check up at the hospital. On Sunday, I was invited by a friend for lunch. It was a good change and I had an opportunity to meet his parents and uncle. They were all in their early nineties and had come to England from Kenya in the seventies, though they sent their children in the 1960s, to study in England. It was a very nice family and I relaxed after a troublesome week.

On Monday, 25 June, Santosh went to Hammersmith hospital for an echo test. I went to hospital with her but thought that there was no need for me to stay with her during this test. I, therefore, went to the emergency department for my own consultation. I saw a doctor who checked me and said that I had abscess which got to be drained. He went to see his senior. I was also seen by a surgeon who told me that the abscess operation would be done at the Charing Cross hospital and the surgeons would be able to do the operation the same night as an emergency. I asked Santosh to go home and I was sent to Charing Cross hospital at about 8pm.

A young surgeon came to see me. I was informed that my operation would take place on Tuesday. I stayed there at night and Akash stayed with Santosh at the house. I mentioned to the hospital people that my wife was sick and I was her carer. I had to put insulin into her body and look after her other interests. One young doctor asked me about my family. I told him that I have a good and large family who always care about us. But we have our own responsibilities. However, I could not have the operation on Tuesday. I, therefore, came to sleep in my own bed. I reached the hospital early the morning on Wednesday at 7am, but had the operation at night at 10pm. I was unconscious for about two hours. I returned to the ward at mid-night and had some sleep.

On 28th June, I was allowed to return home after the dressing. I was given a letter that I would need dressing every day and that I could come to Charing Cross hospital's walk- in- center or go to Parsons Green walk-in center. On Friday we first went to Hammersmith hospital and then to Charing Cross hospital but they told me that the dressing, I needed was not done and that I would have to go to the Parsons-Green- Centre, where a nurse did my dressing. I started to go there every day of the week including Saturday and Sunday. I went there for six weeks. I used to take my own dressing. This routine put a hold on my life. I was unable to do any thing constructive. I used to go to the walk-in –center at about 1pm and would return at about 3pm.

Our telephone went bust in July. We had a break-in at the Delhi house and our relatives tried to phone us. After waiting for four days Vinod and Neetu sent me email, suggesting that I should phone Delhi. There was no major damage done and repairs were carried out soon. On 29th June, my younger brother's elder daughter died during a child birth. This was tragic. I could not reconcile with myself to this tragedy. How could someone die at a caesarian birth in this stane age? I wrote a short letter to Rajendra expressing my condolence and grief. I almost cried and my heart wept. I continued to get my dressing at Parsons Green. My time passed in doing nothing. These two months were very ardent but things started to settle down in August.

On 15th August 2007, people in India and Indians abroad celebrated India's 60th Independence anniversary. Much has happened in these sixty years. Some progress had become visible and the achievements were tangible in economic fields. India, however, still suffered from poverty and ignorance. In some states, villages remained under- developed. While some other States had made economic and social progress. The Southern States had succeeded more than the Northern or Eastern States. Bangalore in Karnataka had become the silicon valley of India. The education has made a stride. India was producing more technical personnel than any other country in the world. The information technology field was enormous. The general education had also progressed.

The middle classes, who believed in educating their children made more progress than the lower classes and villagers. There were more than three hundred million people in India today (2007) who were affluent and owned all the facilities and they identified themselves as middle class. The technical colleges and universities were producing a large number of qualified people of world class. They worked in the United States of America, Europe and other countries The foreign investment into India had increased and foreigners were investing in Indian firms and on the Indian Stock Exchange. Some Indian businessmen had gone multinational and bought foreign firms and operated in Europe, Britain, USA and other states in the world. India had gained respect and Indians were respected more in other countries today, than sixty years ago.

More Indians were flying now to other countries than ever before. India was destined to be an economic and political super-power. India would have to remove and tackle many hurdles. It would have to increase agricultural production and educate people in the villages. It should provide primary education to all and ensure that students get proper education. Some of India's educational institutions were of very high standard especially in engineering and management. But some of the institutions lacked facilities and were unable to provide a good standard of education. There was lack of discipline in many schools and colleges.

The private businesses did not want to pay taxes. They bribed officials to reduce the level of taxation. It was not a sign of a successful developed nation or a successful democracy. Nevertheless, India had sustained democracy in the last sixty years when it had not been possible in neighbouring countries in Asia. It was mainly because of the sound foundation laid by the founding fathers. Gandhiji left the legacy of secularism and respect for all and Nehru wanted every Indian child to be educated.

The five year plans were showing their fruits now. The Indian industry had advanced. They manufactured goods which were imported sixty years ago. The textiles, cars, auto- bikes were manufactured in India today, It was in the Information Technology and Computer programming that India had shined in the world. Many Indians had setup businesses in other countries and were working in the banking and the retail trade. The Indian Stock-Exchange was now affected by the world financial changes. The American financial markets affected the Indian stock prices as they did the British and European stock exchange.

This year, India elected a woman as the Republic's President and a Muslim as the Vice- President. This indicated India's maturity and showed that every citizen of India could make progress and reach the highest position. There were programmes on Indian television showing celebrations of 60 years of independence. The State Chief ministers unfurled the Indian flag on 15th August. The Indian Prime Minister spoke at the historic Red Fort in Delhi. He spoke about the plans for economic and social progress because he was an economist. He did not talk much politics except peaceful relations with neighbours.

There were celebrations on the Indo-Pak border where the citizens of both countries got together. Pakistan was carved out on 14th August 1947, and it had always celebrated its independence a day earlier than India's. It was argued that Pakistan was created because of Mohammed Ali Jinnah's intransigence. It was not fully true. Jinnah was used by the British because they wanted to control a part of India for defence reasons. A strategic Pakistan was created for the benefit of Britain and later the United States used Pakistan for its own purposes.

Actually Jinnah and Gandhiji had the same roots. They both came from Gujarat. It was because of the stubbornness of some Hindus that forced Jinnah's ancestors to become Muslims. MA Jinnah was the grandson of

Premjibhai Thakkar, who in order to support his family, entered into the fish business within the coastal town of Veraval in Kathiawar. His business, however, clashed with the moral ethics of his community who ostracized him. He made enough money in this trade and attempted to rejoin the community. He also expressed the desire to discontinue the fish business.

The community leaders, however, did not accept his request. Premjibhai's son Punjanlal Thakkar (Jinnah's father) was annoyed at his father's humiliation and reacted by adopting the Islam as a religion. He also changed the names of his sons and daughter into Muslim names. However, he continued to use his Gujarati nick-name: Zino which meant "Skinny". Jinno's son Mohammed Ali changed his family name to Jinnah-the nickname of his father. Both Gandhiji and Jinnah were the sons of modern Saurashtra in the state of Gujarat. If Jinnah's grandfather was not kicked out of the community and Jinnah remained a Hindu, perhaps India would have remained united and both India and Pakistan would be celebrating the 60th Independence Day together on the 15th August.

But Pakistan was created for Geo-political reasons, not because of the intransigence of one man or one political party.

CHAPTER 6

International Dimension, 2008-15

After writing about India's 60th Independence Day, I decided not to write any further observations. The year 2008, was extremely busy and we were preoccupied with the ailment of Santosh and her visits to Hammersmith hospital. As soon as we arrived in London on 17 January 2008, she found herself in enormous pain and headache which was of a different type. She used to get pain and hold her head as if it was going to blow up.

On Monday 19th January, she saw the GP who prescribed her some tablets which had no effect. She passed out on the 20th and had to be taken to hospital in an ambulance. That was the beginning of her visits to hospital. In April, she had catherization and was diagnosed with three vessel disease. One of her arteries was 100% blocked, another 83% and the third was 70% blocked.

She was later seen by a cardiothoraic surgeon who arranged for her blood tests, CT scan of the brain, X-ray, Doppler carotid. We were told that she would need a bi-pass surgery but the surgeon felt it was too risky. He referred her to the cardiology department. The doctor there looked at her reports and concluded that angioplasty would not work for her. He, therefore, referred her back to the cardiothoraic surgeon; and also expressed view that she should also be seen by the cardiovascular surgeon because she had narrowing of the artery in the neck. The whole year passed from

January 2008 to January 2009. I felt, we were pushed around and sent from pillar to post without any tangible progress. We awaited action. We visited hospital every week but did not get anything done.

During the year 2008, the world saw an economic meltdown which caused deep recession. Many banks closed down in the United States. The government had to come up with an economic and financial package which had not worked yet. Businesses were closing down at an unprecedented rate. The car industry suffered enormously along with the banking sector and the retail trade. In the United Kingdom, the government recapitalised the banks, nationalized some of the small banks and made capital available for banks and businesses. The share prices (FTSE 100) declined to 3500 or so from the high of 6900. The house prices were down by almost 30% and still there were no buyers. The mortgages were scarce. I had my suspicions when house prices rose by 200% in the past ten years. It was an artificial market because the incomes had not increased in line with house prices. It was unsustainable and yet the house prices continued to rise. All these difficulties rose at the same time. Unemployment had gone up dramatically in the United States and the United Kingdom. There was a saying that troubles do not come in singles but they come in trains. All sectors of the economy suffered.

It had been a global phenomenon and it was not confined to the UK or the United States. Even the developing countries had been affected. The price of crude oil declined from 147 dollars to 45 dollars a barrel. The interest rates were the lowest in centuries. It applied to all the continents and all the countries. The world had become a global village. The demand for goods and services had dwindled. It would take at least two years to come out of the recession and five to seven years for the house prices to start to rise. Some economists had called it the worst recession since the Wall Street crash of 1929. But this recession had affected the main street at the same time.

India and Pakistan had started to improve their relations in the past few years but on 26th November 2008, ten terrorists of Pakistani nationality came from Karachi to Mumbai by boat and attacked the Oberai hotel, the

Taj hotel., the main railway station and the Jewish Centre. It took time for the authorities to acknowledge the enormity and magnanimity of the problem. The terrorists killed 173 people. Some tourists from the United States and Europe were also killed. The police, commandoes and army soldiers took action and killed nine terrorists and caught the tenth. The terror attacks, however, left a carnage. The Central Home Minister and the Maharastra Chief Minister along with some officials resigned. It was the failure of security, and secret services, and other reasons which led to this attack. How could this happen in a big country like India. The navy had failed to stop the terrorists at sea. The police had failed to provide information on their secret plans and there was no co-ordination between the different departments.

The surviving terrorist was interviewed by the police. He provided information on the training and facilities apportioned to terrorists by the organizations in Pakistan including their secret agency the ISI. The Indian government blamed the Pakistan government and demanded action against the terrorist camps and terrorist organizations. But the Pakistan government refused to acknowledge that the terrorists were Pakistanis or the ISI was involved in the Mumbai attacks. This soured the India-Pakistan relations and Pakistan threatened to attack India, if it took action against the Pakistani terrorists or their camps.

Pakistan itself suffered terrorism and Pakistan's former Prime Minister Benazir Bhutto was assassinated in a dreadful attack on her convoy during an election rally. Some two hundred people died in that attack with her. It had been argued that if you dig a grave for others, you yourself dig a hole for yourself. It applied to Pakistan. In order to create problem for India, they produced and trained so many ruffians that they themselves were attacked by those militants. There was a new trend of suicide bombs in such rowdy attacks where a person killed himself in order to kill others in large numbers.

Any- way, the war of words continued for many months. I still thought that India and the Indian government had a responsibility to protect its citizens and Indian Territory. Many questions could be asked. A Commission of

Enquiry should be set up in order to investigate the reasons for an attack in Mumbai. How did the terrorists arrive in the city? Who helped them with the details of the local knowledge? Why did the Indian navy fail to intercept them in Indian territorial waters? Why did the Indian secret services and the police not know of the whole plot? Why didn't they intercept the telephonic conversation between the plotters? Also why was not there a good security check at the hotels and other public places especially when Mumbai had been attacked in 2006, and India had suffered 90 seditious attacks in the past seven years?

I presume, India should set its own house in order and ensure the protection of its citizens from violent attacks. They should look at the home grown terrorism and collect proper information about the foreign thugs. They should plant informers wherever possible and their embassies should collect information on destructive activities abroad. It had been observed that the US and the UK governments had applied some pressure on Pakistan government who failed to acknowledge the problem. It could not take any action because the ISI and the Pakistan army were not under the control of the civilian government which was weak and inexperienced. There was not a single politician in power of any substance. Thirdly, people were mostly emotional. They were told whatever could excite them. People in Pakistan like common people in India wanted to live in peace and harmony with each other. But they could be told that India would attack their country. This argument could rouse emotions and turn them in favour of their government and the army.

The Mumbai attacks of 26th November 2008, were compared with the 9/11 aggression in the United States. At that time the US cities of New York and Washington were stormed by terrorists, the greatest power on earth with a large net work of espionage and secret services had no knowledge about this thrust. After the Mumbai onslaught the world opinion turned against Pakistan and it was sympathetic towards India. The American government conducted the shuttle diplomacy. The US Secretary of State, The Deputy Secretary of State, some Senators and Congressmen visited both India and Pakistan, in order to impress upon Pakistan to stop violent encroachment. The British Prime minister told the Pakistani leaders that 75% of terrorist outbreaks had connection with Pakistan. They had training in Pakistani camps and that the Mumbai attacks had originated in Pakistan. But the Pakistani leaders were either reluctant or unable to do anything in order to put an end to these intrusions. Pakistan suffered an attacks, including a five star hotel in Islamabad. This was a global problem and needed a global solution and co-operation among nations.

In 2008, the US Presidential election took place and for the first time the United States, public elected a black President- Barak Obama who was half Kenyan and half white. This indicated that the United States had changed enormously in the past forty years. In 1968, the civil rights leader Martin Luther King was assassinated for demanding rights for the black and the underprivileged. He was not even a Presidential candidate. He simply wanted people to recognize and respect the character of a person rather than to look at his/her colour. His dream became a reality after forty years in 2008. Obama was supported by white majority especially the younger generation and the liberal middle- class. He had some opposition from the working class white. The African-American population supported him because they were pleased to see a black candidate. Other minorities also voted for him in large numbers. He was very popular and presented his arguments to the general public. The success of his Presidency would depend on policies and economic turn-around as he was faced with enormous economic and financial conundrum.

The world had been in the grip of economic recession. It had affected the developed world more than the developing countries which had suffered in their exports to the advanced nations. The house prices and the share prices remained low in the United Kingdom and the United States at the beginning of 2009. Both sectors had suffered and declined by some thirty percent or more from their peak. I could foresee no sign of recovery this year (2009). It was being predicted that economic recovery should start in early 2010. The government's fiscal and monetary policies had not fully succeeded or convinced people of an upturn. The unemployment level continued to rise in most countries. It would lead to further decline in aggregate demand and economic activities.

Apart from the economic problems, terrorism continued to blot the world. Many nations including Pakistan had now recognized and accepted that most dreadful activities were planned in that country. People became homeless and refugees in their own country and province. The Americans kept their unmanned planes and satellites to watch the Pakistani military actions. The Indian army had also started to watch their Kashmir border by small planes especially designed with the help of the Israelis. But the militant penetration continued into Kashmir and often there were clashes between the ruffian and the Indian army.

The general elections took place in India for the Lok Shabha (the Lower House of the Central Parliament). It was nice to see a peaceful participation by a large number of people including senior citizens and women in Kashmir. The elections in other parts of the country were also peaceful. The economic development, removal of poverty and the fight against terrorism were the main themes at the election rallies. Some 714 million Indians were eligible to vote. The elections were held in five phases on Thursdays in April and May. A large number of candidates stood for the 543 seats. It was typical of India that many political parties surfaced. The BJP and the Congress were, however, the main contestants. Regional parties had ascended as strong participants. They all, however, believed in national unity and economic progress.

It was observed that three trends had sprung up in India in the 21st Century. Some are still traditionalists and looked to the ancient glory. They were proud of the ancient culture and ignored the historical happenings. Surprisingly, on the television the Ramayan and the Mahabharata were made and were being produced by different producers. More research had been done in order to justify the remaking of these epics. The social dramas were also popular on television channels. The second, group looked at the middle ages and economic and architectural progress under the Muslim rulers and the Maharajas. They were, nevertheless, in minority. The third, group consisted of modernizers. They had adopted the Western culture.

The American culture was predominant in India these days. The clothes, food habits and even the language had influenced middle class Indians.

People had adopted English words and English language as their own. Even in discussions in Hindi, they preferred to reply in English. Jeans and burgers had gained popularity. For the younger generation modernization meant Westernization. The gap between the eastern and western cultures had widened. The parents had accepted this change. They rather encouraged their children to wear jeans and eat burger and chips. They wanted to identify themselves with the progressives and the developed people.

On the home front, we continued to go to hospital. We could not go to India in 2008. We, therefore, went to Delhi on 24th February 2009, and thought of staying there for over two months. But after two weeks, Santosh fell seriously ill. We saw five doctors who could not diagnose her problem and lack of hygiene further drove us from their surgeries and hospitals. On 22 March we returned to London and saw our GP who referred her to Queen Charlotte hospital. At the hospital they carried out blood tests, X-Ray, ECG test, ultra sound and finally a biopsy. The surgeons removed the polyps during the operation and the tests showed they were benign. Santosh was discharged from the hospital for this particular ailment. The doctor in the hypertension unit felt that she did not have hypertension but she should be reviewed by the cardiothoracic surgeon. Her kidney had also stabilized and was in good condition. But she did not want to go through the triple bi-pass and was keen on continuing her medicine.

The weather had not been particularly good. It rained for many days in April and May. It was still cold in May. The family members in London and Canada were fine. Sangeeta and Akash got good results in their examinations. Amar started his degree course at Alberta University in Edmonton and Ashish had moved to High school to study Maths and Science along with English and social studies. It was a specialist school in Sciences. He wanted to join that school and continue with his soccer. I had an ECG test and holtor monitoring but everything was normal. I was keeping reasonably healthy and well. I had started yoga exercises after a gap of almost one year.

In Britain, the newspapers published the MPs expenses under the Freedom of Information Act. Some of the expenses were embarrassing and could not be justified and should not have been claimed. The popularity of politicians declined dramatically and some resigned or stated that they would not stand again at the next general election. The Prime Minister was very unpopular in the media. People argued that he should have maintained the moral standards and the standard of the House of Commons and the House of Lords. There was a need to change the expenses system for MPs. An independent committee was set up in order to recommend the changes.

There had been a quieter atmosphere all over the world. In Britain efforts continued to solve the economic problems caused by recession. The level of unemployment and the national debt soared. The interest rates remained low. It was believed that the developing countries led by India and China would be the engines to take the world out of this recession. The Indian and American relations had improved since the Bush administration. For the first time India had bought defense material on a large scale from the United States. The economic, educational and cultural ties had made stride. Some ninety thousand Indian students were studying in the United States in 2009. It was equal to four universities. India should expand its own higher education and open a few more universities rather than depend on foreign countries and spend so much money abroad. Sometimes students faced racial attacks in these countries.

Occasionally, I was disconcerted and looked back to my own experiences in the 1960s and 1970s or even in the 1980s. These had haunted me this year more than at any other time. Still I had been reasonably relaxed and autarkic. I had also watched a large number of Hindi serials and Hindi movies. The Mahabharata had been made by another producer. I noticed that Prime Minister Vidur of Hastinapur (as in the epic) warned king Dhratrashtra that his son Suyodhan later came to be known as Duryodhan was born under inauspicious circumstances and he would be the cause of destruction of the kingdom of Hastinapur.

The efforts should, therefore, be made to destroy the child in order to save the kingdom. This advice was rejected by the king. Later many mistakes were repeated by the king and the prince in the old city. Some of the mistakes were repeated because of the advice of Shakuni, the king of

Gandhar and uncle of the prince. Shakuni was determined to destroy the Kauravs because he did not like that his sister was married to a blind king Dharatrastra. This episode, nonetheless, reminded me that there were three types of people. In the first category, were those who could visualize the future events and make an attempt to avoid the catastrophe? They also learnt from the mistakes of the others. They did not commit the same mistake. They were called wise people. In the second category were those people who faced a problem and solved it. They avoided any further conundrums. They were identified as clever people. Thirdly, there were those who repeatedly committed the same mistake and never learnt from the mistakes or the situations. They were known as fools.

It all depended on the level of understanding and their commitment. Certain principles applied in understanding a task and accomplishing the objectives. In this connection also there were three categories of people. There were those who never started a new task for the fear of failure. They lacked confidence in themselves and their abilities. Secondly, there were people who started a new function but gave up as soon as they faced any problems. They lacked an ability to fulfill their objectives and commitments. Thirdly, there were those who never gave up until they had accomplished their aims and objectives and finished the work they initially undertook. They were committed people and always succeeded. They were also ambitious and made contribution to society in one way or the other.

The month of July, was wet. It rained almost every day in England. I continued to go out for a walk or shopping. There had not been any problems in the country, though many British soldiers died in Afghanistan in this month.

Jaswant Singh, a Member of Indian Parliament, who had been Foreign Minister and Finance Minister in the vajpai government, published a book – Jinnah, partition and independence of India. This brought an up roar in the Bhartiya- Janta party (BJP) and the Sangh pariwar. Mr Singh was expelled from the party. It was maintained that Jinnah had been praised in the book, while Nehru and Patel had been criticized. The party leaders argued that Jinnah was responsible for the partition of the country. It caused dislocation of millions of people and about one million Indians were killed in the communal violence. In expelling Jaswant Singh from the BJP, the party hierarchy behaved like feudal village elders and not the leaders of a modern political party.

The fundamental question, however, remained whether a single person was responsible for the partition of India and for the creation of Pakistan. A very large number of books had been written on both the partition and the independence of India and Pakistan. I have done research on these subjects and published The Indian Independence Movement in Britain, 1930-49, and V K Krishna Menon- A biography. I have gone through the Transfer of Power documents, the British Cabinet papers and the British Prime Ministers files at the British Library, the Public Record Office, the Bodlein Library Oxford and many other libraries and archives in Britain and New Delhi.

I presume, there were three different themes in Mr. Jaswant Singh's book, a biography of Jinnah, the question of partition of India and India's independence. No single person could be held responsible or praised for the accomplishments or failures in these areas. Moreover, there were many parties in the freedom struggle. The British imperialists wanted to hold on to power for as long as they could. Even when it had become impossible to control India by force and the British government led by Clement Attlee had decided to relinquish India in 1947, the conservative party led by Churchill and many ICS- (Indian Civil Service) officers of British origin wanted to hold on to the British rule in India. When it became impossible they created mischief and did nothing to control disorder in the country. They hoped that under such situations the Indian leaders would ask them to stay on to continue with their administration of India.

As late as June 1947, Gandhiji offered Jinnah the Primeministership of undivided India and he agreed for avoiding the partition. But it was the Congress party led by Jawaharlal Nehru who made a political argument stating that the Muslim League led by Jinnah was a minority party and the Congress was a majority party in the Indian legislature. How could the leader of a minority party become the Prime Minister of the country?

Nehru himself wanted to become the first Prime Minister of independent India.

In the June 1947, the Indian leaders came to London in order to negotiate the final settlement. Mountbatten, who was the Viceroy of India, went to see Churchill who was leader of the opposition in British Parliament. Churchill asked Mountbatten to keep a part of India under British control. Mountbatten assured Churchill to carry out his wishes. Despite this double dealings, Mountbatten often argued that he could have avoided the partition of India. Partition had become the British policy in order to grant India its independence. Moreover, when the state of Pakistan had become a reality with Sindh, Baluchistan, North-West Frontier and West Punjab in the West and East Bengal and Sylhatte district of Assam in the East of India, all the provincial governors were British who created fear in the minds of people. Consequently, disorder and violence often broke out between different Indian communities. The partition of India was a precondition of the conservatives led by Churchill in order to support India's Independence Bill in 1947.

The British-Indian-administration and the army refused to stop the violence. Consequently, people decided to move from their homes in India or Pakistan in order to save their lives. Some of the Muslims from east Punjab, Uttar Pradesh and Bihar moved to the new state of Pakistan and the Hindus and Sikhs came from the west Punjab and Sindh. The population in south India was not affected. It was the British government officials who sent a printing press to Karachi to publish the Dawn newspaper. It was critical of the Congress party and wrote against India. The two communities, which had lived in peace in India for centuries, were now killing each other. It took time to stop the violence. Initially, it was felt that the partition of India would be temporary and the two sides would come together when sanity returned.

Nevertheless, geo-politics and shortsightedness of both Indian and Pakistani leaders, the partition became bitter and permanent. The power blocs led by the United States of America and the Soviet Union created their areas of influence. The US and Britain controlled Pakistan indirectly and provided defence and financial support which was often used against India. India also did not seriously attempt to improve relations with Pakistan as a good neighbour. Surprisingly, in the course of time, India's relations with Britain and the United States improved enormously but its relations with Pakistan were not very cordial when these should have been better because of geopolitical, historical and cultural reasons.

I hope and trust that Mr. Jaswant Singh might have made that attempt in his book by recognizing the role of the Muslim League and Jinnah in the independence movement. But it blew on his face because a substantial number of Indians blamed Jinnah and the Muslim League for partition and the aftermath-carnage. The Muslim League refused to join the Indian Constituent Assembly in 1946. The Muslim League, however, joined the interim government led by Nehru and Liaqat Ali Khan who wanted to prolong the interim government because there was no centralized administration for the state of Pakistan. It was vital to have a working administration in place before the creation of the new state. If that situation existed, perhaps the carnage of killing and the unplanned movement of people would have been avoided. It had, nonetheless, become a policy of the British imperialism to divide the country. The division of a nation left enormous problems as could be seen in the partition of Ireland, Palestine and of course India.

No single person or party could be held responsible for the consequences of history and politics. In expelling Mr. Jaswant Singh from the Bhartiya Janta party, its leaders had repeated the actions of the Thakkar's in Gujarat who ostracized Premjibhai Thakkar, Jinnah's grandfather. The BJP's action was no different from that of those community heads of the past.

In October 2009, we went to India to stay there for ten weeks. We discussed our programme with children. Azad felt that he should come over to Delhi for two weeks to spend the valuable time with us and that he would return with us to London on 28th December and stay over-night before returning to Edmonton.

We reached North-East Delhi on the 20th, and decided not to look for a cleaner to clean the house but to visit our sisters in order to celebrate Bhaidoj (a festival after Diwali to bring brothers and sisters closer) belatedly. We did that and spent esteemed time with both our sisters. The next day, we brought a man to clean the house. He did a good job and finished the work on time. Then we went for our customary shopping of food supplies. I started to go to mother dairy to buy milk in the mornings. Vinod used to talk to us in the evenings. He often asked if we needed any help. We made many visits to Sadar Bazar and Chandni- Chowk to purchase goods or to roam around. We had few visits from relatives and made fewer visits to them. Morning walk was good but I missed the yoga practice and exercises though I managed to do a few minutes of kapalbhati each day.

We became busy during Azad's visit we invited a couple of families for dinner on a Sunday and went to dinner to their houses. I also visited my younger brother a couple of times. He had developed some health problems. Otherwise he was fine. Something has stolen his happiness We were told that a man tried to climb on our roof terrace. We therefore, decided to make the house more safe and secure. Though there was no way any one could steal from our house. There was only furniture. We consulted an iron monger who suggested for putting two iron doors- one on the roof terrace and the other at the balcony entry of the small room over the garage. He did that work but took a long time to do it. In India there was no value of time or promise. Even a businessman could not keep his word. They could not visualize the problems that might arise. It looked as if they simply wanted business and then would decide to carry out the work leisurely. This was against business ethics and business principles especially on the delivery of goods and services on time.

The other problem which haunted me and took away many sleep nights was that someone, whom I had respected and loved so much attempted to grab and get hold of our house. This hurt me most. I discussed it with some relatives who did not believe in the first instance and then questioned why did he try to do that? It was due to sheer jealousy. It was a bad move. We forgave these people for their unforgivable behaviour in the past but we had not forgotten what they did in the earlier years. We were grateful to the Almighty God for keeping us sane and helping us in our bad times. There were many people who had helped us in London and in India but not those who wanted from us.

The pollution and overcrowding were the main problems in Delhi. We did not enjoy the Metro rides this year as we had done in the past. My eyes used to get hot and I felt burning in the eyes. People in Delhi did not want to work hard. They had become corrupt and lazy. One news that dominated the newspapers and the television media was about the ex-chief minister of Jharkhand State in Eastern India, who stole and embezzled four thousand crore rupees from the state treasury and invested that money all over India and in other countries of Europe and Africa. The investigating authorities arrested him and his colleagues but he pleaded innocence. This was not new.

Many modern Indian politicians were corrupt and inefficient. There was no nationalism in them. They hindered progress rather being vehicle for development. They were illiterate or less educated, deeply rooted in caste system and provincialism. India would take many decades to become a developed country. There was no moral in politics and administration. Building a few roads or flyovers in Delhi or a few multi-storied houses did not make a country developed. The education standard was very low. Hardly any training was provided on the jobs. It had created an inefficient work force. They were keen to become rich, own a house and a car and become middle class. But they did not want to work for that.

Anyway, on returning to London on 28th December 2009, we found London cold and wet. It further snowed in early January. Because of lack of salt and grit the roads remained treacherous. People did not use their cars for days. Schools remained closed. The whole of the country was still cold and in the grip of snow. It might snow further in the next few days. It was the coldest weather since 1981. The lowest temperature reached -22.7 Celsius. We remained house bound and kept our heating on, all the time. I spent time watching television programmes and reading novels. I did not have much constructive work to do.

On 15th October 2010, I completed forty five years of my stay in London. It had been suggested that I had not changed much in these 45 years except that I had grown a little older, lost my hair, use glasses and have developed a few ailments like the diabetes and controlled hypertension. I have had hernia operation, prostate operation, knee operation and abscess removed a few times. I have suffered with syncope twice in two years when my blood pressure became low. Lack of blood circulation led me to unconsciousness. I had all sorts of tests and saw a neurologist and a cardiac doctor. Later I discovered that syncope was due to iron deficient anemia.

Today, it was a warmer day compared to the day I arrived for the first time. It was due to pollution and gas house effect. England was no more an industrialized country. It depended on service industry. At this juncture, the country was in the middle of recession with a huge budget deficit. Today the conservative party was in power with Lib-Dems as coalition partners. The Labour party had a government in 1965. Presently, I was a retired man. That day I was in the company of a fellow from Delhi. Today I was in the company of my wife.

So much has changed in these forty five years. The children grew up and moved on to live their own lives. I kept in touch with my grandchildren. Often talk to myself, if I had great grandchildren what would they say how they would talk and laugh. It was for fun only. My wife did not like me thinking that far ahead. I hardly was in touch with my extended family except for a nephew. Others have grown older and looked to their own interests and financial gains rather than maintaining social relations. My thinking was different from theirs.

I had kept in touch with some friends, I made during these forty five years. After fully retiring at the University, I had not visited the campus again. I walked around local High Streets and parks. My needs were still not much and I lived a simple life. Sometimes, I did not do the things which could be done. I was satisfied and sometimes emotional. I often recalled the same incidents which perturbed me. It was a psychological effect. My memory was still sharp and I could remember some of the minutest details of earlier years. I was surprised that people hardly changed in their behavior and attitudes.

The City of Parks had also witnessed innumerable changes in these forty five years. In the 1960s, I used to roam around the square mile when I worked at the Department of Customs and Excise at Mark Lane. In 2006, I got lost while returning from the Liverpool Street station. The city's architectural structure had altered beyond recognition. A number of tall buildings had sprung up when there was only one NatWest bank's Head-Quarter of that height. Nevertheless, the city still served as a financial center and the Bank of England was within its bounds.

Many international banks and Investment banks had moved to the Canary Wharf, a new financial hub in the east end of London. It was a derelict place caused by the decline of docks and London Port activities. The Canary Wharf had been joined by the Jubilee line of the London-Under-ground and the Docklands Light Railway (DLR). Beautiful and large stations had been built on both sides of the River Thames.

The parks themselves had seen some changes. Many local parks were losing parts of their land in order to build flats and houses. Yet, it was possible to relax, walk, jog and play tennis and weekend-football in some areas. The children's play areas were visible in most local parks. Young babies and children swing, slide and play other games. These had also become meeting places for families with young children.

The month of October 2010, saw the holding of the Commonwealth Games in Delhi. As typical with the British media, they were looking for drawbacks and focused on a scene of dirty washrooms. The games were, however, very successful. The sports persons enjoyed participating and staying in Delhi. They revealed their approbation. The facilities were world class and better than ever seen in the past. The opening ceremony was fantastic with cultural display. It was watched by four billion people. 71 countries participated in the games. India won many medals. The new generation would use the sport facilities. Delhi hardly had a swimming pool and tracks. It had now added to Delhi's beauty and fame. India's economic progress was good but needed the distribution of resources fairly for the benefit of all Indians.

In November 2010, we went to India for two months. We needed that break after many visits to hospitals. We had a clearance from the renal department and the cardiology doctor who suggested that a change and sun-shine would do Santosh some good in order to provide vitamin D. We did not notice many changes in our neighbour-hood either socially or environmentally. I used to go to bring milk with Vinod and we often discussed sensibly social and political problems in India. Vinod could not visit us very often as he had done in the past years. He was extremely busy.

We visited old-Delhi four times and Connaught place just once. I spent time reading newspaper and watching television. We visited our relatives whenever we could. They were kind and helpful. Once or twice people tried to talk about money, incomes and our expenditure which annoyed me. Why did they need this information at micro level except to express their selfish interest? But they showed as if they were there to help us. I had never required any assistance in any form. One thing, I discovered about new Indian attitude was that whenever people visited their relatives and friends, they were offered all sort of food. I was contented with that and took whatever I wanted to consume. But some people wanted to be served by hand otherwise they would say that there were things on the table to show. They did not ask them to eat or offered the food by hand to be picked up by them. This was strange. Once or twice I refused to eat at host's insistence and was ready to walk out from their house. They often got angry with my reaction. They could call me a rude person. I could not, however, change myself and my habits.

As usual, I often went back to the memory lane. I was a man of principles from my childhood. I was not surprised when I stuck to my ways and probity. I also recalled that I had been told off and chided in abusive language by my family. On the other hand people with whom I had worked, they had paid me compliments. There was no shortage of recognition of my contribution to society and especially to young people in education field. I could quote three important one's at a gathering one evening. The very first compliment came in 1964, when I was visited in Delhi by an ex-colleague from Chirawa High School, where I taught for more than three and half years but I had to leave all of a sudden because of family reasons. My friend and colleague told me that the Headmaster of the school had told the teachers that seven of them could not do when KCArora had done all that work alone. I had organized examinations, conducted cultural activities and edited the school magazine apart from doing other jobs and full-time teaching.

The second compliment came when I left the General Education department at South West London College, Tooting. The Head of Department sent me a note stating 'kc, no one can challenge you on the results'. I had often produced hundred percent results at that college and other places during my teaching career. The third compliment came from the Chancellor of Greenwich University, who quietly told me that he was aware of all the good things I had done at the University and in writing and publishing books and articles. I felt jubilant when I recalled all these incidents that my time and life had not been wasted. I knew that I did not think of money all the time as some of my family members would like me to do and help them financially. I was an academic and believed in culture which was well above monetary resources.

I thought of society, politics and real people who could work within a frame work. Perhaps I was a little Westernized or British in this approach. I believed in the rule of law, equality of opportunity for everyone. I would like Indians to feel Indians and not based on caste, creed, language or provincialism. If something affected the majority of people, I would be glad to discuss it. If it affected only me and others had no role, I would like to avoid it.

It was our own decision not to reveal to all in the neighbourhood, a date of our departure for London. When we told that we were going back to England on 25th January, they were not surprised but asked us why did we not tell them much earlier or was it a sudden decision because of health reasons? One or two people did not question much but the majority did not like our method of returning to London. They wanted to know every detail in advance which I could not provide.

On 7th April 2011, I wrote some notes after a brief interval. Many events had taken place in the first three months of this year. In Britain, the government introduced changes to retirement age and pension rights. It was expected that the pension age would gradually, rise to sixty seven. The compulsory retirement age had been scrapped. People could work beyond seventy if they wished and were capable of working. There were fears among employers that some employees might not be able to work in their advanced age but they could not be fired. I thought there should be flexibility on both sides. Employers should not be forced to keep employees, who were unable to contribute to the organization. On the other hand the able and willing people should be allowed to contribute to economy and society.

In India corruption and lethargy was at its peak. One could not get any work done without paying bribery. It was so open that workers counted the extra earning at the end of the day. The corruption among politicians and officials had become intolerable. There was a movement among the masses to get rid of this disease. Some people had moved money out of the country and deposited in Western banks. This brought drain in the economy. Some had become very rich, while poverty had increased in many states. There was a demand to bring the nation's money back to the country, in order to invest on rural as well as urban projects. The central government had power and authority to make laws and negotiate with foreign banks and governments to repatriate the Indian wealth. The central government had, however, taken no action.

General public and pressure groups started to converse whether the politicians and leaders were also involved in sending money out of the country. There had been meetings and demonstrations against corruption and for repatriation of money which stood at many billions of rupees or even dollars. At the beginning of April 2011, some eminent people started hunger strike in order to show their disgust and anger against the government inaction. An awakening had taken place among the masses and the movement had reached in different states of India. Some action could be forthcoming.

However, being aware of the Indian psyche and behaviour, something variant would emerge on the scene and people would forget about corruption. It was vital to be vigilant and active in order to get rid of this disease. There was a need for political will, commitment, courage, perseverance and patience. In other words real leadership was required not by any one person or one group but organized leadership which should be filtered down from central government to state government and villages and cities. Everyone should remain alert and active for a long time. There should be an administrative structure. Award and punishment should be given in order to eradicate improbity.

Only the awakened masses could accomplish this objective. There was a need for the masses to be educated in this area. The education system should also be changed because the education system and the educators had become unscrupulous. The students had no respect for their teachers. Selfishness had become quite common. People thought of themselves only. There was no respect for elders or neighbours or to their property. There was jealousy among the masses. They were unhappy with other people's success or accomplishments and wanted to have everything for themselves. Let us see how the future turns out to be.

On the international scene, there had been turmoil in the middle- east. It started with North Africa. It was a kind of revolution. The political leaders in many countries did not want to give up their positions which had been dictatorial for many decades. They had become Presidents for life and ignored all the rules of democracy. In some nations including Egypt the President resigned after some opposition and demonstrations. But in Libya, Gaddfi refused to go and the struggle continued for eight months. Finally he was caught in a hole and killed by a gunman. Libya was rich in oil. It produced 2% of world crude oil. In the name of democracy the Western powers started air strikes which led to the loss of lives of civilians and damage to property.

It was strange how the developing countries remained psychologically underdeveloped. They should realize and understand that the system of family rule or permanent rule by one person could not sustain forever in this age of information and high technology. There should be elections at regular intervals and leaders should leave after five or ten years. The circumstances could change soon and dramatically. People could not cling on to one system or one person for long. There should be changes in policies as well as politicians. India, Britain and the USA had elected many Prime ministers and Presidents while only one person ruled for thirty or forty years in the Middle-East. The world had moved towards globalization. There were certain precepts which applied to all the people and all countries in the world.

In India the level of shoddiness has increased over time. In a typical Indian fashion Anna Hazare, a social worker, went on hunger strike, demanding an Ombudsman. A Committee had been set up with members of the central government and some citizens in order to draft the powers and functions of such an authority. This had not solved any problem and the demand of the public led by Ramdev, the yoga guru had started to seek changes in Indian governmental activities and functions. The main demands remained for the removal of corruption, and the recall of Indian money from abroad, and the use of Indian languages in higher education including the medical and engineering courses.

The aim was to provide equality of opportunity for all Indians and to remove poverty from cities and villages in India. These objectives were consonant with the modern values and the United Nations Charter. There had been an increase in the use of English language which had taken away some of the opportunities of the poor. The poverty had increased despite all the five year plans and economic development. Money and political power had concentrated in a few hands. The majority of Indians barely survive.

The present revolts and demonstrations by the general public whether led by a sadhu or a social worker or lawyers and academics were of historical significance. If we looked at the events of the 19th and early 20th centuries, we discover and observe, that sluggishness and indolence among Indian rulers led to foreign invasion. The rulers though revolted against the foreign imperialism in the 19ᵗʰ Century, the lack of defence power and defence preparedness led to their defeat. The British took over the reins of administration in 1858, and united the whole of India. They also introduced modern education which created a professional middle class. These professionals later revolted against the foreign rule. This revolt was, nevertheless, based on liberal values and liberal ideology. They demanded self- rule for Indians themselves. This opposition was, however, less violent because the Indians did not have weapons or trained army. India accomplished political freedom in 1947, because the British were not in a position to hold on to the empire. A social revolution took place by constitutional methods. Many political leaders came forward from the lower communities as well.

The independent Indian government started economic planning, education, agricultural and industrial development. It did not, however, improve the condition of the poor villager. Now in the year 2011, there was a silent revolution taking place in order to improve the conditions of the majority of Indians who were still poor and lived in villages. This revolution should now pass from the middle classes to the working people. The accomplishments were still to be seen because the Indian society was very introvert and stagnant In this awakening, however, some people were working for the benefit of the majority The general public was providing funds and organizing meetings. Still the Satyagraha of 4ᵗʰ June 2011, in Delhi, led by Swami Ramdev, was brutally crushed at midnight by the police on the orders of the politicians. What happened on the night of 4ᵗʰ June was unbelievable. The next day, I watched the program. There was a good atmosphere with songs, prayers and yoga exercise. At Ranleela ground in Delhi, at 1.10am (night) the police attacked the gathering, including women and children and dismantled the tents without prior warning. They tried to take away Ramdev who escaped in a woman's dress. There was stampede. People were beaten with lathi (bamboo sticks), smoke bombs were thrown by the police. The whole of India was amazed. But the British media did not show this on the news. The Astha TV, NDTV, ZEE TV and Star News showed everything that happened on that night.

Some People argued that such things happened in 1975, when emergency was declared by the Congress government. In June 2011, the lawyers went to the Supreme Court. The Supreme Court asked the Indian Central government, the Delhi government and the Delhi police to explain why such a drastic action was necessary, which led to attacking the innocent people many of whom were sleeping at that time.

Many people, except the Congress party leaders deplored the police action though no one tried to make political capital out of it. It was also an attack on Indian culture. Even the British imperialists accepted the Satyagraha, as a means of expressing discontent because it did not hurt anyone. The Satyagraha (truth-force) was a moral weapon to demonstrate to the other party that they were wrong and should reconsider their policies for the good of the country.

The Indian government and the Indian politicians had lost all morality. It was an extreme form of immoral action to take away money abroad, not to perform administrative responsibilities and to beat up people who expressed their discontent. The Satyagraha moved from Delhi to other places. The accomplishments of satyagrahis might be minimal at that stage but there was a ray of hope that a change in government at the next general election could show some light and bring back the issues for consideration and solution.

The black money and the flight of Indian money abroad had led to inflation, unemployment and the decline in value of rupee. As the corrupt people amassed, their money abroad and converted rupee into dollars, the supply of rupee increased and demand for foreign currency increased. The value of rupee declined and became less attractive. There was a time when rupee was equal to one pound. Now it was equal to seventy or eighty rupees or in even one hundred and two rupees in 2013. The British economy was not hundred times better than the Indian economy. It was an artificial exchange rate. In the 1930s, one pound was equal to five US dollars. Now it was equal to one dollar sixty cents because the American economy was stronger than the British economy and the US dollar was used to buy oil and in international trade. Thus the demand for dollar had increased.

In the early 19th Century, the British imperialists kept their currency strong for prestige reasons. In India the situation was entirely adverse. There was no patriotism or nationalism among the politicians or people. They had developed inferiority complex. The had lost all trust in their own system and had, therefore become pervert. Ramdev and other satyagrahis, who wanted to enlighten nationalism and national pride, had been suppressed.

This incident highlighted the dissimilarities between the East and the West, between ancient Indian manners and modern methods borrowed from nowhere. It represented neither the democracy of the West nor the culture of the East. In the West, the democracy was paramount. The demonstrations were permitted to take place. The public could display their discontent peacefully. In the East the Sadhus were respected and young and old were shown sympathy and regard. But this was the representation of autocracy or self- imposition of feudal system. India was still under the grip of feudalism and caste system. It was far from democracy in social and personal life. The ruling parties at the Centre and the States suppressed the masses as happened in feudal and imperialist systems in the past. It was to be seen if the objectives of the social workers for a Lokpal (Ombudsman) at the center; recall of black money from overseas, improvement in administrative system, removal of corrupt and ignorant workers and Indianisation of education could be accomplished.

The only result of the pervert system had been the decline of education standards. In the Asian education and academic standards in 2011, India came at the bottom. Only one institution in Bombay came 187th out of 200 institutions surveyed. The teaching standards, achievement by students and research in Universities by staff remained low or negligible. The teaching staff was ill prepared to teach with high standards. The student discipline was bad or worse, the teaching methods were unbelievable. Most of the modern subjects were taught in Indian Universities and colleges but standards were poor in all respects.

The use of English language or rather the misuse of English language had not helped. It had produced a few call- center workers for the West but it had not produced high class scientists of international standards and social scientists of great repute. No wonder some clever students from rich families had gone to study in Australia, the United Kingdom and the USA. Despite the fact that they faced social, academic and financial problems and they certainly missed their families and friends. Their overall performance and personality development was not perfect as it could have been if they studied in their own environment.

In October, we decided to go to India and bought our tickets. We planned to leave London on 20 November but due to bad weather the plane was diverted to Manchester airport. We were sent back home. There was no arrangement by the Jet Airways to inform us properly or to make arrangement at a hotel. A couple of foot soldiers were walking around. They simply said that we should go home and check with the airline the next day. They did not note our telephone numbers or provide any further information. It was very irresponsible by an international airline. However, I phoned my cab company to take us home to Chiswick.

The next day, we went back to the airport, deposited our luggage and waited for the plane. The plane left on time and we reached Delhi airport the next morning. We hired a paid taxi and reached home by midday but decided not to clean the house that day. The next morning we collected a worker to clean the house. He found it a big job and left. Vinod went out again to fetch another worker who was a little more mature. Although he arrived late he said that he would skip his lunch break and continue to work nonstop and he would finish before 6pm. If he managed to finish the work before that, he would go home. We wanted him to do the job. We, therefore, agreed. He worked nonstop and finished at 4pm. I paid him two hundred and fifty rupees. He said that he was a professional tailor from Uttar Pradesh. But he did not have a job. So he was doing odd jobs. Any way it was his business to do whatever he wanted to do. We felt relaxed when he cleaned and washed the house floor.

We went shopping and purchased our food supplies as usual. We started a normal living. We were visited by many of our relatives. One of them performed a drama. His son-in- law had decided to stay in Canada. He wanted to talk to Azad. I gave him Azad's telephone number. Another relative also came to visit us that week. I could not remember which day. He was a jealous and angry man those days. He gave me an impression that he was an unhappy person and that he had missed out on certain things. Even at his age, he wanted things for himself and could not bear the progress of others. This time he was annoyed with farmers especially in villages in Uttar Pradesh. He said that these people had only about ten acres of land but had become carorpati (multimillionaires). I could not understand why he was talking to me about them and what had they done to infuriate him. I simply ignored and asked him about his health and the welfare of his children. He left in about twenty minutes. I decided not to visit him any time soon.

However, I went to visit him before returning to London in February 2012. He did not ask me to sit down but I sat down in a plastic chair. He started to criticize Azad and his in-laws. He said that Azad was not aware with the Indian culture because he left India at the age of four. His relatives were not nice people. He often told many people that he had done so much for us and we had not returned the favours. He never explained what had he done for us. On the contrary, I realized that he had taken money from us on many occasions and he asked me to send clothes from London for his friends and family. He used our house to put building material and his son's car was parked in our garage for over a year, making the place dirty. But what surprised me most, was that he told one of his close friends that he had done so much for us and we did not send any gift on his daughter's wedding, and we sent some money at the wedding of our sister's daughter. His friend advised that I should be constructed in the wall. When my mother and sister heard about it, they were annoyed and asked his friend, why did he want me to put in the wall when I had a young family? My sister took the threat literally. Surprisingly after many years this man hugged me at a festival. But the fact was that they were jealous with my success. There was a saying that failure was orphan and success had many parents.

I had the impression that he was no more my type of man. This man looked to me as a person with primitive instincts of craving and hunger. He had refused to grow psychologically and socially. My observation was that demand for money was made in order to satiate hunger. He always thought of acquiring or grabbing money from any source. Craving instinct also created demand or lust for money. People like him also develop other qualities like anger, greed, jealousy, disrespect, duality, enmity, maliciousness, contempt and hostility along with selfishness, snatching and rapacity.

On the contrary, there were other people who had overcome the primitive instincts and had developed high culture. They were inclined to respect others and would not attempt to find fault in them. They also had understanding, love, large-heartedness, affection, kindness, courteousness, welfare, patience, calm, creativity and a desire to help people in need. If they committed any errors of judgment or became trapped in turmoil, they would repent and make sure that the mistake was not repeated.

Santosh was ill most of December 2011 and January 2012. She had fever, pneumonia, constipation and hypo six times. We went to visit Doctors many times, had ultra sound and blood tests. She would get up but become sick again. We did not visit many people or places this time. We went to Sadar Bazar and Chandni-Chowk twice. I went to Connaught place two times. Once in order to change the time of our departure from Delhi to London and the other time for some other work. On returning to London, we discovered that Santosh had headaches and giddiness. She fell down a couple of times because of low blood pressure. We went to the diabetic clinic and hypertension unit at Hammersmith hospital. She was not fully well but continued to cook and do house work.

On the international scene, it was Syria in the Middle East, where leadership had turned against its people. The same story was being repeated as in North-Africa. The politicians and the government had attempted to suppress the uprising for freedom and democracy. The general public had been beaten up, houses destroyed. People had become refugees in their own country or started to flee to the neighboring nations. Young children had lost their parents especially fathers. The women had lost their sons and husbands. It was like Bosnia. Men and boys were picked up by the army and killed. It was pathetic. The World community had not done much yet, though there was a cry for justice.

My life had been comfortable. We did not have much to do. I suffered from acidity and kept on spitting at night. The spit turned into mucus in course of time. Sometimes I had sleepless nights. I visited my doctor who prescribed me medicine which did not work at all. The Ayurveda life plan suggested that medicine did not work in acidity and mucus. It propounded that I should avoid milk and dairy products and take ginger and honey, also walk in the morning and evening. I should not lie down immediately after food and I should take food three hours before going to sleep. I stopped milk and cheese. The mucus receded. I realized that I was allergic to milk product. The Chest X-ray and stool test did not reveal anything. Santosh had developed breathlessness. She did not like walking and had become home bound except when it was essential.

I started to read a personality psychology book in order to look into the behaviour of people from an academic point of view, and to discover Peoples motives behind interference. It had been argued that personality was influenced by culture. The Western culture of Europe and the United States laid emphasis on individuality and freedom of the individual and the Eastern culture of Asia, Eastern- Europe and South America were affected by community. The social norms, customs and traditions were important for these people, than an individual. People tend to be self-aware and leaned towards the family. A child learnt what he could do and what he could not do. There was always a social comparison with a group. The self of a person included attributes such as thoughts, feelings and desires. There was also an objective self- awareness whereby a person reacted to others and drew their attention. There was a positive and a negative side in a person. The self -esteem was the total of the positive and the negative reactions of all aspects of self -concept. The people had low and high esteem of themselves. I found that some people unnecessarily interfere in other's lives.

It had also been suggested that the personality was affected by and expressed through social institutions, social roles and expectations and through relationships with other people. Many traits interact with each other. Such as dominance vs submissiveness; love vs hatred. Whether a person was co-operative or not, whether a person was reliable, agreeable and easy to get along with others.

Apart from thinking about human behaviour, we had our Chiswick house renovated in March 2012. In June we decided to go to Canada to spend some time with the children. We wanted to fly direct from London to Edmonton for our convenience. We left London Heathrow airport just after 4pm and reached at Edmonton airport at 6pm because Edmonton was seven hours behind London. The food was horrible and not tasty at all. Otherwise the service was good and the flight was pleasant. Edmonton airport though small, it had a long walk from the landing place to the exit. We had to walk on foot which was not pleasant after a long journey.

Azad, Meenakshi, Amar and Ashish came to receive us at the airport. We went home in their new van which was a seven seater car. There were some visible changes and developments to be observed. We reached home and soon settled down. We slept in the basement bedroom which Azad had built since our last visit in 2004. The washroom was convenient. There was also a television which we did not watch. Ashish attended his examination and Azad used to go to his office. We stayed at home and watched television. Amar took us to stores and food shops. Ashish also drove to the town centre once and Amar brought us back. They both shared a blue car.

I continued to suffer from acidity reflux. I used herbal medicine but it had no effect. I stopped using dairy products, had green tea or black tea. My reflux got worse at night when I coughed a lot and kept on spitting mucus. We were in the basement. So I did not disturb any one. Azad took us to a friend's house for dinner. He told me that they had created a group of twelve like-minded families who organized dinner once a month. One family arranged dinner at their house but food was brought in by all the families. They decided in advance who was to cook what? There was always enough food for everyone. It did not put burden on any one person or family to prepare food. It was also a way of getting together in that country. They had something in common and shared their food, which I thought was a very good system of meeting people who were all professionals and educated. Their children got on well with each other and enjoyed the evening.

Amar and Ashish had quite a few friends. They hung out at each other's house but also went to cinema and the town center together. We went to town center one day. After watching fare, we went to an Iranian restaurant. I went with Amar and Ashish to malls a few times but did not do any shopping. I kept in touch with Saneh who informed me of the position in Chiswick. Once or twice we spoke to Akash and Sangeeta who had completed her first year degree course at Loughborough University. On 27th July, we watched the opening ceremony of the 2012 Olympic Games in London. I enjoyed it very much. Sangeeta wanted to buy tickets for the hockey game tickets for 10th August. But I refused. We would be tired at that time after returning from Edmonton on 8th August.

In Edmonton we used to go for a walk in the evening. There was a huge park in the area. Quite a few other Indian families lived in this neighbourhood of North West Edmonton. They exchanged greetings by saying 'sat shri akal'. Azad wanted to have a break at a resort. He, therefore, organized a holiday with effect from Sunday 22 July to Thursday 26 July. Both the families (including Akhilesh's) went in their own cars. It was a one thousand kilometers distance lake resort known as 'LA KASA.' It took us thirteen hours to reach there through the mountains, plains and the mountain edges. The road was zizzag. We could not even see a few yards distance and had to negotiate the curves and the edges. Azad, Meenakshi and Amar took turns to drive through. We reached La Kasa at about 8pm. We stayed at a self-contained house which was good. It had three bed rooms and a large reception room with a kitchen on the right corner. We had break- fast and dinner there. Twice we went to the lake, where the children enjoyed themselves by boating and swimming. At the resort house we watched a couple of movies. We returned on Thursday, through another route and saw Calgary in passing. The road was slightly better and wider but in the early drive we had to come though mountains and valleys.

In the next week, we did not have much to do. Azad had returned to work. Amar and Ashish had their own lives and spent a lot of time outside the house. We were preparing to return to London and informed Saneh to that effect. There was no change in our programme. During my loose conversation with Azad and Meenakshi, I expressed my surprise at the disposition of people in India in general and extended family in particular. I could not reconcile with myself at the frame of mind and conduct of these people towards us. Sometimes I considered that if there could be someone to take over the responsibility, I would get cut off from India altogether.

By the end of the 20th Century, politics was being replaced by economics. India was no more a begging bowl of the world. It produced food and sold to other countries. Indians were running call centers for American banks and companies. People of Indian origin had gained respect. Pakistan on the other hand descended towards chaos and terrorism. It was not helping Americans in Afghanistan. Many Americans had been killed in the 26/11 blasts in Mumbai. Pakistan refused to deal with its terrorists. It was, therefore, natural for the oldest and the largest democracies to come closer. People of Indian origin in the United States and Presidents Clinton, Bush and Obama contributed in this progress. The US administrators were more receptive to India's needs in the 1990s and the 21st century than ever before. The United States was also looking for a giant in Asia to compete with China economically and politically. India became a natural ally in this project.

Despite India's corruption and maladministration, Indians had gained some respect in other countries. The advanced developing countries had formed an organization known as BRICS on the name of these countries for their own co-operation and development. The international institutions led by the Western powers had not served their objectives of increasing trade and investment. Brazil, Russia, India, China and South Africa (BRICS) meet regularly in order to increase business between them and to help the other developing countries of Asia, Africa and South America.

Something else had just cropped into my mind. Mumbai had faced many terrorist bombings but the well-known film industry and their actors had never suffered any interruption. People of Pakistan enjoyed the Bollywood films. I wonder if the terrorists also watched Hindi movies. The other topic which interested me was education. Education played a vital role in a person's life. It affected the society as a whole. It had been suggested that literature was the mirror of society. The literature represented all written and unwritten work in all the subjects including languages, sociology, psychology, economics and sciences. The current economics literature and books reflected the economic environment and explained the economic problems. The literature influenced the minds of people.

An education system also portrayed society and was designed to alter the social environment. In India today (2013) emphasis was being laid on technical education in order to ensure economic progress needed to meet the demand of the society. The current generation was full of knowledge of technology. Intelligent and clever students went to engineering courses and computer programming courses. It looked as if the Indian education was geared to meet the demand of the Western corporations in order to run their call centers cheaply. The all-round education to develop the character of students and prepare them for life and employment had become a rarity. The ethics and morality had disappeared. This system had led to corruption and social decline.

The people (not everyone) had become deceitful. If a man had worked hard and gained economic security, others wanted a share of his wealth. People thought, what the others had, should be theirs without enquiring how the other guy worked rigorously for it and reached where he was today. These cunning people were happy if others were poor or had less. Once the hard working people acquired the benefits of their effort, the lazy and jealous come into action to pull them down. They did not try to understand that the Western nations and their people had worked extremely strenuously and life was still difficult in these countries. They had the fruits of their honesty and labour.

The American and European education was also of a very high standard. It prepared students for adult life and employment. A recent survey showed that 17 universities in America were the best out of 25 universities. One

Swiss university and 6 British universities were also in the same category. The Oxford University stood third, next to Harvard this year. The university graduates could take independent decisions which were vital for management positions and to run business and government organizations.

On 1st August 2012, we celebrated the festival of Rakshabandhan. I had to tie the rakhi myself as I was in Canada on that date. We had been in Edmonton for almost seven weeks. Edmonton had grown over the years. More houses, stores and parks had been built near the North-West part of Edmonton. I had walked around this area and travelled with Amar to the city center, the University of Alberta, the NAIT- North Alberta Institute of Technology (where Amar and Ashish were studying). Edmonton, however, was still an open place, as were Alberta and Canada as a whole. There was a lot of space for a small population. A few days ago at a gathering, someone asked me how I compared Canada with England. I liked the wide roads and empty space in Edmonton but London had its own character. It was easy to walk and travel in London. It had easy access to shops, libraries, museums and parks which attract me. Moreover, I had lived in London for 47 years by that time.

In Edmonton, I had visited shops and malls with my son and grandsons. I became dependent on them for transport. In London, I travelled by bus or underground because I gave up driving in 2004. I was happy in the company of my family but I would still like to live in London most of the time. It was not easy to change habits at that age or stage.

On 31 January 2013, I wrote that it was my first note of the year and written after a long break. We returned from Canada on 8th August 2012 and soon settled down to the London routine. We rested for a few days but later the business was as usual. We did not have any special plans to go anywhere, though we went to Hounslow almost every week preferably on Thursdays or Sundays to walk around the High Street. We decided to refurbish our house and redecorate the bed rooms and the hallway. We removed the wall papers and discovered that there were cracks in the walls. I tried to repair in my own way but it looked bad and did not solve the problem. We, therefore, decided to get the walls and ceilings plastered or skimmed.

Azad suggested that we should not paint ourselves but ask a builder to do the whole job. We, therefore, asked a few builders to give us quotes. It came from twelve hundred pounds to plaster three rooms to two thousand eight hundred pounds to skim the rooms and the hall way. We worked out the cost and thought that it should not cost more than one thousand four hundred pounds for skimming. The painting would be extra. Soon we found that the back bed room's ceiling could not be repaired and needed replacing before plastering. We, therefore, agreed with one of the builders to do the whole job for one thousand seven hundred pounds and three hundred and sixty pounds for painting the rooms and the hall way area with gloss paint on doors and windows. The work commenced on 8th October. Due to sickness of workers, it prolonged for two months. On that day the builders moved our bed to the reception room on the ground floor. We could not have stayed in the damp, while the work was going on the first floor.

One of the friends suggested that we should also do the other work at the same time as we were planning to get a new kitchen in the new-year. We went to look for kitchen units at the Moldens and B&Q DIY. We opted for the B&Q kitchen in oak colour with one and half sink unit and gas and electric cooker. The work commenced in early November and everything was fitted before the old kitchen was removed. We, therefore, continued to cook at the house. We did not buy ready-made food from shops because I was allergic to quite a few foods. When we removed the kitchen we also decided to remove the small wall in order to make it a kitchen diner.

We had the entire area redone and the door was moved inwards. We asked an engineer to look that the small wall was not holding the 1st floor wall. He confirmed that there was no problem in removing the wall. All this work took about two months and another three weeks to look for carpets for which we shopped around and finally asked the Kingsley Road, Hounslow carpets to fit carpets for us. They did it in the first week of January 2013. We moved our bed to our bed room on 8th January, three months after we were moved down to the reception room. It took us another week to put our things in right order and to return to normal living. We did not have any commitments in London apart from a few hospital appointments for Santosh. She was mostly fine but complained of back pain. The weather had been cold and rainy in London. It snowed in early January. We were not disturbed in our routine and continued to go to Acton and Chiswick High Road.

Something startled me about maintaining relationship between various groups of people. Be they friends, brothers, sisters, parents or children. If it was based on selfishness and self-interest it could not last forever. The selfish people saw what they could gain from the other party. If they did not benefit from relationship, they would not want to maintain the connections. It had happened to me on many occasions. They were frank in telling me that if I could not help them with money and time, they would have nothing to do with me. They had never been helpful to me yet expected me to assist them in many ways.

In 1960, I wrote in my Hindi poem that 'love was not love that altered when alteration it found'. It was also argued that love or affection was a sacrifice and giving to others rather than demanding from them. I did not know what perception my family and friends had of me. They expected something distinct of me than I provided. I knew, I was an uncomplicated man and had always wished to live a quiet life. I was, however, creative, intelligent, better adjusted, independent minded and unconventional though not a rebel to oppose social system.

Still the others wanted me to be obedient and always listen to them, consult on matters which did not concern them, and had nothing to do with them. They thought I was an earning machine and did not know how to save or spend money. They also expected me to work for the good and benefit of them, their children and friends. I should brush aside my own needs, wishes and demands along with those of my family. They had been rude to me and my family but they desired me to be good to them and their children. I must stress here that a person's performance depended on his level of intelligence, skills and creativity. The creativity was not confined to arts, music and drama but it was an ability to act efficiently and develop interests in many fields as well as to be prepared to do new things and develop new ideas. People could be both intelligent and creative or they might excel in intelligence or just creativity. I have acquired success in many fields where as the others had not been so lucky and, therefore, jealous with my accomplishments.

In 2012, a new party emerged in India. They called themselves Aam Admi Party (AAP). (Party of the common men) The convenor was Arvind Kejriwal, a qualified engineer but he also passed the IAS (Indian Administrative Services) examination and became Assistant Commissioner in the Inland Revenue or Tax Office. He did not like the routine work and joined Anna Hazare, a social worker and became a social activist himself. Soon he realized that problems were not being solved and the government had not done anything on the appointment of Lokpal or the Ombudsman in order to fight bribery and corruption. Kejriwal thought that if he entered politics and won an election, he would be able to pass the Lokpal bill. He became quite popular in Delhi. Like minded educated young men and women joined him. He was popular among the poor and working class. He was secular in his conduct. His party members wore a cap, written AAP on it. In the Delhi Assembly elections in 2013, the AAP won 28 seats but not enough to form a government. The BJP had 31 seats and the Congress had 8 MLAs. The Congress decided to support AAP and persuaded Kejriwal to form a government.

He did introduce a few changes in order to reduce the cost of water and electricity for the poor. He used to hold meetings in the open space and street corner or Ramleela ground. After a month, his government introduced the Lokpal Bill in order to reduce corruption and decided to take action against the past leaders, the police and the bureaucrats. He would have many Congress leaders under investigation. However, the Congress withdrew its support and the BJP attempted to divide the AAP's MLAs. One of them did indeed refuse the party whip. But it was on the question of Lokpal that the AAP Chief Minister Arvind Kejriwal resigned on 49th day of his rule. There was shouting by the BJP that they ran away from responsibility. The BJP itself did not form a government. The Assembly was not dissolved. Yet, the Delhi administration passed under the President's rule. The AAP had one objective – removal of corruption. Whereas, politics are about many phases of social life including- political life. The AAP had not declared its social policies, education or health, industrial policy, foreign policy and defence policy along with a host of other commitments on taxation, removal of poverty, transport facilities. The AAParty was behaving like a pressure group. The members of the Aam Aadmi Party started as a pressure group with Anna Hazare. They should have stayed as a pressure group for a little longer and fight election later.

Alternatively its members should have joined the existing parties closer to their thinking and philosophy and then they should have attempted to reform from within and take over the leadership in order to fight local, state and national elections and implement their policies in government with the help of their fellow legislators.

In India, the Lok- Sabha (Lower House of Central Parliament) elections were to take place in April and May 2014. A large number of political parties had emerged to take part in the elections. Many politicians changed parties. Some were angry that they had not been given tickets to fight election from their chosen constituencies. Narendra Modi, the Gujarat Chief Minister and the BJP Prime Ministerial candidate was expected to win and become India's Prime Minister with the help of the smaller parties. They would form an NDA (National Democratic Alliance) government. They had not declared their policies except that they would work for the National Development and equal development in all areas and all states. The Congress did not have any experienced leader to become Prime Minister. They wanted to continue the Nehru- Gandhi dynasty.

A large number of political parties and candidates took part in the election, with almost 800 million voters. These were acrimonious elections I had ever seen. The political leaders were mudslinging at each other. They argued about secularism without understanding the meaning of the word. The Gandhi-Nehru dynasty still wanted to rule India whether they had the ability or not. There was no Congress leader of national stature. They, therefore, relied on Rahul Gandhi because he had a dynastic name. His appeal was not heeded. The BJP's Narendra Modi held meetings in all states and all parts the country, and he presented policies for economic development. The other party leaders opposed to him either because he was from the lower caste, or he was the Chief Minister when violence broke out in 2002 in Gujarat. They opposed him arguing that he would work for the welfare of the Hindus only and ignore the welfare of Muslims.

He maintained that he would follow the constitution and that every citizen was equal in India. The development would reach all communities and parts of the nation. Still attempts were made to stop him from becoming Prime Minister. The so called secular parties had been corrupt and inefficient and they had no economic and social policies to offer. I found it strange that an election was being fought on personality and not on policies or honesty and hard work. The caste and communal card was played vigorously in these elections. Many candidates had criminal records. Yet they were allowed to participate in the elections. The election results would come out on 16th May which would reflect the public's verdict.

The Indian elections results for the Lok- Sabha provided a clear majority for the Bhartiya Janta Party (BJP). Narendra Modi became prime Minister. It was his policies for economic development which appealed to people. It was for the new government to achieve a reasonable growth rate in order to provide employment to general public. The new Prime Minister had appealed for foreign investment, because there was a lack of investment in India. Apart from shortage of investment the developing countries faced a large gap in relevant research based knowledge which created policy challenges. For policy formation local knowledge and research was essential. The policy makers should have access to research and statistics for economic growth and social development. There was a need for effectiveness and the government's ability to raise revenue in order to provide public services. These services should be run by high caliber civil servants. Good public servants would also strengthen public institutions. There was also a need to develop sectors for production function. Efforts should be made to provide energy especially in poor rural areas in order to improve the economic life of the residents in villages.

X   X   X   X

In Britain general elections took place in May 2015. When the election results were declared for the Westminster Parliament, the Conservative Party won an overall majority and formed a government under the Prime Minister David Cemeron. The Liberal party was reduced to eight MPs from fifty six in the previous parliament. Their leader resigned his position. The Labour party also lost some seats and failed to gain in other areas. Although a few new MPs were elected. Its leader also resigned. But real change was seen in Scotland. While the Conservatives, the Liberals and the Labour party lost many seats, the Scottish National Party (SNP) gained. It now (1915) had 54 MPs at Westminster Parliament. Although its main purpose was to achieve freedom for Scotland, it started to participate in British elections in 1967, when it won the Hamilton by-election for Winnie Ewing. In 2015, a charismatic person, Nicola Sturgeon, emerged as its leader. She also had a national appeal. Many people in England were impressed by her oratory and arguments. She was convincing and appealed to people to vote for her party. Indeed people in Scotland voted for her party and elected a large number of MPs. This party already had a majority in the Scottish Parliament.

After writing about the British elections, I did not write anything about Britain, India or the world, despite all the problems in the Middle- East, especially in Syria and the attacks by terrorists in many countries. This turned out to be a barren period with unproductive consequences for my writing. I started to go to Gym in Acton for physical exercises and the use of bike and tread-mill. One of the instructors asked me to write about the social aspects of gym. I wrote a few words and passed on a copy to him.

The Social Aspects of Gym:

The Every One Active Gym, in Acton, aims to provide facilities for physical exercise for people of all ages in the neighbourhood and the surrounding boroughs. It was not only the technical apparatuses available for those who come to the gym that made an impact on people, it was also the personal touch, individual attention, friendly environment and other aspects of socialization that brought smile and laughter on the faces of those who came to use these facilities. The whole environment had been created for the socializing aspect and demeanour among those who were strangers only a few days earlier. The group practice in the studio was designed to bring participants together for multi-activities, where elderly people enjoyed walking sideways or doing push- ups against the wall.

The instructors gave individual attention, which brought pleasure and happiness to those who came to take part in all kinds of tasks. It also led to fun and friendship. The involvement in conversation made this place distinct from other premises. For most participants the activities were designed in order to meet individual needs based on their state of health. The instructors essentially endeavored to assist in people's health conditions related to diabetes, arthritis or high blood pressure. Quite a number of them had been referred to this gym by their GPs. The improvement in their condition was monitored as was the lack of amends. The social and psychological factors brought amelioration and betterment in their physical wellbeing.

This was accomplished by creating an environment conducive to establishing trust and understanding between instructors and participants who achieved their personal best through encouragement and motivation. In this, the personal instructors and personal training played a very significant role. Regular exercise augmented self-confidence, prevented depression and reduced stress. It, therefore, lead to emotional and social benefits. It increased focus and a new kind of social relationship and companionship. It had been suggested that meeting, others without personal self-interest, was the foundation for establishing true friendship and developing mutual support – which was the main objective of this gym in Acton.

x   x   x

I had an opportunity to write my observations on 15 October 2015, as it was the 50th anniversary of my arrival in London. On this day, however, I was not in the City of Parks but was in Edmonton, Alberta, Canada. I spent most of the day at the Royal Alexandra hospital. While my grandson Ashish had his sinus operation, I waited in the guest room. He went into the operation theatre at 11.30 am and came back at 2-30 pm to the ward.

Then I sat with him. He was still sleepy. I, therefore, went to collect his medicine from the Pharmacy on the 1st floor. We came home at 6pm. It was a busy day.

A great deal has happened in these fifty years, since 1965. When I left Delhi on 15th October 1965, Santosh and children and a large number of relatives came to see me off. During this half a century, I lost a great deal and gained enormously. I lost my wife Santosh. I had been left lonely, if not alone. I have my children and grandchildren to comfort me and support me in many ways. They were now grown up and had their own lives. I paid my tribute to Santosh and had reproduced my views in the Appendix rather than making a part of this narrative.

The weather was sunny, in Edmonton. Though a little windy. I was at ease, despite my knee pain which woke me up at night. I had to take injections at regular intervals. Sometimes I could not go to sleep once I woke up. I was mentally alert and could read and write. Walking was strenuous. I was still in touch with some relatives in India. Others had their own affairs to attend. I hardly receive letters or phone calls from them.

In Edmonton, I used to go for a walk with Azad or by myself. I stayed with Amar and Ashish most of the time at home and continued to speak to Saneh and Akash in London on phone. I returned to London on 19th November to live my own life of reading, writing and walking on the streets of West London.

CONCLUSION

I had always wished to live on certain principles, which had not been easy. I had to face a number of problems. I came across all sorts of people during this journey which was full of struggle for survival and progress. There were people who always wanted to take advantage of me for their financial and social gains. There were people who could not see me progress or succeed and tried to drag me down. Even if they would not gain or benefit out of my miseries or decline. They wanted to see me at a lower status in order to keep themselves at a high level.

When I arrived in England to start a new life, I stayed in West London's North Acton, for a few weeks before moving to live at Hanger Lane. Later I lived in South London, Hackney and Manor Park in East London. But I returned to West London in 1977, in order to live in Bedford Park. These years witnessed changes in London's population structure, though population density remained the same. The ethnicity had altered. In 1965, Poland was a part of the Eastern-bloc dominated by the Soviet Union. Now it was in the European Union. Over one million people from Poland had moved to live in England. A substantial number now lived in London. We saw quite a few construction workers on our street, repairing houses and building loft rooms. There was more acceptance of ethnic minorities now, than it was in the 1960s.

On Monday, 30th September 2013, I was walking from the Kew station to the National Archives. All of a sudden, I felt exhilarated and happy, thinking that I was a contented man, academically as well as professionally.

Coming from a small village background of Northern India, from where I walked out of my Primary School at the age of nine, I acquired seven qualifications from seven different Universities. BA from Agra, BT from Punjab, BSc Economics (Honours) from London University, the Advanced Diploma in Education from Brunel, MA from City of London Guildhall, M Phil from the London School of Economics and Political Science and finally PhD from Greenwich University. It was all very satisfying. I applied all my knowledge and qualifications into practical use. Apart from teaching successfully for forty years when hardly any of my students failed, I was also a course director for BABA Part 1 and Research Coordinator for BABA part 2. I taught at all levels from School to colleges of Further Education and Higher Education, Polytechnic and University. I taught at GCSE Ordinary level, Advanced level, BTEC, Degree and Masters Courses.

The 1990s, was the golden period of my writing. I published my MPhil thesis on the 'India League and India Conciliation Group as factors in Indo-British Relations' with a title, 'Indian Nationalist Movement in Britain, 1930-49, in the year 1992. In 1993, the University of Greenwich published my pamphlet on 'The Decline of Cotton Industry in 19th Century India'. In 1994 and 1995, I published a few articles in journals and newspapers. It was during this period, I did research on many themes and in 1996, my book the 'Steel Frame, Indian Civil Service Since 1860' was published. 'Imperialism and Non-Alignment', came out in 1998 and 'VK Krishna Menon- A Biography' was published in the same year. I started to work on the 'Stagnation and Change-Economic Impact of British Raj in India'. I made a substantial progress and also found a publisher in Wales but because of the family circumstances, I could not complete this book. In the year 2000, Hamilton& Co. published my Economics book for First year degree course.

My life had been a race. Not a sprint or long distance race but a hurdle race, where I had to cross many hurdles and jump many fences through flood plains, river lets, farms, plain land and in the air. It was not a struggle to accomplish my aims and objectives but a constant race in order to reach the final goal. My first recollection goes back to early 1940s, when

I told my mother that I would like to go to school. But it was not until 1946, when one of my siblings left the village primary School, that I was admitted to a nursery class where I stayed for two years. In July 1948, I was promoted to First year of the Primary School. For reasons stated earlier, I had to leave the village school in August and went to city in order to study at a High School. However, my admittance in that school was not immediate. A cousin had to get clearance from the District Inspector's office at Bulandshahr. I was a big fish in the small pond as a class captain at my village primary school, but became a small fish in the big pond when I suddenly moved to secondary school at Khurja, where I learned new subjects in a new language-English. It was not easy to adjust in a new environment. But I bounced back after a year in that school. I crossed all hurdles and confronted impediments. When I fell sick in 1952 and 1958, I had to face problems and solve them myself. Others were there to create conundrum, although, they pretended to be my well-wishers.

When I received admission at SMJ School Khurja, in 1948, I learned English language and indeed passed my English language examination but could not follow the other subjects. I could understand the subject matter but when it came to doing the examinations, I could not recall much of the material and could not write the answers in details. There was a gap in my learning. I had not completed my Primary education and had not grasped the skills and techniques for examination answer writing. Consequently, I failed most of the subjects except English, Wood Work and Art. For Wood Work practical I could not lift the tools or make anything. But the theory was fine. There was a saying that the failure was the foundation of success. In July 1949, I found myself in the same class with new students and a couple of old ones who also failed in their examination. In the new class, I dropped Wood Work. I wanted to study Music but the music teacher refused to accept me as there was a shortage of musical instruments. I, therefore, had to content myself with Art. I was not good at Art either, but my teacher was a good man, very polite and kind faced.

I soon grasped my subjects. In the mid-term examination, I scored highest marks in many subjects and my overall percentage was the highest in the class. I was declared first in the class. I started to learn. I forgot the past hindrances. Because of my high marks and good position in the class, I was given half-rate concession in my school fee. My father did not appreciate the saving of just three rupees a month but I was allowed this concession for the next four year of the secondary education. This set in motion my learning process.

When I arrived in England in October 1965, I knew only one person, whom I had briefly met in Delhi. I wrote to him a couple of times from India but he did not reply to my letters, thinking that I was not worth it. As if he was much older and much superior in his thoughts. He took me around to Southall, (a London Suburb) to visit people of Indian origin who claimed that they had good jobs in India, as college professors. But in England they had to work in factories. They tried to convince me that I had no chance of getting a teaching job in England and that I had been given a visa to work in factories. He said that he would be glad even if I obtained a job to clean the roads. He made every attempt to instill inferiority complex in me. This, however, displayed his own prejudice, and the lack of understanding of me. After a few days, I moved to live at Hanger Lane. But one day, I went to visit him. We were sitting near the Chimney- fire place, He told me that he was surprised that I received a Visa to come to England. He did not expect that. When he wrote to my brother to ask me to apply to the British High Commission in New Delhi, he was simply teasing me because he thought that I was a lazy person and would never make an effort to immigrate to the United Kingdom. Still, I did not challenge him on his views.

Some other members of Indo-Pak community, however, expressed the view that I should get an office job soon if not a teaching job. Anyway, I worked in a factory for a few months to earn some money and then moved to work at an office at Shepherd Bush and later at HM Customs & Excise at Tower Hill in the City of London. So far getting a teaching job was concerned, I became a teacher in Newham in 1973, and stayed in full time teaching until 2003, and part- time visiting lecturer at the University from 2004 to 2007.

I taught a number of subjects including History, Geography, Social Studies, Mathematics, Economics, Law and Politics at various levels from Little-Ilford School, in the Borough of Newham, to University of Greenwich. Prior to coming to England in 1965, I taught English, Hindi, Social Studies and Mathematics in India. In 1958-59, I was trained to teach English and Hindi at Bhiwani, in Haryana state of India. I used my skills and co- operative humble manners to edit the School magazine at Chirawa High School and did research with others at the Inner London Education Authority on 'Equal Opportunities for Ethnic Minorities in Work-Related NAFE.' I wrote on a variety of subjects which included Gandhi's Communal Individuality, anti-imperialist pressure groups like the India League and the India Conciliation Group, Non-Aligned Movement, North-South economic relations, the Indian Civil Service, The Treasury Control of Public Expenditure in Britain, Biography of VK Krishna Menon. I jotted down my own experiences and Observations, which were the sources of this book.

I felt that my ambition had been accomplished and my objectives achieved. The purpose of my life had been fulfilled. I was a happy man despite all the obstacles. A number of people helped me at various stages in positive ways. I also turned the negative attitude of people into positive action. I mixed with all kinds of good people but ignored the jealous and negative thinkers who could be impediments in my life and work. I changed with the changing circumstances and progressed with time. Britain also changed with time and progressed from being a sick man of Europe to one of the most developed economies in the European Union. In order to accomplish this Britain had to give up its old industries in the fields of textiles, shipbuilding and mining and moved towards high tech industries and research in many areas including stem cell.

My observation was that the disagreements and physical attacks at an individual level or between the states could find their roots in ideological differences. People thought differently in accordance with their situations and circumstances. There could be genuine deviation between family members or neighbours. They could find it impossible to accommodate each other. These ideological disparities find expression through words, in an attempt to find fault in each other and sticking to their own points of view. They might criticize openly or in private. This could, however, lead to shouts and verbal attacks. If they were unable to control themselves, they would physically attack each other and inflict bodily harm. This could happen to people or between nations. It was, therefore essential to understand each other's views and arguments in order to live peacefully.

People should attempt to examine their interest logically and should not try to undermine others. They should show respect to people and nations, their philosophy, culture and history. This was vitally important for co-existence and survival. They should endeavour to seek co-operation rather than conflict, reconciliations, and not to impose their opinion and policies on others.

APPENDIX

MY LIFE WITH AND WITH OUT SANTOSH RANI ARORA

Having lived in India, for two and half years in my absence, Santosh Rani and children arrived in London on 5th April 1968. I went to Heathrow airport to collect them. We stayed in a room at New Cross Road, South London, for a week. Then we moved to a two room flat in Dalston, Hackney. These places were not very attractive, yet she did not express discontent or displeasure. It was our place albeit rented. We settled down to a routine and Santosh adjusted herself to the new environment as if she had lived there for a lengthy span. She was friendly to people who lived in that multi-occupied, multi-storied house. She started to wear shirt and slack along with her Indian saree. She also began to do shopping by her-self at the local shops and at Dalston market.

She never moaned or lamented of discrimination or prejudice in London because she had bitter experience of impropriety, wrongness and unjustifiability in her own families in India. She did not come across any particular injustice or bias in England. During our conversation in the last few months of her life, she revealed some wearisome affliction and distress which had taken place almost fifty to sixty years earlier. But they came to her mind repeatedly and made a psychological impact. Some of her experiences were hurtful and brought tears to our eyes. On the contrary some feelings crystallized her joy and cheerfulness. She was especially pleased to recall her friend and colleague Manjeet who gave her sarees at the time of her sons' birth and Manjeet's husband Jeet used to gift her cardigan at Christmas and sweets at Diwali. Santosh often stressed that they treated her as a family member and Manjeet called her aunty. She also praised her own father who provided her five almonds whenever she had a cold or she sneezed.

The other incident she narrated took place in 1968/69, when she became friends at Sharma Fashions with an English lady whose name was Elsie. Santosh and Elsie were together many times on the High Street. On a Saturday, Elsie met us at the main road. She gave half- crown each to Saneh and Azad because she saw Santosh's children for the first time. Santosh and Elsie were comfortable in the company of each other. The other lady Santosh became friends, with was a West-Indian. They both went into a shop. The shopkeeper was surprised to see a young Indian woman with a well-built Jamaican woman. Santosh told the shopkeeper that she was her mother. He asked whether her father was an Indian or a white man. That could be the reason that a Jamaican woman had an Indian looking daughter. This, however, showed Santosh's respect for all races and people whoever loved her and respected her.

Because of such pleasantness, she forgave those who had been provocative and unrighteous to her. But she never forgot their misdeed. She ignored those people who were not worth a thought or company. She did not like selfish or users who took advantage of her gentleness. Neither did she ask anyone to do anything for her. Whenever an individual did something for her, she paid for it or gave them chocolate and cigarettes.

Santosh Rani was a very simple person. She never bought expensive clothes or went to eat-out. She wanted to save for the future. Together and separately we had faced enormous problems and poverty in our earlier years. We did not want to return to the old days. We were both forward looking and worked for the betterment of our lives. She worked hard since she left school at the age of eleven. When she was young, she would have preferred to study and carry a bag. Nevertheless, she compensated this by encouraging her children to study and refrain from domestic work (both our children received Master's degree and also added other professional qualifications). Santosh always supported me. It was due to her sustainability, I managed to study in London and continued to gain degrees and write books. I used to read my books in bed and even make notes by putting the writing board on the pillow. She used to say that I should read or write, so that she could sleep. She felt safe and comfortable in her bed when I was there.

She appreciated my writing skills and the diary writing which I called "My Observations". She wanted me to publish my notes as a book and make my views public. She preferred to hear all I wrote on a day. Initially she was surprised that I could write without reading any books because she had seen me making notes from books for my degree examinations as well as for research. However, these notes were about my own experiences and observations and a psychological analysis and expression about events and people's thoughts and behaviour.

She was not too religious but used to pray at home, lighting ghee diva and agarbatti (incense sticks). She went to temples in Southall and Hounslow every now and then. She used to contribute a small sum and also offer money in the boxes and at veneration (arti). She loved celebrating Karvachowth, Diwali and Rakhi festivals. She always bought Indian sweets, made fried food or Dal-Rice as the custom suggested. Santosh followed my family traditions and never talked about her own family customs except that they did not celebrate Rakhi. Though, I wrote above that she was not too religious. In one sense, however, she was religious, because she conducted the rituals and truly followed religious teachings.

In this age of turmoil, selfishness, differences, anger and mutual conflict, she remained calm and serene. She never harmed or thought ill without exception. Despite the fact that many people had hurt her socially, psychologically and mentally, she forgave her opponents and tolerated their tartness. She bent a little in order to avoid conflict or create scene. She followed the dictum of the Gita, "Sukhe Dukhe Sameh Kratava, Labha Labho, Jaya Jayo"; People should not change their conduct and behaviour and remain the same in pleasure and in pain, in gain and loss, in victory and in defeat. Their feelings should remain unaltered. Santosh practiced that to the last minute, which made her a precious and rare species.

Santosh enjoyed her family life. Her happiness was at its peak when she became a grandmother. She took the grandchildren to the park to play and to have picnic. She took them to school and brought them back home in the afternoon. She used to watch them play football at school. She cooked food of their liking, even when she was unable to function effectively and stand straight in the kitchen. In the last days of her life she made curry and rice for Amar in Delhi.

Santosh loved London and relished being a Londoner. She felt comfortable in Chiswick and the surrounding areas- visiting Acton, Shepherds bush, Wembley, West Ealing, Southall and Hounslow. She travelled by bus and gave up the use of trains in 2013. She casually used taxi and minicab.

She used to wake up at 6.30 am, would shut the bedroom door, so I could sleep a little longer. She would clean her teeth and have a bath. If we were to go out, she would wear different clothes to the ones if we were to stay at home. She used to sit in the kitchen with her green tea- drinking it. She would not watch television in the morning but wait for 9 am in order to listen to Ravi Sharma on the Sunrise-Radio or Lyca-Radio in recent months. She used to have breakfast at 9.30 am, so she could start to take her medicine. She would take four tablets at 10 am, then the new three tablets at 12 noon. She never missed her tablets and took them herself with water in a steel glass which she kept on the kitchen table. She kept another steel glass in the bedroom. She took her warfarin tablet exactly at 6 pm and would wait for the exact hour. She would not drink water or tea half an hour before that.

She continued to go shopping at Sainsburys' in Chiswick, Morrison's at Acton and Quality stores at Hounslow for Indian food supplies. She bought clothes in December 2014, at Bonn Marche', Marks& Spencer and Primark in Hounslow. During these High Street walks or staying at home, we were mostly together. One day we decided to go to Acton and left home. Later I felt that we might do some unplanned shopping. I asked her to wait at the pavement outside the house while I went to kitchen to collect the shopping trolley. She returned to the house and briefly said 'Mai aa gai' (I am back) indicating that she did not want to stay on her own even for a few minutes.

During the past two years or so, Santosh had lost confidence in herself. She could not take decision. She often asked me 'Tum Batayo', you tell me what you think about things, going out etc. I used to say, it is difficult to live a man's life, now I have to decide for both of us. Thus, living two people's lives. The decision should be for the benefit and good for both of us. We did not want to impose or take wrong decision affecting any- body. That was my dilemma. But once a decision had been taken, she did not ask to alter it. Neither did she criticize it. She took it as an advice and acted upon it.

In hindsight, we could stress that Santosh was not enjoying during the last few months of her life. She used to get breathless. She never complained but often pondered over the past happenings. She missed her grandchildren when they were not around or did not phone her. She was pleased to see Amar and Ashish when they came to London from Canada in the summer of 2014. She cooked for them, made panipuree for them. She was happy and joyful in London in the company of her family. She was mentally alert but her body had started to deteriorate. She was not the same Santosh Rani as she had been in the first forty years of her living in England. The last seven years were inordorous and unpleasant if not tedious. In September and October 2014, she went to doctors or hospitals for twenty five times. In London, nevertheless, there was always a hope that she would get better and return home, not necessarily to the same routine but she showed her presence in the house and where-ever she went.

She was sometimes asked in India whether she liked India or England. She told them that she was at ease at both the places. Perhaps she was a bit diplomatic on this question. She often fell sick in Delhi, especially during the past six years. She wanted to return to London and indeed returned earlier than planned in 2009, when she could not get treatment in Delhi.

Santosh made a number of trips to India after her arrival in London for the first time in April 1968. We sometimes reached Delhi airport at night but waited there for the daybreak before going home. There I used to go with some- one to hire a cleaner and she would wait at the house. After cleaning the house, we used to go for shopping for food supplies. During our stay in Delhi, we would visit Chandni Chowk, Sadar Bazar and Connaught place in order to buy clothes, hosiery, belts and artificial jewelry. In total she made twenty five journeys to India and three to Canada. She travelled 250,000 miles by air.

Our visit to Delhi in February 2015, however, became her last. Never to return to her favorite place- London. She fell sick within a week of our reaching Delhi. At first we thought of returning to London as soon as possible but she wanted to stay for a few more days. On Thursday 19 February, she became breathless and had to be taken to a local doctor who advised her to be hospitalized. We took her to Max hospital where she stayed for a week. She recovered a little and returned home on 27 February. But she fell sick again. She was breathless. Her feet, hands and face had started to get swollen. She refused to go back to hospital. We, therefore, arranged for an oxygen cylinder and an oxygen mask by her bed side. She had lost appetite and did not eat solid food. She took some dal (lentils) or (porridge) dalia.

Everything, however, comes to an end. Her diabetes had become uncontrollable, though she used to take her medicine on time and insulin as advised. She started to feel unwell in April 2000, and in June, she had to be taken to hospital in an ambulance. Later we discovered she had a stroke and her memory was temporarily feigned. After this incident she started to go to hospital many times in a month. She was seen by a diabetic specialist, a renal consultant, a cardiologist and at lung function unit. She had to go for the INR test every month, podiatioay every three months and eye specialist two to three times a year. She had diabetes for twenty five years and had developed further complications over the years. Her lungs were weak. Her kidney and heart had become frail. Her admission to Max hospital in Delhi did not help to recover from her breathlessness for which she was admitted.

In the year 2008, she was advised to undergo a triple bypass (a graft). But she refused to have the major surgery for fear of going into coma. Her arteries had become blocked. She had a moderate heart attack in April 2014. She was in hospital for twenty five days and again advised for the surgery which she refused. She came home in May. After that she was often quiet and unwilling to go out, saying that she did not was to walk around.

The last two days of her life were very touching. Yet, she did not indicate that she was to leave this world soon. She was sleepy most of Wednesday. She did her routine teeth cleaning, washed her face, and had tea, a bite of toast and a few crisps. We were planning to return to London on Thursday, 5th of March and had booked our flight. She asked me to pack her clothes and medicines. For the journey she wanted to wear trousers, a new top and pink cardigan. She wanted to bring the old shawl along with the new one. She expressed a desire to wear the old sandals because her feet were swollen. We also arranged for small oxygen cylinders for the journey.

During the day time on Wednesday, 4th March, she stayed on the couch. Sometimes lying down, and at other times trying to sit for a little while. After 10 pm, she said that she wanted to go to the bedroom. I assisted her to walk from the living room to the bedroom. She wished to use the washroom before going to bed. She removed her denture, washed them and tried to put them back into the mouth. I asked her to put the dentures in the cup, which she did. She wiped her hands and face with a towel. I helped her to the bed. She almost fell on the bed. I removed the bed cover and asked her to stand for a second. She came to the feet side of the bed and slipped on to the floor. I entreated her to be brave and that we were going to London, the next day. She questioned, are we going tomorrow?

She could not move and collapsed into my arms. When I could not hold her as she was getting heavy, I called Sonu to come and help me in order to put Santosh on the bed. Sonu arrived within minutes. We both helped her to the bed. She said 'Mujhe Seedha Lita Do'. Help me to lay straight – vertical on the bed. This we did. I then asked her whether she wanted me to put her oxygen on. She made no reply. I thought she was either sleepy or had fainted. I touched her. She was ice cold. I called Dr Surendar from

240

the neighbourhood. He felt her nerves, throat, opened her eyes and mouth. Her tongue had turned blue. The doctor declared her dead. Santosh Rani was gone within seconds of her lying down on the bed where she died peacefully at 10.30pm on 4ᵗʰ of March 2015. She had been unwell for so long, yet she passed away so quickly without relaying any message or making demand to see someone near and dear.

I could not believe that Santosh Rani could depart so expeditiously and in that manner. She was a brave person and a fighter. However, she could not fight any longer. Her weapons of tablets, insulin and oxygen did not help in time of need and deserted her. Moreover, the tablets could do only that much as Dr. Kooner at Hammersmith had said. The Delhi pollution hastened her demise. 'Mujhe Seedha Lita Do' were her last words. She did not go into coma or deep sleep as she had feared, could be the effect of the GRAFT. Nonetheless, she was sleepy for the last two days. Her memory was sharp to the last minute. Her voice was fine and audible. She knew what she was doing and what she was saying.

Santosh was a gentle and kind woman, hardworking, compassionate and tolerant, always thinking of the others, doing something for them. She was very forgiving. She used to say 'Jane Do', 'Kya-fayeda'. Let it go. There is no advantage in confrontation or criticism. She had accumulated so much positive energy, which she did not want to waste on people who showed apathy and indifference. She felt that energy should be directed towards constructive action and planning for the future in order to improve people's lives. She was soft spoken. Obeyed like a soldier. Respected elders and loved young ones. She wanted to live for her grandchildren whom she dearly loved and would do anything for them. She had enormous energy for work especially for cooking for the family, more particularly for the grandchildren. She knew what they wanted. She would make yogurt curry and rice, dal, chapatti and soft parathas and sweet purees at Diwali. In the last few years, she stopped cooking and eating greasy food. She preferred parathas to purees even at Diwali festival. She enjoyed green tea, ginger tea and cinnamon tea during the day time. She used to make tea herself but sometimes asked me to make tea for both of us.

We mourn the death of Santosh Rani but celebrate her life and her addition to enriching our lives and giving us the pleasure of her company for so many years. Looking after us, nursing us in need, going to hospital with me, doing shopping and accompanying me for a walk to parks, which she herself enormously enjoyed until the year 2000. She did not care for money but never wasted a penny. She understood the value of financial resources. She always kept plenty of food supply at the house and would buy essential goods in advance. She always said that there should be no shortage of things in our house.

We all feel the agony of her absence and miss her devotion and dedication and other qualities. Nevertheless, her contribution and conduciveness towards our accomplishments and advancement would essentially be enshrined in our memories and treasured forever.

My Life Without S. R.

When I went back into the memory lane and discovered that I was alone, at the age of thirteen, cooking my own meal. Then again when I arrived in London at the age of twenty six, I found myself on my own. I could not mix with other people because of ideological and practical differences. However, after having lived a family life with my wife and children for so long (1968 to 2015), I again became forlorn and dreary at the age of seventy six, because of the loss of my dear companion and friend who was also my wife. When she was with me, I did not need a friend. We had discussion on all sorts of themes including human behaviour and our own experiences over the years. We would analyse them in details and attempt to seek comfort in this explanation.

My life would not be the same as it was with S.R. (Santosh Rani). In March 2015, we were busy in the aftermath of her death. But when Azad and Meenakshi left for Canada on 30th of March, I realized the enormity of my loneliness and felt the void. I often woke up at night at 3 pm or even earlier and could not go to sleep for hours. I often read a book or drank tea at that odd hour. There had never been a deep sleep in the month of April. Whenever, the scene of her death came to my mind, my heart ached.

I did not cook meal for days and weeks. I lived on bread. Often thinking, she would not have allowed that. If she was present, she would have accompanied me to the dentist, I would have taken her to the hospital appointments. In the meantime, I have read a few books, watched a few programmes on television. But I did not enjoy them anymore. When I thought of preparing food or living on my own at this age, I felt uneasy and could not bear to go on like that for long. I still liked our house in Chiswick, where I have lived since August 1977. I did not know how I would conduct myself and what the future holds for me. I get visits from Saneh, Akash and Sangeeta whenever she was in London and phone calls over the weekends from Azad, Amar and Ashish. Sangeeta phones me almost every day. Enquiring how I spent my day. I still took my morning tea, breakfast, lunch and dinner but it is with bread or readymade roties.

I had changed a little. I was eating, less savories and no Indian sweets. But I still took biscuit with tea in the evenings. I would never be able to live a normal life because S.R. and I were mostly together during the past forty seven years. Santosh used to sleep and I used to read or write in bed. That routine has gone, because this house had lost fifty percent of its population. I had not yet reconciled with the fact that S.R. was no more and she had gone forever. When I thought, of the events of her life, tears came to my eyes and I did feel the woe and sadness. There was no answer to my questions except that people had variant notion towards the events in life.

It was, however, the conversation that I missed most. I often felt that I would like to speak to people and listen to them. I woke up in the morning; there was no one to talk with. Then I listened to TV voices. I had not watched much of Hindi programmes, or films and have lost interest in Hindi news. Because of the general election in Britain, I watched the BBC news and listened to politicians and the expert analysis by the journalists. I did not take much interest in India or Indian affairs because it was the pollution of Delhi, ignorance of doctors, along with their inefficiency and greed for money that snatched a person who was so precious and dear to me and my family. They did not express or demonstrate their feelings but they missed her veritably and painfully.

In the future we would perhaps be guided by SR's ways of living and conduct. We would make efforts to forgive and definitely forget certain behaviour. There was no point, on sticking to the views and actions, which rendered no constructive results but became barriers to advancement and progress. Neither was there any advantage in antagonizing people, even when they had diverse methods of living and expressing their opinions. People should live as they wished in a democratic system. I should also attempt to return to my routine, remain busy and seek comfort in reading and writing which interested me and Santosh would have preferred my system.

DR Keshava Arora April 2015

Printed in the United States
By Bookmasters